Nietzsche and Zen

Nietzsche and Zen

Self-overcoming without a Self

André van der Braak

LEXINGTON BOOKS

A division of

ROWMAN & LITTLEFIELD PUBLISHERS, INC.
Lanham • Boulder • New York • Toronto • Plymouth, UK

Published by Lexington Books
A wholly owned subsidiary of The Rowman & Littlefield Publishing Group, Inc.
4501 Forbes Boulevard, Suite 200, Lanham, Maryland 20706
www.rowman.com

10 Thornbury Road, Plymouth PL6 7PP, United Kingdom

First paperback edition 2013

British Library Cataloguing in Publication Information Available

Library of Congress Cataloging-in-Publication Data

The hardback edition was previously cataloged by the Library of Congress as follows:

Braak, Andre van der, 1963–
Nietzsch and Zen : self-overcoming without a self / Andre van der Braak.
p. cm. — (Studies in comparative philosophy and religion)
Includes bibliographic references (p.) and index.
1. Nietzsche, Friedrich Wilhelm, 1844–1900. 2. Zen Buddhism—Philosophy.
3. Philosophy and religion. 4. Self (Philosophy) I. Title.
B3318.B83B73 2011
193—dc23 2011017036

ISBN 978-0-7391-6550-8 (cloth : alk. paper)
ISBN 978-0-7391-8444-8 (pbk. : alk. paper)
ISBN 978-0-7391-6884-4 (electronic)

™ The paper used in this publication meets the minimum requirements of American National Standard for Information Sciences—Permanence of Paper for Printed Library Materials, ANSI/NISO Z39.48-1992.

Printed in the United States of America

In memory of Niek Pierson (1953–2007)

Contents

Preface

For a good understanding of this study on Nietzsche and Zen, it is important to first elucidate three crucial characteristics. First, it is situated within the field of comparative philosophy and follows a cross-cultural hermeneutical approach. Second, it uses a conception of philosophy that is non-propositional: it views philosophy as a form of *áskēsis*. Third, it situates itself within the discussion whether Nietzsche can be seen as a soteriological thinker.

COMPARATIVE PHILOSOPHY

As globalization spreads ever farther across the planet and dialogue between global cultures increases, it is becoming more and more apparent that cultural exchange has been at the heart of the Western philosophical tradition itself. The Greek tradition, long considered the very root of the Western philosophical tradition, has Asian origins. Many Western thinkers from the modern era have invoked non-Western philosophy (often in a skewed way) to provide an alternative standpoint from which to criticize Western institutions and practices. In the eighteenth century, for example, Voltaire hailed Confucianism as a truly rational religion, free of the superstition that could be found in Christianity. In the nineteenth century, Schopenhauer and others idealized the mystical philosophy of the Indian Upanishads and Buddhism.

From the beginning of the twentieth century, the academic discipline of comparative philosophy has taken root. In his history of this discipline, J. J. Clarke distinguishes three historical phases, which can be loosely connected to three methodological approaches.[1] The first approach was the universalist one. The universalists attempted a grand synthesis between East and West. They grossly schematized and simplified the various traditions: the West was rationalistic and materialist, the East was intuitive and spiritual. This universalizing approach was characterized by a "will to truth": a will to find the one overarching perspective under which all philosophical traditions can be subsumed. The second approach, comparativism in a more restricted sense, has been more modest. It has aimed to compare the views of Western and non-Western philosophers, mapping out similarities and differences. The comparativists abandoned the ambition of a great synthesis and more modestly compared doctrines from individual thinkers.

Over the past decennia, cross-cultural hermeneutical philosophy has gained influence as a third approach. The thinker most often associated with philosophical hermeneutics, Hans-Georg Gadamer (1900–2002), was a well-known proponent of intercultural dialogue and a major source of inspiration for the study of cross-cultural philosophy in the West. Philosophical hermeneutics stresses the importance of interpreting philosophers within their temporal and cultural context and of keeping in mind that every interpretation constitutes another recontextualization. The aim is not to arrive at some static "objective truth" about reality, but to expand the range of possible interpretations, and in this way to contribute to the ongoing conversation of global philosophy. Philosophical hermeneutics recognizes a plurality of different traditions and stresses that one's own tradition needs to be continuously both reinterpreted and strengthened in light of its exposure to what is foreign to it.

Cross-cultural hermeneutics aims not so much at comparison per se, but at deconstructing fixed perspectives and opening up a plurality of interpretations, in order to enhance the fullness of our understanding. Within this approach, it can even be misleading to speak in essentialist terms about "Western" or "Chinese" or "Japanese" philosophy, as if these were clearly demarcated philosophical traditions with their own unique characteristics (which are then considered to be the essence of Western, Chinese, or Japanese thought). From the cross-cultural hermeneutical point of view, there is just one philosophy, which has been practiced at various times and places around the world. From this perspective, comparing Nietzsche and Zen is not fundamentally different from comparing Nietzsche to Plato. Such comparisons can assist in the emerging global conversation of philosophy and can be mutually enlightening. Philosophical positions and approaches that are minor in one tradition can be dominant in another.[2]

This study's methodological approach can be characterized as "doing intercultural philosophy the Nietzschean way." In offering a critical interplay of opposing perspectives, a "hermeneutics of difference" is established, leading to a multiplication and proliferation of horizons.[3] In the global context of interculturality today, hermeneutics must undergo a fundamental change, according to some. Since every hermeneutics has its own culturally sedimented roots and cannot claim a universal acceptance unconditionally, the fundamental principle of intercultural hermeneutics is the view that an interpretation is always determined in terms of culture. Therefore, intercultural hermeneutics attempts to always recognize and respect the "foreign" element.[4] Fostering a cross-cultural dialogue between Western and Asian philosophical traditions can help to provide the kind of regeneration that these traditions are in dire need of or, as Froese puts it, "cultural dialogue provides a possibility for reinfusing our world with meaning and preventing the kind of stagnation of ideas that leads us to assume that the cosmos itself is meaningless."[5]

The French sinologist Francois Jullien stresses that, through the detour of non-Western philosophies, we can regain access to lost or underemphasized dimensions of our own Western tradition:

> However taken it may be with surpassing itself, Western philosophy never questions itself except from within. However radical it may wish to be, this criticism is always relatively integrated, remaining within the limits of an implicit understanding from which certain positions may emerge. There is always that on the basis of which we question ourselves, which, for that very reason, we cannot question.[6]

To step back from the Western tradition and criticize it from without can allow us to assume a more truly global position. Cross-cultural philosophy is, therefore, especially valuable and helpful in undercutting assumptions about one's own tradition.

Jay Garfield has noted that comparative philosophy has too often functioned as an arm of Orientalism, where Western scholars appropriate the expertise on non-Western traditions. Moreover,

> comparative philosophy often imports hermeneutical and philosophical methods to the study of non-Western texts that succeed in distorting or simply missing the significance of those texts or the meaningfulness of their claims and arguments in the contexts of their home cultures. In addition it has been noted that the interpretative lens privileged in most comparative philosophy is distinctly Western [. . .] the Western texts, views, and arguments are typically taken as the standards against which non-Western texts are compared.[7]

Garfield goes on to suggest that a more promising approach would perhaps be to elucidate forms of Western thought through the lens of non-Western ways of thinking. In one of his essays, Garfield retells the development of Western Idealism from the perspective of the Indian Cittamātra school.[8] Methodologically this study is indebted to his approach.

NON-PROPOSITIONAL PHILOSOPHY AS WAY-SEEKING RATHER THAN TRUTH-SEEKING

One such assumption within Western philosophy is that philosophy is a propositional discipline that aims at the establishment of true doctrines. But such a conception of philosophy has not been dominant in all philosophical traditions. In the Chinese tradition, the notion of philosophy as aiming at the establishment of true doctrines (a Truth-seeking paradigm) has historically been superseded by the notion of philosophy as a way of life (a Way-seeking paradigm).

Such a Way-seeking paradigm can also be found in Buddhism. It is a religious and philosophical tradition that focuses more on practice than on doctrine. In religious studies, a distinction is made between orthodoxic religious traditions that put an emphasis on correct belief in theological and philosophical doctrines, and orthopraxic ones that emphasize correct practice.[9] Buddhism stresses orthopraxy rather than orthodoxy. It is therefore characterized by a kind of spiritual pragmatism that is intensified in Zen. As the thirteenth-century Japanese Zen master Dōgen wrote, "a Buddhist should neither argue superiority or inferiority of doctrines, but only be mindful of authenticity or inauthenticity of practice."[10]

As Pierre Hadot has argued, in ancient Western philosophy such a Way-seeking paradigm was common. Philosophy was practiced by the ancients as a form of *áskēsis*—a practice of continual self-overcoming and self-transformation. With the rise of Christianity in the West, philosophy became an orthodoxy, a quest for correct doctrine. Philosophy was no longer practiced as a way of life because the Christian way of life was already established as the only true one. Philosophy became a theoretical practice aimed at the justification of the revealed truths of Christianity.[11] In the Chinese tradition, the reverse occurred: Truth-seeking philosophies (such as the Mohists for example) were relegated to the countercultural margins of the tradition.

Hadot writes about *áskēsis* as a means to "*let* ourselves be changed, in our point of view, attitudes and convictions. This means that we must dialogue with ourselves, and hence we must do battle with ourselves."[12] *Áskēsis* makes use of techniques of the self that are as much bodily as intellectual. These exercises were designed to bring about "a conversion which turns our active life upside down, changing the life of the person who goes through it."[13] It should not be confused with asceticism. Michel Foucault comments on the difference between asceticism and *áskēsis*: "Asceticism as the renunciation of pleasure has bad connotations. But the *áskēsis* is something else: it's the work that one performs on oneself in order to transform oneself or make the self appear that happily one never attains."[14]

Richard Rorty writes about such a different kind of philosophy as *edifying philosophy*, a term he borrows from Gadamer. In such a philosophy, the will to truth is replaced with the will to edification. Philosophy should be seen as a conversation beyond the exchange of views:

> The attempt to edify (ourselves or others) may consist in the hermeneutic activity of making connections between our own culture and some exotic culture or historical period, or between our own discipline and another discipline which seems to pursue incommensurable aims in an incommensurable vocabulary. [. . .] [This] activity is [. . .] edifying without being constructive—at least if "constructive" means the sort of cooperation in the accomplishment of research programs which takes place in normal discourse. For edifying discourse is *supposed* to be abnormal, to take us out of our old selves by the power of strangeness, to aid us in becoming new beings. [15]

This study is situated within Rorty's notion of philosophy as edifying philosophy. However, this does not mean that it leaves the search for truth entirely behind:

> The contrast between the desire for edification and the desire for truth is, for Gadamer, not an expression of a tension which needs to be resolved or compromised. If there is a conflict, it is between the Platonic-Aristotelian view that the only way to be edified is to know what is out there (to reflect the facts accurately—to realize our essence by knowing essences) and the view that the quest for truth is just one among many ways in which we might be edified.[16]

The Truth-seeking paradigm is also an assumption that Nietzsche rejects and tries to undo by means of his revaluation of all values. Nietzsche's philosophy is not propositional in the sense of aiming at discovering objective truths about reality. In opposition to the modern Western conception of what it means to practice philosophy, Nietzsche aims to revive the Greek way of philosophizing as a way of life. Nietzsche's *áskēsis*, however, seems in some points to go beyond the *áskēsis* that Hadot describes. Some have claimed that his Dionysian philosophy in fact constitutes a soteriology, a teaching of religious liberation.

NIETZSCHE AS A SOTERIOLOGICAL THINKER

From 1890 to 1920 Nietzsche was often interpreted as a religious thinker. In her book on Nietzsche, Lou Salome represented him as such.[17] Several varieties of Nietzschean religion blossomed.[18] The German sociologist Ferdinand Tönnies, who had been an admirer of the early Nietzsche of *The Birth of*

Tragedy, complained about this phenomenon in his book *The Nietzsche Cult*.[19] Since the Second World War, however, the secular Nietzsche interpretation has dominated the field of Nietzsche studies.

The past years have seen a renewed interest in Nietzsche as a religious thinker. But the nature of his religious thought has been interpreted in widely divergent ways. Tyler Roberts has described Nietzsche as a "postreligious thinker." In 2000, two collections of essays, *Nietzsche and the Gods* and *Nietzsche and the Divine*, appeared. Julian Young sees Nietzsche as a religious reformer who never let go of his youthful ideal of a Dionysian communitarianism. Alistair Kee describes Nietzsche's religious thought as a clash between his own Dionysianism and Christianity.[20]

Does Nietzsche preach a soteriological doctrine? Gilles Fraser thinks he does: he has interpreted Nietzsche's thought as an anti-Christian soteriology.[21] Bruce Benson, on the other hand, interprets his Dionysian piety as an anti-soteriology.[22] He notes that the Pietism that Nietzsche grew up with emphasized a childlike trust in God rather than doctrinal correctness. It approached Christianity as a practice of faith, not as an agreement with a set of propositions. Nietzsche calls his own Dionysian philosophy "the highest of all possible faiths," which he baptizes "with the name of Dionysus" (TI 9, 49).[23] In chapter 8 I will examine this question further.

The debate in the literature whether Nietzsche's thought can be considered a soteriology or not is perhaps clouded by the fact that the English word *soteriology* implies a *soter*, a savior. In the Buddhist tradition, the equivalent to soteriology is conceptualized as a path to liberation (*mārga*). Robert Buswell and Robert Gimello suggest, in their introduction to a collection of essays on the Buddhist *mārga*, that this concept might prove useful in cross-cultural studies, and that

> it may have scope and theoretical potential sufficient to allow us eventually to speak—with due caution and proper nuance—of Christian mārga, Jewish mārga, Islamic mārga, and so forth. Perhaps the study of Buddhism may be enlisted to illumine those other traditions in ways in which their own categories alone do not [. . .] because we think that [. . .] the concept of "the path" has been given in Buddhism an explication more sustained, comprehensive, critical, and sophisticated than that provided by any other single religious tradition.[24]

As Buswell and Gimello argue, the term *mārga* is somewhat analogous to "soteriology" but without the theistic connotations. Perhaps, therefore, it could be fruitful to speak of a Nietzschean *mārga*, a Nietzschean path of self-overcoming.[25] The concept of *mārga* is also suited for approaching the question of Nietzsche's soteriology because it helps to move the attention from doctrines to approaches to wisdom, from Nietzsche's philosophical views to the *way* he philosophizes, his practice of revaluation of all values, and his philosophical *áskēsis*.

A dialogue with Zen can be very helpful in such an undertaking. Zen is a prime example of a non-propositional philosophical tradition, full of deconstruction and iconoclasm. One of the reasons that Zen might arguably be the most suitable Buddhist tradition to clarify Nietzsche's soteriology is that it rejects the standard Buddhist soteriology; it could be called a skeptical soteriology or even an anti-soteriology.[26] Although Zen emphasizes practice and experience, seemingly endorsing the *mārga* paradigm, its rhetoric is very strongly anti-*mārga*. Zen rejects gradualist practice aimed at a goal. Therefore, the path and the goal become one. Zen's strong anti-*mārga* rhetoric, combined with a strong emphasis on the necessity of practice and continual self-overcoming, also runs through Nietzsche's work. We could therefore speak of a Nietzschean *mārga*—keeping in mind that this would be as much a non-path as the Zen *mārga*. This study aims to elucidate such a non-path through the dialogue between Nietzsche and various representatives of the Zen tradition.

NOTES

1. J. J. Clarke, *Oriental Enlightenment: The Encounter Between Asian and Western Thought* (London/New York: Routledge, 1997), 119–29.

2. J. N. Hoffman, *Wahrheit, Perspektive, Interpretation. Nietzsche und die philosophische Hermeneutik* (Berlin/New York: de Gruyter, 1994), 252–306, comments that Nietzsche has long been excluded from the cosmos of Gadamer's hermeneutics. This may be because his theory of interpretation, his understanding of language, and his uncovering of power relations behind interpretations all oppose Gadamer's hermeneutical universalism and optimism. Where Gadamer speaks of the importance of prejudices for interpretation and understanding, Nietzsche speaks of perspectives and valuations.

3. Fred Dallmayr, *Beyond Orientalism: Essays on Cross-Cultural Encounter* (Albany: State University of New York Press, 1995), xi describes a hermeneutics of difference as a form of deconstructive dialogue, where dialogical exchange respects otherness beyond assimilation. See also Dallmayr, *Beyond Orientalism*, 39–62.

4. R.A. Mall, *Philosophie im Vergleich der Kulturen: Interkulturelle Philosophie, eine neue Orientierung* (Darmstadt: Wissenschaftliche Buchgesellschaft, 1995).

5. Katrin Froese, *Nietzsche, Heidegger, and Daoist Thought: Crossing Paths In-Between* (Albany: State University of New York Press, 2004), 5.

6. Francois Jullien, *Detour and Access: Strategies of Meaning in China and Greece* (New York: Zone Books, 2000), 371.

7. Jay. L. Garfield, *Empty Words: Buddhist Philosophy and Cross-Cultural Interpretation* (Oxford/New York: Oxford University Press, 2002), 152.

8. Garfield, *Empty Words,* 152–69.

9. Catherine Bell, *Ritual: Perspectives and Dimensions* (Oxford/New York: Oxford University Press, 1997), 191–97.

10. Dōgen, *Shōbōgenzō, Bendōwa*. Quoted in: Hee-Jin Kim, *Dōgen on Meditation and Thinking: A Reflection on His View of Zen* (Albany: State University of New York Press, 2007), 22.

11. Pierre Hadot, *Philosophy As a Way of Life* (Oxford: Wiley-Blackwell, 1995).

12. Hadot, *Philosophy As a Way of Life*, 91.

13. Hadot, *Philosophy As a Way of Life*, 83.

14. Michel Foucault, "Friendship as a Way of Life," in Michel Foucault, *Foucault Live: Collected Interviews, 1961–1984*, ed. Sylvère Lotringer, trans. Lysa Hochroth and John Johnston (New York: Semiotext[e], 1989), 309.

15. Richard Rorty, *Philosophy and the Mirror of Nature* (Princeton: Princeton University Press, 1980), 360.

16. Rorty, *Philosophy and the Mirror of Nature*, 360.

17. Lou Salome, *Friedrich Nietzsche in seinen Werken* (Vienna: Carl Konegen, 1894).

18. See Steven E. Aschheim, *The Nietzsche Legacy in Germany: 1890–1990* (Berkeley: University of California Press, 1990).

19. Ferdinand Tönnies, *Der Nietzsche-Kultus* (Leipzig: O.R. Reisland, 1897).

20. André F. M. van der Braak, *Hoe men wordt, wat men is. Zelfvervolmaking, zelfoverwinning en zelfvergetelheid bij Nietzsche* (Budel: Damon, 2004); Bruce Ellis Benson, *Pious Nietzsche: Decadence and Dionysian Faith* (Bloomington/Indianapolis: Indiana University Press, 2008); Gilles Fraser, *Redeeming Nietzsche: On the Piety of Unbelief* (London: Routledge, 2002); Weaver Santaniello, *Nietzsche and the Gods* (Albany: State University of New York Press, 2001); Richard Schacht, ed., *Nietzsche's Postmoralism* (Cambridge: Cambridge University Press, 2000); Jim Urpeth and John Lippitt, eds., *Nietzsche and the Divine* (Manchester: Clinamen Press, 2000); Julian Young, *Nietzsche's Philosophy of Religion* (Cambridge: Cambridge University Press, 2006); Tyler Roberts, *Contesting Spirit: Nietzsche, Affirmation, Religion* (Princeton: Princeton University Press, 1998); Alistair Kee, *Nietzsche Against the Crucified* (London: Trinity Press International, 1999). See the overview of some of these works by Michael Skowron, "Rezensionen: Neuerscheinungen zu Nietzsches Philosophie der Religion und der Religion seiner Philosophie," in *Nietzsche-Studien* 36 (2007), 425–39.

21. Fraser, *Redeeming Nietzsche*; see already Ulrich Willers, *Friedrich Nietzsches antichristliche Christologie. Eine theologische Rekonstruktion* (Wien: Tyrolia Verlag, 1988).

22. Benson, *Pious Nietzsche*.

23. Nietzsche's friend Franz Overbeck wrote an essay in which he diagnosed the problem of the theology of his time as being too concerned with theory and not enough with practice. Nietzsche most likely agreed. In *The Antichrist* 39, Nietzsche speaks about Christianity as not a faith, but a doing—another state of being (AC 39). Nietzsche is against Christianity as an orthodoxy.

24. Robert E. Buswell, Jr. and Robert M. Gimello, eds., *Paths to Liberation: The Mārga and Its Transformations in Buddhist Thought* (Honolulu: University of Hawai'i Press, 1992), 2.

25. Buswell and Gimello, *Paths to Liberation*, 2f.

26. Benson characterizes Nietzsche's religious thought as an anti-soteriology (Benson, *Pious Nietzsche*, 9).

Acknowledgments

This study could not have been completed without the generous support of the Stichting Pierson Filosofie. I am very grateful to them for providing time for research and writing through their financial support. Chairman Bruno Nagel has especially been a source of much encouragement and good advice throughout the project.

This work has been in progress since 2004. It was born during a short stay at the Nanzan Center for Religion and Culture in Nagoya, Japan. Thanks to Tom Kasulis and Jim Heisig for their encouragement of the project. Over the years, my colleagues at the Comparative and Continental Philosophy Circle (David Jones, Bret Davis, Jason Wirth, Brian Schroeder, Ann Pirrucello, Tim Freeman, Michael Schwartz) have provided much support and encouragement.

This study followed on directly from my Nietzsche dissertation ("How One Becomes, What One Is"). Paul van Tongeren, my Ph.D. supervisor, continued to encourage me to extend my research into a comparative direction. The monthly seminars of his Nietzsche Research Group in Nijmegen have provided since 1998 a very lively philosophical environment for my Nietzsche research. I have greatly benefited from being able to present early versions of several chapters of this study in the seminars. I am grateful to Paul Carls and Wolter Hartog for their detailed reports of those seminar meetings, and to Isabelle Wienand for helping me to review the French language material on Nietzsche and Buddhism.

Thanks to Michael Skowron for reading an early draft of the entire manuscript. The anonymous reviewer for Lexington Books (who revealed himself, through his style and his acquaintance with the topic of Nietzsche and Zen, to be Graham Parkes) provided excellent suggestions for revisions and stylistic restructuring.

My own philosophical *áskēsis* has included the practice of Buddhist meditation since 1981. Gassho to my Dutch Zen teachers Nico Tydeman and Ton Lathouwers for their continuous support and encouragement. Teaching Zen (especially Dōgen) to the students of Zen Center Amsterdam has provided much inspiration for writing this book. Thanks to Henny van der Veere, lecturer in Japanese Religions at Leiden University, for his continuous deconstruction of Zen myths during several Classical Chinese reading groups.

An early version of some of the material in chapter 6 and 7 appeared as "Nietzsche and Japanese Buddhism on the Cultivation of the Body: To What Extent Does Truth Bear Incorporation?" in *Comparative and Continental Philosophy*, volume 1.2 2009, 223–251 (c) Equinox Publishing Ltd 2009. I am grateful to Equinox Press for permission to reprint that material here.

Key to References

Nietzsche citations refer to the following editions of Nietzsche's writings:

Sämtliche Werke, Kritische Studienausgabe (KSA). Edited by Giorgio Colli and Mazzino Montinari. Berlin/New York: de Gruyter, 1967–1977.

Sämtliche Briefe, Kritische Studienausgabe (KSB). Edited by Giorgio Colli and Mazzino Montinari. Berlin/New York: de Gruyter, 1986.

Werke, Kritische Gesamtausgabe (KGW). Edited by Giorgio Colli and Mazzino Montinari. Berlin/New York: de Gruyter, 1967–.

Letters will be cited by KSB volume followed by page number. All translations are my own, except those from *Thus Spoke Zarathustra* and *Ecce Homo*, where I have used the following English translations:

Thus Spoke Zarathustra: A Book for Everyone and Nobody. Translated by Graham Parkes. Oxford: Oxford University Press, 2005.

Ecce Homo: How To Become What You Are. Translated by Duncan Large. Oxford: Oxford University Press, 2007.

Unpublished texts are cited as KSA, followed by the numbering of Nietzsche's notebooks.

Even though I have worked mostly from the German text, I shall use the following English titles and abbreviations to indicate Nietzsche's published writings. Numbers following the abbreviations refer to sections, rather than pages.

AC	The Antichrist
BGE	Beyond Good and Evil
BT	The Birth of Tragedy
CW	The Case of Wagner
D	Daybreak
DW	The Dionysian World-view

EH	Ecce Homo
GM	On the Genealogy of Morality
HAH	Human, All Too Human
JS	The Joyous Science
NCW	Nietzsche Contra Wagner
PPP	The Pre-Platonic Philosophers
PTAG	Philosophy in the Tragic Age of the Greeks
SE	Schopenhauer as Educator
TI	Twilight of the Idols
TU	The Untimelies
TSZ	Thus Spoke Zarathustra
WS	The Wanderer and His Shadow

For Zen koans and stories, I have used the following translations:

Addiss, Stephen, Stanley Lombardo and Judith Roitman, eds. *Zen Sourcebook: Traditional Documents from China, Korea, and Japan.*

Sekida, Katsuki, transl. *Two Zen Classics: The Gateless Gate and the Blue Cliff Records.*

Citations from Linji are from the following edition:

Taishō shinshū daizōkyō, ed. Takakusu Junjirō and Watanabe Kaigyoku, 100 vols. Tokyo: Taishō issaikyō kankōkai, 1924–1932.

I have used the following translation:

Watson, Burton, transl. *The Zen Teachings of Master Lin-Chi: A Translation of the Lin-chi lu.* New York: Columbia University Press, 1993/1999.

Citations from Dōgen are from the following edition:

Dōgen, Kīgen. *Shōbōgenzō*, edited by Mizuno Yaoko. Tokyo: Iwanami, 1990.

For the fascicle *Genjōkōan*, I have used the translation of

Davis, Bret. "The Presencing of Truth: Dōgen's Genjōkōan." In *Buddhist Philosophy: Essential Readings*, edited by William Edelglass and Jay L. Garfield, 251–259. Oxford: Oxford University Press, 2009.

For all other fascicles, I have followed the translations in the following work (except where indicated otherwise):

Kim, Hee-Jin. *Eihei Dōgen—Mystical Realist.* Tucson: University of Arizona Press, 2004 (original edition 1975).

As a reference, I have used two other translations:

Waddell, Norman, and Masao Abe, transl. *The Heart of Dōgen's Shōbōgenzō.* Albany: State University of New York Press, 2002.

Tanahashi, Kazuaki, ed. *Moon in a Dewdrop: Writings of Zen Master Dōgen.* New York: North Point Press, 1985.

Introduction

A Summary of Arguments

Buddhist philosophical traditions can be seen as "emerging traditions" that call for an engagement with Western philosophical thinkers. Nietzsche is a prime candidate for such an engagement. He can be considered a transcultural thinker who aimed to revitalize Western culture by using his self-proclaimed "trans-European eye" (see chapter 1). Nietzsche was one of the few Western philosophers with an interest in non-Western philosophies, especially Buddhism, even if his familiarity with Buddhism was limited to early Buddhism[1] and his understanding of Buddhism was marred by nineteenth-century preconceptions of Buddhism as a "cult of nothingness," as Roger-Pol Droit has called it.[2] In line with these preconceptions, Nietzsche rejected the early Buddhism that he knew as a life-denying nihilism (see chapter 1).

Nietzsche's thought has been extensively received and commented on by Japanese Buddhist philosophers. But although the comparison between Nietzsche and Buddhism has had a long history in Japan, it is fairly recent in the West. Only since the 1980s have some affinities, albeit unintended or "ironical," between Nietzsche and Buddhism been pointed out in comparative studies.[3] Although these studies focused on the early Buddhism that Nietzsche himself was familiar with, Graham Parkes has convincingly argued that the later Mahāyāna Buddhism (that only became well-known and fully appreciated in the Western world after 1900) is a much better candidate for a fruitful comparison with Nietzsche's philosophy. According to Parkes, Nietzsche might have considered the Mahāyāna Buddhist philosophical ideas much to his own taste.[4] In China, Mahāyāna Buddhism met the Daoist tradition, which led to the emergence of Chan Buddhism (better known in the West under its Japanese name Zen), which is, according to Parkes, perhaps closest to Nietzsche.[5] As Parkes notes elsewhere:

> This is surely a most fertile field for Nietzsche studies, the common ground between the hermit of Sils-Maria and the life-artist-sages from the Chan and Zen traditions. The first wave of Zen to reach Western shores struck mainly *littérateurs* and religious types, now that Nietzsche is finally coming into his own is the time for a more philosophical engagement with thinkers of those Asian traditions, in which dialogue based on correspondences between both sides aims at precise elucidation of the divergences. Time, finally, for more of us to cast a trans-European eye over Nietzsche's legacy.[6]

Although Nietzsche as a philosopher and Zen as a Buddhist religious tradition seem to be widely divergent in their concerns, I aim to show that whereas Nietzsche is more religious than previously thought, Zen is more philosophical and skeptical than previously thought. However, this study does not aim to make a Zen master out of Nietzsche, and neither does it present a Nietzschean Zen to its readership. As Nietzsche remarks, "Seeing things as similar and making things the same is the sign of weak eyes" (JS 228). A crucial difference between Nietzsche and the Zen tradition lies in their respective relationship to practice. On the one hand, both are praxis-oriented: philosophy is not a theoretical or speculative enterprise, but a form of spiritual practice. On the other hand, what distinguishes them is Zen's emphasis on the practice of sitting meditation, zazen. Other important differences have to do with historical and cultural context. Nietzsche was very much a nineteenth-century German thinker, concerned with cultural criticism and the question of decadence, neither of which have much to do with the Zen tradition.[7]

Exactly the differences between Nietzsche and Zen make for a rich interplay of interpretations and perspectives that can open up new avenues for investigation in both Nietzsche studies and Zen studies. The "and" in Nietzsche and Zen should therefore be read both ways. This confrontation of two language games of widely different cultures calls into question the familiar identities of both Nietzsche and Zen.

OPENING UP THE NIETZSCHEAN TEXT

Derrida has spoken about a kind of interpretation that is not merely a "doubling" commentary on a text, but also an opening up of a text.[8] This study aims to open up Nietzsche's texts, his concepts, the way he *does* his philosophy, especially with regard to the religious or soteriological aspects of his thought. In this way it aims to contribute to a fuller and richer interpretation of Nietzsche's philosophy. Although Nietzsche the skeptical thinker is usually emphasized in Nietzsche research, his skepticism actually serves his project of self-overcoming.

A confrontation with Zen can help to open up perspectives on Nietzsche's thought beyond skepticism because it takes us beyond the "familiar" Nietzsche. There are some gaps in most Nietzsche interpretations that could be fruitfully addressed by means of a comparison with Zen. As Roger Ames has observed, since Nietzsche is part of our own Western philosophical tradition, we all too easily expect him to share with us some unannounced assumptions. The exoticness of Zen can help us to get behind what we initially take to be familiar in Nietzsche only to discover that he, too, is very exotic indeed.[9] Nietzsche's famous declaration of the death of God has often been misunderstood as a radicalization of the Western Enlightenment. But Nietzsche's "philosophizing with the hammer" served for him as a preparation for a revaluation of all values, a return to a life-affirming mode of existence, and even a new way of speaking about the divine.

Nietzsche was a transcultural thinker who used comparisons with non-European philosophical traditions in order to question what we call our "own." He not only used non-Western philosophy to criticize his own Western tradition, but he also attempted to go beyond it to a more global "world philosophy." (It is therefore fitting that he has been read widely in non-Western cultures, especially Japan and China). A comparative study with a non-Western philosophical tradition does justice to Nietzsche's own aspirations to go beyond Western philosophy. Nietzsche can be considered a transcultural thinker with a self-described trans-European and even trans-Asiatic eye. Therefore, to read Nietzsche himself with a trans-European eye (an East Asian eye, even further removed from Europe than the Near Asian and Indian eye that Nietzsche had in mind) can further elucidate Nietzsche's work.

ZEN

What is known in the West as the single entity of "Zen" in reality comprises a varied and heterogeneous collection of Buddhist traditions in China, Japan, Korea, and other East Asian countries, that span about 1500 years. After the death of the historical Buddha (traditionally placed at 480 BC, but according to recent research perhaps as late as 400 BC, which would make him a contemporary of Socrates), his message was spread by several schools. This early Buddhism is the Buddhism of the Pali Canon, which survives today in the school of Theravāda Buddhism in Sri Lanka, Thailand, and Birma.

In the first centuries CE, Mahāyāna Buddhism arose, most likely as a reform movement against a scholasticism that had set in. Its *Prajñāpāramitā* sutras (sutras of the wisdom beyond wisdom) claimed that all views, including Buddhist views, were "empty" (*śūnyatā*). This was the philosophical climate in which Nāgārjuna was born, one of the most important figures in the early development of the philosophical tradition of Mahāyāna Buddhism. He is the founder of the Madhyamaka school, a rich skeptical tradition, startlingly similar to the Western skeptical tradition, in respect of its aims, methodology, and philosophical problematic.[10] Nāgārjuna's radical ontological and epistemological skepticism deconstructed the dogmatic philosophical systems of some early Buddhist Abhidharma schools (see chapter 4).[11]

The Mahāyāna teachings were transmitted to China by Indian Buddhist monks. One of them was the legendary Bodhidharma (d. 532?),[12] who is revered as the founder and first patriarch of the school of Chan or Zen.[13] Bodhidharma's successors combined Indian Mahāyāna Buddhism with indigenous Chinese Daoist elements. In combining Nāgārjuna's philosophy of emptiness with the Daoist thought of Zhuangzi, they opened up the possibility of a thoroughly this-worldly affirmation of life, an amor fati beyond good and evil, that replaces early Buddhist renunciate morality. In the Song dynasty, Zen became the established form of Buddhism in China. This is when it was brought to Japan by several monks, among whom the thirteenth-century founder of the Sōtō Zen school, Dōgen (1200–1253).

ZEN AND THE WEST

In an interesting twist of fate (or karma), Nietzsche and Zen have suffered similar misrepresentations in their reception throughout the twentieth century. Initially, both were misrepresented as an anti-philosophical mysticism and a panacea for an ailing Western culture. Steven Aschheim has documented the many Nietzsche cults throughout Europe that claimed Nietzsche's thought for their own brand of spirituality.[14] Zen was presented to the West as a universal mysticism that contained the core of all religions without cultural baggage, especially through D. T. Suzuki (1870–1966) and the members of the so-called Kyoto School, a collection of Japanese thinkers who attempted to engage Zen with Western philosophical thought in order to arrive at a world philosophy for our times.[15]

Zen was seen as an anti-ritualistic tradition that focused on the experience of enlightenment (*satori* or *kenshō*). Because of this, it has exercised a fascination over Western philosophers, theologians, psychologists, and spiritual seekers. It has been hailed as a universal religion, founded on individual experience rather than conformity to church structures, meditation rather than ritual, critical investigation leading up to "the Great Doubt" rather than belief in religious dogmas. For many intellectuals, Zen served as a perfect replacement for a Western Christianity that was perceived as outmoded. It was viewed as an exponent of the mystical East, as epitomized, for example, in Eugen Herrigel's bestseller *Zen in the Art of Archery*.[16] Kyoto School member Kitarō Nishida (1870–1945) described the Zen enlightenment experience as a "pure experience" prior to the subject-object distinction. Nishida's concept of pure experience was based on his reading of a.o. William James (to which he was introduced by Suzuki). And although Nishida dropped his notion of "pure experience" in his later work, Suzuki adapted it as the central hermeneutic principle in his presentation of Zen to the West.[17]

Just as Nietzsche's thought was misused by the Nazis, Zen thought was misused by the Japanese government in an effort to justify its war efforts. Both were seen as philosophies "beyond good and evil" that justified violence. Western Zen priest Brian Victoria published in 1997 *Zen at War*, documenting nationalism and war crimes by Japanese Zen masters and throwing doubt on the universality of Zen spirituality.[18] A 1995 publication, *Rude Awakenings*, stressed the need for a critical self-examination within the Zen tradition itself.[19]

In the fifties, Zen was embraced by artists and intellectuals like Jack Kerouac, Allen Ginsberg, and Alan Watts, who formed the Beat Zen Generation. They embraced a kind of romantic and even "Nietzschean Zen" beyond good and evil, a radical iconoclasm that went beyond all conventions. In the sixties, Western counterculture claimed both Nietzsche and Zen in their protest against rationalistic Western culture. Nietzsche's "God is dead" was echoed by the Zen dictum "if you meet the Buddha on the road, kill him." Zen was one of the non-Western philosophies that was invoked as a way of criticizing Western culture.[20] Over the past decades, however, historians of the Zen tradition have stressed the role of embodiment, practice, and ritual in Zen, deconstructing the idea of Zen as a spiritual tradition aimed at a mystical experience of enlightenment.[21] Currently, Zen studies is at a crossroads, looking for a new paradigm and a new hermeneutics.[22] Contemporary hermeneutical and postmodern interpretations of Zen emphasize its theories of language and interpretation, enabling many useful and fruitful confrontations with Nietzsche's thought. Especially postmodern Nietzsche interpretations could do much to further de-mystify Zen and disclose its significance as a philosophical tradition.

Elsewhere, I have argued that the conflict between what I called the "Romantic" and the "historicist" Zen reception could be fruitfully approached from a cross-cultural hermeneutical perspective.[23] A hermeneutical approach to Zen would not so much look for the "real Zen" (whether conceived as a Romantic ineffable truth or an objective historical narrative) as for what Zen has been and can be to world citizens of the twenty-first century. One's interpretation of Zen cannot but be shaped by one's own pre-verbal understandings of what "truth," "self-overcoming" and "enlightenment" mean, and the contexts and conditions within which it is possible to have "an enlightenment experience."

So, whereas Nietzsche and Zen have been strange bedfellows throughout the twentieth century, perhaps in the twenty-first century a dialogue between them can open up new and liberating insights into the philosophical *áskēsis* that can be discerned in their thought, but that has, in both cases, been undervalued and underemphasized. Even though Zen has been presented to the West by some as an anti-philosophical mysticism, the Zen philosophy contains a philosophical *áskēsis* as well. As Thomas Kasulis notes, the Western popular notion that Zen resists philosophical explanation is more Western than Japanese.[24]

SELF-OVERCOMING WITHOUT A SELF

For Nietzsche, philosophy as *áskēsis* is connected with the notion of self-overcoming. In *Ecce Homo*, he discerns a path of self-overcoming that is reflected in his works, leading up to "*what* I am today, *where* I am today—at a height where I no longer speak with words but with lightning bolts" (EH III TU, 3). For example, he views *Human, All Too Human* and *Daybreak* as overcoming his addiction to idealism and Wagner. About *Human, All Too Human*, he says, "I liberated myself from what in my nature *did not belong to me*" which constituted "progress—*towards myself*" (EH III HAH, 1). Today, many Anglo-American Nietzsche interpreters fail to see this aspect of Nietzsche's philosophy, or choose to ignore it. But recently, this aspect of Nietzsche's philosophy has received more attention. Several studies have appeared that argue that Nietzsche can profitably be read as advocating such a philosophical *áskēsis*. Bruce Benson interprets Nietzsche's *áskēsis* as being aimed at realizing a Dionysian piety: a way of being that fully embraces life. Horst Hutter focuses on the specific ascetic practices that serve as a means for Nietzsche for overcoming decadence. Richard White shows how Nietzsche in his writings sought to provoke a personal sovereignty. Tyler Roberts reads Nietzsche's *áskēsis* as an attempt at postreligious philosophical practice.[25]

The peculiar and paradoxical thing is that both Nietzsche and Zen also deny that any such thing as a self ultimately exists. Their self-overcoming is therefore a self-overcoming without a self. As far as Zen is concerned, this may be obvious: the idea of non-self (*anātman*) is crucial to all Buddhist traditions. But also for Nietzsche, what we call a self is ultimately a fiction. Although in *Schopenhauer as Educator* Nietzsche writes about aspiring to one's true Self, in his later work, self-overcoming turns into self-overcoming without a self, expressed through the cipher of Dionysus, the Greek god of ecstatic self-transcendence. This study will investigate what such a "self-overcoming without a self" could possibly look like. It engages Nietzsche in dialogue with four main representatives of the conglomerate of traditions that we call Zen:

1. The Indian founder of Madhyamaka Buddhism, Nāgārjuna (ca. 150–250 CE), who is, although chronologically a predecessor to Zen, nevertheless traditionally regarded as a patriarch of the Zen tradition. Although Nāgārjuna certainly was a historical figure, not much is known about his life, nor about the exact role he played in the transition from early Buddhism to Mahāyāna.[26] He is widely considered to be the most influential Buddhist philosopher after the Buddha himself.
2. Linji Yixuan (d. 860), one of the classical Chinese Chan masters of the Tang Dynasty, has been the most influential Zen master in further Zen traditions in China, Japan, and Korea. He has been accorded the highest praise within the Zen tradition. According to translator Burton Watson, he is "the oldest and most authentic voice that has come down to us from the early tradition of Chinese Chan or Zen, the fullest exposition of its teachings."[27] Linji has contributed to Zen's reputation for iconoclasm. He famously declared that the Buddhist goals of bodhi (awakening) and nirvana (enlightenment) were hitching posts for donkeys. His most famous injunction is "if you meet the Buddha on the road, kill him." The followers of Linji stressed that Zen was "a separate expression outside the teachings, beyond words and letters," which has co-determined the Western image of Zen as a radical antinomianism and iconoclasm.[28]
3. The thirteenth-century Japanese Zen master Dōgen strongly criticized Linji for his antinomianism and iconoclasm. He stressed that enlightenment is not beyond words and letters but always takes place within words and letters. He also stressed the importance of the body. In some ways, Dōgen can be seen as a Zen Buddhist Nietzsche, critically examining and unmasking cherished notions within the Zen tradition. As a Japanese "master of suspicion," he deconstructs orthodox Zen perspectives on language, thinking, practice, and most of all, enlightenment.[29]
4. The Japanese Zen Buddhist philosopher Keiji Nishitani (1900–1990) studied with Heidegger from 1937 to 1939 and attempted to integrate Zen with Western philosophy. He wrote a study on nihilism, in which he devoted several chapters to an interpretation of Nietzsche's thought informed by his Zen Buddhist background.[30] However, as a contemporary Zen philosopher who attempted to connect Zen Buddhist thought to Western philosophy, Nishitani focused on certain aspects of Zen thought that he thought would be of greater relevance to Westerners.

SUMMARY OF CHAPTERS

Part I (chapters 1 through 3) will set the stage for a cross-cultural dialogue between Nietzsche and Zen. Chapter 1 will briefly recap Nietzsche's own relationship to Buddhism, his status as a transcultural thinker, the way he practiced transcultural philosophy, and why comparing Nietzsche to a non-Western philosophical tradition is in line with his own philosophizing. Chapter 2 will review the research on Nietzsche and Zen so far (give an overview and summarize the basic findings) and indicate where the present study can be situated within the field. Chapter 3 will set out the basic argument and the hermeneutical approach of this study. It will argue that both Nietzsche and Zen can be interpreted as philosophies of self-overcoming. Such a process of self-overcoming has famously been described by Nietzsche in terms of the three transformations of the spirit into camel, lion, and child. However, in this study the Mahāyāna Buddhist hermeneutic of *upāya* will be applied to interpret these transformations as moving from an other-oriented to a self-oriented to a world-oriented way of experiencing reality and the process of self-overcoming itself.

Part II (chapters 4 through 7) will elucidate various practices of self-overcoming. Chapter 4 addresses self-overcoming from an other-oriented perspective. From such a perspective, self-overcoming is connected to a will to truth and takes place in the context of the ascetic ideal. Both Nietzsche and Nāgārjuna criticize their own philosophical tradition for such a will to truth and ascetic ideal. Their critical views with regard to truth (epistemological skepticism) and reality (ontological skepticism) seem to culminate in epistemological nihilism, but as it turns out, they consider it possible to overcome this nihilism. Nietzsche differentiates between a weak, nihilistic skepticism and a strong skepticism that refers to a new truth practice. Nāgārjuna differentiates between conventional and ultimate truth. His notion of emptiness serves as a conventional truth that allows for the realization of ultimate truth. The identity of samsara and nirvana makes room for a radical affirmation of life.

Chapter 5 explores a new truth practice that is aimed not at discovering static truths about reality, but at becoming a truthful person, a "Master of Truth." Such a magisterial conception of truth can be found both in Nietzsche and the Zen tradition, where Nāgārjuna's philosophy of truth is worked out in a Chinese context. In this conception, truth is not representational (knowing that) but performative (knowing how). It is a quality of persons, not of propositions; truth refers to a personal embodiment.

Chapter 6 focuses on practices of embodiment. According to Nietzsche, in matters of knowledge and truth, incorporation plays a very important role.

The constellation of one's physiological drives determines how one views the world and to what extent one is able to refrain from not only distorting one's perception, but to step outside the representational model of knowledge. From such a perspective, the only way for self-overcoming would be to "educate the drives," which would in fact amount to a self-education of the body. Such a self-cultivation of the drives allows one to incorporate truth, become a Master of Truth, and be able to digest "higher" perspectives than before. The Zen tradition presents not only a well-worked out perspective on the theory of such a self-cultivation through the body, but also describes various somatic practices as part of this self-cultivation. For Dōgen, such a somatic practice takes the form of zazen, sitting meditation practice. Nietzsche's self-cultivation and self-overcoming of the body will be compared to Dōgen's notion of zazen as a somatic practice.

Chapter 7 discusses the self-overcoming of the ego. From a naturalistic, non-anthropocentric perspective, self-overcoming refers to an optimal way of functioning without the friction of the conscious "I." There is no unique individual soul that can be liberated, but the multiplicity of drives (taken as an orchestra) performs a beautiful concert. Every drive knows what to play without needing a conductor. The later Nietzsche uses the metaphor of self-forgetfulness to point to self-overcoming. In the post-Zarathustra works we find many passive and even fatalistic formulations suggesting a process of ripening, pregnancy, organic growth, and the absence of struggle, emphasizing the allowance of transcendence and openness. All conscious attempts at self-cultivation actually only interfere with this process. Even the willful attempt at self-overcoming must overcome itself: the self-overcoming of self-overcoming. Dōgen's notion of "forgetting the self" will be used to elucidate such a perspective.

Part III (chapters 8 through 10) addresses the question of a possible end point of self-overcoming. In chapter 8, Nietzsche's ambivalent use of the notion of redemption will be compared to Zen's deconstruction of Buddhist enlightenment.[31] Nietzsche is well-known for his critique of Christian redemption as a symptom of decadence and resentment. But in his work, especially in *Thus Spoke Zarathustra*, an attempt can also be found to define a positive (although skeptical) form of redemption and liberation, centered around incorporating the thought of eternal recurrence and relinquishing an ego-centered perspective. However, in both Nietzsche and Zen there is a tension between an apophatic critique of such a state of liberation and attempts at a kataphatic construction of liberation.

In chapter 9, one of such kataphatic constructions, Nietzsche's notion of the child, will be investigated in dialogue with Dōgen. From a child perspective, self-overcoming is no longer directed toward any particular goal. For

Nietzsche, this constitutes a restoration of the innocence of becoming. In Zen, a similar dynamic can be observed, which Dōgen expresses as the oneness of practice and realization. Chapter 10 investigates Nishitani's interpretation of Nietzsche's child stage as the self-overcoming of the will to power. According to Nishitani, Nietzsche's views on self-overcoming eventually fall short of the Zen Buddhist perspective because he remains mired in the notion of will to power. I will critically discuss this conclusion.

In Part IV (chapters 11 and 12) I argue that, especially in his recognition of the need for a self-overcoming of philosophy, Nietzsche comes closest to the spirit of Zen. Chapter 11 addresses one of Nietzsche's notebook fragments on the notions of exoteric and esoteric in order to advance the argument that Nietzsche regards the will to power as an exoteric notion, an instrument to facilitate the realization of an esoteric Dionysian philosophy. In Buddhist terms, the will to power serves as *upāya*.

The practice of philosophy now comes down to a revaluation of values. In chapter 12, I will interpret Nietzsche's revaluation of all values as a philosophical *áskēsis*. Nietzsche's immoralism and self-overcoming of morality, which are associated with such a revaluation, have been interpreted as "beyond good and evil," just as Zen has been interpreted as antinomian. However, a look at Dōgen's views reveals how "beyond good and evil" can be combined with "the non-production of evil."

NOTES

1. See Thomas H. Brobjer, "Nietzsche's Reading about Eastern Philosophy." *Journal of Nietzsche Studies* 28 (2004): 3–27.

2. Roger-Pol Droit, *The Cult of Nothingness: The Philosophers and the Buddha* (North Carolina: University of North Carolina Press, 2003).

3. Freny Mistry, *Nietzsche and Buddhism: Prolegomenon to a Comparative Study* (Berlin/New York: de Gruyter, 1981) and Robert G. Morrison, *Nietzsche and Buddhism: A Study in Nihilism and Ironic Affinities* (Oxford: Oxford University Press, 1997). Morrison claims that ironically enough, Nietzsche's thought can be interpreted as akin to the early Buddhism that he was familiar with and rejected as a form of passive nihilism. He therefore calls his comparative study "A Study in Ironic Affinities." Another recent collection of essays on Nietzsche and African American thought, Jacqueline Scott and A. Todd Franklin, eds., *Critical Affinities: Nietzsche and African American Thought* (Albany: State University of New York Press, 2006), bears the title "Critical affinities." This study will argue that the affinities between Nietzsche and Zen are more critical than ironic, since they both focus on unmasking and revaluing crucial notions within their respective philosophical traditions.

4. Graham Parkes, ed., *Nietzsche and Asian Thought* (Chicago: University of Chicago Press, 1991), 15.

5. Parkes, *Nietzsche and Asian Thought*, 14.

6. Graham Parkes, "Nietzsche and East Asian Thought: Influences, Impacts, and Resonances," in *The Cambridge Companion to Nietzsche*, eds. Bernd Magnus and Kathleen M. Higgins (Cambridge: Cambridge University Press, 1996), 377.

7. Young, *Nietzsche's Philosophy of Religion*.

8. Benson, *Pious Nietzsche*, xi.

9. Roger T. Ames, "Nietzsche's 'Will to Power' and Chinese 'Virtuality' (*De*): A Comparative Study," in *Nietzsche and Asian Thought*, 132.

10. See Jay L. Garfield, "Epoche and *śūnyatā*: Skepticism East and West," *Philosophy East and West* 40/3 (1990): 285–307.

11. Mahāyāna Buddhism, the term *Hīnayāna* is used pejoratively to refer to those early Buddhist traditions that developed a systematic soteriology (in particular the Sarvāstivādin school). Hīnayāna therefore does not refer to the contemporary Buddhist schools that base themselves on the early Buddhist Theravāda school. Their positions are much more nuanced than the (caricaturized) Hīnayāna views.

12. Very little contemporary biographical information on Bodhidharma is available, and subsequent accounts became layered with legend, but most accounts agree that he was South Indian Tamilian and was a Pallava prince from the kingdom of Kanchipuram, the third son of King Sugandha. Bodhidharma left the kingdom after becoming a Buddhist monk and traveled to Southern China and subsequently relocated northwards. The accounts differ on the date of his arrival, with one early account claiming that he arrived during the Liu Song Dynasty (420–479) and later accounts dating his arrival to the Liang Dynasty (502–557). Bodhidharma was primarily active in the lands of the Northern Wei Dynasty (386–534). Modern scholarship dates him to about the early sixth century.

13. Chan is the Chinese transliteration of *dhyāna*, the Sanskrit term for meditation. In Japan this Chinese term was transliterated as Zen, in Korea as Son. Since the term *Zen* has become well-known in the West, it will be used in this study.

14. Aschheim, *The Nietzsche Legacy in Germany*.

15. E.g., Daisetz Teitaro Suzuki, *An Introduction to Zen Buddhism* (Kyoto: Eastern Buddhist Society, 1934). See André F. M. van der Braak, "Enlightenment revisited: Romantic, historicist, hermeneutic and comparative perspectives on Zen," *Acta Comparanda* 19 (2008): 87–97; Dale S. Wright, *Philosophical Meditations on Zen Buddhism* (Cambridge: Cambridge University Press, 1998).

16. Eugen Herrigel, *Zen in the Art of Archery* (London: Routledge, 1953). For a critical discussion of this work, see Shōji Yamada, "The Myth of Zen in the Art of Archery," *Journal of Japanese Religious Studies* 28/1–2 (2001): 1–30 and Shōji Yamada, *Shots in the Dark: Japan, Zen, and the West* (Chicago: University of Chicago Press, 2009).

17. But Zen was also approached very critically. Arthur Koestler criticized the deliberate obscurity of the Zen texts in his book *The Lotus and the Robot* (New

York: Macmillan, 1961). The Japanese novelist Yukio Mishima portrayed the Zen monastery in his novel *The Temple of the Golden Pavilion* (New York: Knopf, 1959) as a power-infested, authoritarian community. In line with this critical approach, the Chinese historian Hu Shi approached Zen as merely one religious sect among others and attempted to describe the Zen tradition within the context of larger political and social developments in the Chinese historical tradition.

18. Brian Daizen Victoria, *Zen at War* (New York: Weatherhill, 1997).

19. Jim Heisig and John Maraldo, eds., *Rude Awakenings: Zen, the Kyoto School, and the Question of Nationalism* (Honolulu: University of Hawai'i Press, 1995).

20. In a related development, Japanese Zen masters (roshis) came to teach in the West (Yasutani, Maezumi, Shunryu Suzuki, Sasaki), and their Western students became roshis as well (Richard Baker, Robert Aitken, Philip Kapleau, Dennis Merzel, Bernie Glassman, Daido Loori). They emphasized not so much Zen philosophy, like the Beat Zen generation, but Zen as a religion, which included traditionally and culturally mediated meditation practices, such as the sitting practice of zazen and koan practice and all kinds of ritual.

21. In the seventies and eighties, the Japanese Zen scholar Yanagida Seizan gave a new impulse to the philological research of Zen texts. Together with Western students, he carefully researched many Zen texts that had been discovered in the early twentieth century in a cave in Dunhuang. Their results led to a questioning of many established Zen myths and to critical considerations about the nature of the spirituality of Zen.

22. In a recent publication, Steven Heine has attempted to clarify the conflict between the two competing perspectives on Zen that he calls "the traditional Zen narrative" and "historical cultural criticism." See Steven Heine, *Zen Skin, Zen Marrow: Will the Real Zen Buddhism Please Stand Up?* (Oxford: Oxford University Press, 2008). As Heine points out, the Western study of Zen Buddhism has all too often been a reflection of the preoccupations of Western modernity. The critical approach to Zen is part of a reaction to the wider phenomenon of Orientalism, the stereotypical approach of Western scholars to Oriental culture based on thinly disguised, hegemonic agendas. Whereas the colonial West has tended to portray the East as generally inferior and degenerate compared to Western civilization, the field of religious studies (more dominated by the temperament and outlook of Romanticism) has often shown a seemingly opposite pattern of thought. The spirituality of the East is considered superior to Western varieties (reverse Orientalism). Those two opposed perspectives are both a gross distortion, Heine notes: "Buddhism is seen either as a sublime and quaint form of meditative mysticism, based on mind-purification and self-transformation, or as the hollow shell of a sequestered ancient cult that broods on death and decay yet thrives on monastic political intrigue" (Heine, *Zen Skin, Zen Marrow*, 4).

23. Van der Braak, *Enlightenment Revisited.*

24. Thomas P. Kasulis, *Zen Action/Zen Person* (Honolulu: University of Hawai'i Press, 1981), ix.

25. Horst Hutter, *Shaping the Future: Nietzsche's New Regime of the Soul and Its Ascetic Practices* (Lanham, MD: Lexington Books, 2006); Benson, *Pious Nietzsche*; Richard J. White, *Nietzsche and the Problem of Sovereignty* (Urbana/Chicago: University of Illinois Press, 1997); Roberts, *Contesting Spirit.*

26. See Joseph Walser, *Nāgārjuna in Context: Mahāyāna Buddhism and Early Indian Culture* (New York: Columbia University Press, 2005).

27. Burton Watson, transl., *The Zen Teachings of Master Lin-Chi. A Translation of the Lin-chi lu* (New York: Columbia University Press, 1993/1999), ix.

28. This image has been constructed largely through the writings of D. T. Suzuki. But as recent studies by Welter show, the Linji interpretation has taken place through the lens of Japanese sectarian scholarship. As more and more historical material becomes available, it is even unclear which part of his writings can actually be attributed to the historical Linji. See André F. M. van der Braak, "Toward a Philosophy of Chan Enlightenment: Linji's Anti-Enlightenment Rhetoric," *Journal of Chinese Philosophy* 37/2 (June 2010): 231–47.

29. Since the 1970s, the field of Dōgen Studies has exploded with various schools of thought not only in Japan, but also in the West. The orthodox Sōtō Zen academia interprets Dōgen according to the Sōtō orthodoxy in a religious way. In Japan, resistance has arisen from the thinkers of the so-called Critical Buddhism movement, who want to liberate Buddhism from its reactionary status and call for its modernization. In their opinion, Dōgen should primarily be interpreted as an intellectual thinker, not as a meditation master. Western Dōgen studies treat him primarily as a philosophical thinker. For an overview of the various approaches to Dōgen, see Hee-Jin Kim, *Eihei Dōgen—Mystical Realist* (Tucson: University of Arizona Press, 2004), xv–xxii.

30. Nishitani Keiji, *The Self-Overcoming of Nihilism* (Albany: State University of New York Press, 1990).

31. Nietzsche uses the term *Erlösung* which can be translated as either redemption or salvation. In this study, I will use "redemption." See the discussion in chapter 8.

Part I

Setting the Stage

Chapter 1

Nietzsche's Buddhism

> I could become the Buddha of Europe, which actually would be the opposite to the Indian one.[1]

Nietzsche paid, as one of the few Western philosophers, quite serious attention to Buddhism. Johann Figl has documented that for Nietzsche, from an early age on, non-European cultures played an important part in the development of his thought, a development described by Nietzsche himself as "gradually becoming more extensive, transnational, European, trans-European, Oriental [*morgenländisch*]" (KSA 11, 41 [7]).[2]

Thomas Brobjer and others have demonstrated in detail how much Nietzsche actually read about Buddhism, which is, although more than his contemporaries, not as much as one would expect based on Nietzsche's own writings.[3] During his period at Schulpforta, Nietzsche was taught comparative Indo-European studies and comparative study of religions, which also included Buddhism. During the time that he worked on *The Birth of Tragedy* (1870–71), he read the book by C. F. Köppen, *The Religion of the Buddha*, and Max Müller's essays on comparative science of religion.[4] In 1875, Nietzsche read the *Sutta Nipata* from the Buddhist Pali Canon,[5] and in 1882, 1884, and 1888 he read Hermann Oldenberg's classic *Buddha: His Life, his Teaching, his Community.*[6] The term *Buddhismus* occurs 173 times in his work, sometimes in a performative sense and sometimes to elucidate his own positions.[7]

NIETZSCHE'S VIEW OF BUDDHISM

Whereas Nietzsche's early mentors Schopenhauer and Wagner were admirers of Buddhism, Nietzsche was more critical. He rejected early Buddhism as a life-denying, nihilistic answer to the problem of suffering, opposed to his own Dionysian, affirmative philosophy. This is connected to the general perception of Buddhism in his time. As Roger-Pol Droit shows, the nineteenth-century European philosophical imagination saw Buddhism as a religion of annihilation calling for the destruction of the self. In actuality, says Droit, such portrayals were more a reflection of what was happening in Europe at the time (the collapse of traditional hierarchies and values, the specter of atheism, and the rise of racism and social revolts that shook European societies) than an accurate description of Buddhist thought.[8] Nihilism was on the rise in Europe, and Buddhism was seen as a representative of it. Generally no clear distinction was made between early Buddhism and later Mahāyāna Buddhism, and those who did make a distinction considered Mahāyāna as a later degeneration of Buddhism to a kind of folk religion.

Between 1880 and 1887, Nietzsche used the term *Buddhismus* to diagnose the development of nihilism in European culture. He wrote about the inevitable development of a new European Buddhism: a longing for nothingness as a result of decadence. Nietzsche called this a "passive nihilism." Therefore, although he praised it as an aristocratic and non-moralistic religion, he rejected Buddhism as yet another form of nihilism: a philosophy that is hostile to life, that considers life a disease to be cured from.

In *Daybreak* 96, Nietzsche is quite positive about Buddhism. He compares his own time with that in which the Buddha appeared. Only now, he says, Western culture is ripe for a religion such as Buddhism in which self-liberation [*Selbsterlösung*] takes the place of redemption by an external redeemer. Later, he becomes more negative about Buddhism. As a cultural critic, Nietzsche designates the nihilism that permeates European culture as a longing for "nothing," a no longer wanting to act, a "Buddhism of action" (KSA 12, 2 [127]). Nietzsche sees that "Buddhism increases silently everywhere in Europe" (KSA 12, 5 [71]), a passive nihilism and pessimism, a hatred against life. Nietzsche resists such a European Buddhism, although there are also places where the coming of a European Buddhism is described as a possibility, an instrument of culture, a result of the eternal recurrence as the most scientific of all hypotheses (KSA 12, 5 [71]). As a pessimistic philosophy it can function as an indispensable hammer in the hands of the new philosopher (KSA 11, 35 [9]).

For Nietzsche, the Buddha was a great physician that had a great therapy for suffering on offer—a therapy that even worked, rather than the superstitions of

Christianity—but whose views on health Nietzsche considered to be opposed to his own radical affirmation of life, with all joys and sufferings included. "I could become the Buddha of Europe," we read in his notebook fragments, "which actually would be the opposite to the Indian one" (KSA 10, 4 [2]).

Nietzsche compares Christianity and Buddhism in *The Antichrist* 20–23.[9] Although for him both belong together as nihilistic religions, Nietzsche considers Buddhism here as far superior because as a "positivistic religion," it is "a hundred times more realistic" (AC 20). It knows the true causes of suffering and offers a physiological therapy for suffering that works. Christianity, on the other hand, interprets suffering as sin (an imaginary concept according to Nietzsche), and offers no therapy, but only faith, hope, and love as a bandage. Buddhism reaches its goal in contrast to Christianity, which considers the highest form unattainable, a gift, grace. As Nietzsche summarizes, "Buddhism doesn't promise but delivers, Christianity promises everything but *doesn't deliver anything*" (AC 42). Whereas Buddhism fights resentment, Christianity originates from it. Nietzsche refers to the famous quote from the Buddhist writing the *Dhammapada*: "Not through enmity does enmity come to an end."[10] Buddhism knows gratitude rather than rancor (KSA 13, 14 [91]).

Nietzsche's comparison in *The Antichrist* 20–23 strikes many commentators as an unfair one. He takes Buddhism as an ideal type, focusing on its founder, Buddha, as an idealized figure, and compares it to the historical manifestations of Paulinian Christianity (leaving founding figure Jesus aside).[11] Indeed, Nietzsche's remarks on Christianity and Buddhism are in no way an objective attempt at a comparative science of religion based on scholarly sources. Although Sommer traces various of Nietzsche's remarks on Buddhism to Max Müller's essay *On Buddhism*[12] and Oldenberg's book *Buddha*, Nietzsche's methodology is very different from that of Max Müller, who transposed the comparative method from linguistics to the science of religion.[13] Nietzsche's aim, rather, is to show how two nihilistic religions have found very different strategies to deal with decadence, whereby he stresses the similarities between the Buddhist therapy and his own. His description, for example, of Buddha's hygiene (fresh air, exercise, balanced diet, no alcohol) matches his own recommendations in *Ecce Homo* (EH I, 6).

QUESTIONING ONE'S "OWN" FROM THE PERSPECTIVE OF THE FOREIGN

Eberhard Scheiffele discusses a crucial aspect of Nietzsche's hermeneutics.[14] By inhabiting "strange" or "foreign" perspectives on what seems old and familiar, Nietzsche seeks again and again to render strange what we consider to be our own. Scheiffele focuses not so much on Nietzsche's perspectivism as an epistemological theory, but on his perspectival *way* of thinking. A primary feature of Nietzsche's "perspectivism in action" is "the estranging [*das Fremdmachen*] of what is one's own by questioning it from behind [*Hinterfragen*], from the perspective of the foreign."[15] Nietzsche's "hermeneutics of suspicion" aims to get behind the tradition by stepping out of its horizon and subvert it by questioning it from behind. Nietzsche tries to get behind his own tradition through a reversal of perspectives.

On the one hand, Nietzsche stresses that in an encounter with what is foreign, we make it our own by incorporating it. This idea of incorporation [*Einverleibung*] plays a central role in Nietzsche's thought (see chapter 6). On the other hand, however, Nietzsche takes what we consider to be our own, in all its apparent familiarity, and makes it foreign by critically approaching it from foreign perspectives. Nietzsche sees himself on the one hand as a philologist who is able to read the text of European culture better than anyone else, and on the other hand as a physician of culture, intent on saving Europe from the viral infection called Christianity (in this role he forcefully denounces Christianity and European culture).[16]

As Scheiffele remarks, although Nietzsche usually ranks the foreign higher, his concern lies for the most part with his "own." Through comparison with the foreign he exposes deficiencies and weaknesses that can't be observed from within one's own horizon.[17] Nietzsche's work hardly contains any remarks on Buddhism that are not somehow related back to Christianity or European culture. He is not interested in Buddhism for its own sake: he appropriates it as part of his hermeneutical strategy of criticizing his own from the perspective of the foreign. Nietzsche's partial and idealized description of Buddhism is nothing more than an instrument for him.

Nietzsche's interest in Buddhism doesn't aim at an objective understanding of it. He is not interested in purely scientific investigation into foreign cultures, nor is he interested in establishing a science of comparative religion. He is not all that interested in the foreign itself: it only allows him to take up a standpoint from which to look back at his own European culture.[18]

NIETZSCHE AS A TRANSCULTURAL THINKER

According to Figl, Nietzsche's development as a philosopher of culture runs from monocentric (the perspective of his own German or European culture) to polycentric (a legitimate plurality of great cultures).[19] Initially he attempts to revitalize German culture through a confrontation with ancient Greek culture. But later on, Nietzsche not only aims at transcending German culture by becoming a "good

European," but even aims to transcend European culture through a comparison with non-European cultural perspectives. In 1884 he writes in his notebook, "I must learn to think *more orientally* about philosophy and knowledge. *Oriental* [*Morgenländischer*] *overview of Europe*" (KSA 11, 26 [317]).

In a letter from 1888 to Paul Deussen, Nietzsche boasts of his "trans-European eye" that allows him to see the parallels between Indian and Western philosophy: "It belongs to the most essential fostering of my freedom from prejudice (my "trans-European eye") that your existence and work remind me again and again of the one great parallel to our European philosophy" (KGW III 5, 221).

Nietzsche often comments that he uses this trans-European (or even trans-Asiatic) eye to gain a critical distance from which to criticize and enhance his own European culture. Therefore, he can be considered a transcultural thinker who confronts European and non-European perspectives with each other in order to go beyond cultural assumptions and limitations. Figl describes Nietzsche's hermeneutical approach as a transcultural hermeneutics.[20] According to Figl, in the development of his transcultural hermeneutics, Nietzsche makes use of two methods: genealogy and comparison.[21] In his genealogical approach, Nietzsche deconstructs fixed cultural self-interpretations by deriving them from their origins. His comparative approach adds further argumentation and aids in the process of deconstruction. The two methods are therefore connected.

In *Human, All Too Human*, Nietzsche speaks about his contemporary culture as an age of comparison in which the various world views, morals, and cultures can be compared and experienced side by side (HAH I, 23). Through comparison it becomes possible to incorporate more perspectives and to loosen one's attachment to one's own culturally bound perspective. One way to do this is to

> become a stranger to one's time and float back from its shore onto the ocean of past world views. Looking back at the shore from there, one surveys its entirety for the first time, and when one approaches it again, one has the advantage to understand it better as a whole than those that never left it. (HAH I, 616)

As part of a similar hermeneutical strategy, Nietzsche criticizes European culture and religion by embarking on a journey into non-European territory, from which he can survey the European tradition. Nietzsche speaks about the need for travel in order to gain knowledge:

> Direct self-observation is not nearly sufficient for us to know ourselves: we require history, for the past continues to flow within us in a hundred waves; we ourselves are, indeed, nothing but that which at every moment we experience of this continued flowing [. . .] To understand history [. . .] we have

> to *travel* [. . .] to other nations [. . .] and especially to where human beings have taken off the garb of Europe or have not yet put it on. But there exists a *subtler* art and object of travel, which does not always require us to move from place to place [. . .] He who, after long practice in this art of travel, has become a hundred-eyed Argos [. . .] will rediscover the adventurous travels of his ego [. . .] in Egypt and Greece, Byzantium and Rome, France and Germany [. . .] in the Renaissance and the Reformation, at home and abroad, indeed in the sea, the forests, in the plants and in the mountains. Thus self-knowledge will become knowledge of everything [*All-Erkenntniss*] with regard to all that is past. (HAH II/1, 223)

According to Figl, Nietzsche's transcultural hermeneutics serves to express a new affirmative philosophy, based on a new transcultural anthropology. As a physician of culture, Nietzsche searches for a new image of what healthy man can be, unrestricted by the limitations of European culture: "Knowledge of non-European cultures and religions serves the conception of an anthropology that not only questions the European moral tradition, but ultimately aims at a transcultural image of man and society."[22]

This transcultural horizon is, according to Figl, an essential characteristic of Nietzsche's philosophy. Only when one steps out of the horizon of one's own situation can one see its overall structure. Not only does one gain distance in this way, one is able to achieve a new perspective from a greater height. The existential confrontation with the foreign serves Nietzsche's own affirmative philosophy. Nietzsche acknowledges that some of the flaws of the Western philosophical tradition are perhaps irremediably connected to the structure of Western language families. In *Beyond Good and Evil*, he speculates that in non-Western languages it may be better possible to avoid some of the superstitions that Western thought has fallen prey to:

> It is precisely where a relationship between languages is present that we cannot avoid, thanks to the common philosophy of grammar—I mean thanks to the unconscious mastery and guidance exercised by the same grammatical functions—everything has been prepared from the beginning for a similar development and order of philosophical systems, just as the road to certain other possibilities of interpreting the world seems sealed off. [. . .] There will be a greater probability that philosophers from the region of the Ural-Altaic language (in which the idea of the subject is most poorly developed) will look differently "into the world" and will be found on other pathways than Indo-Germans or Muslims. (BGE 20)

Japanese is generally counted among the Ural-Altaic languages, which Nietzsche may have known as a philologist with some interest in Japan.[23] As Parkes notes, the Japanese language indeed lacks a well-developed concept of the subject, which may be conducive to styles of philosophizing in which the metaphysical subject is absent.[24] Rolf Elberfeld has called attention to the grammatical form of the middle voice in the Japanese language, which allows for philosophical expressions that do not assume the division of subject and object.[25]

This study aims to take up the challenge of *Beyond Good and Evil.*

NOTES

1. KSA 10, 4 [2].

2. Johann Figl, "Nietzsche's Early Encounters with Asian Thought," in *Nietzsche and Asian Thought*, 51–63; Johann Figl, "Nietzsche's Encounter with Buddhism," in *Void and Fullness in the Buddhist, Hindu and Christian Traditions. Sūnya-Pūrna-Pleroma*, ed. B. Bäumer and J. Dupuch, 225–37 (New Delhi: D. K. Printworld, 2005); Johann Figl, *Nietzsche und die Religionen. Transkulturelle Perspektiven seines Bildungs- und Denkweges* (Berlin/New York: de Gruyter, 2007).

3. Brobjer, *Nietzsche's Reading about Eastern Philosophy*. Mistry, *Nietzsche and Buddhism*; Morrison, *Nietzsche and Buddhism*; Mervyn Sprung, "Nietzsche's Trans-European Eye," in *Nietzsche and Asian Thought*, 76–90. See also Thomas H. Brobjer, "Nietzsche's Reading About China and Japan," *Nietzsche-Studien* 34 (2005): 329–36.

4. Carl Friedrich Köppen, *Die Religion des Buddha. Vol. 1. Die Religion des Buddha und ihre Entstehung* (Berlin: F. Schneider, 1857); Max Müller, "Über den Buddhismus," in *Essays, Bd. 1: Beitrage zur vergleichenden Religionswissenschaft* (Leipzig: Engelmann, 1869), 162–204. Nietzsche borrowed Köppen's book from the Basel library on October 25, 1870. It presented Buddhism especially as an ethical empiricism, and was one of the most widely read and commentarized works on Buddhism in Europe in the 1860s and 1870s. See Droit, *The Cult of Nothingness*, 133f.

5. He probably read the abridged translation into English by Sir Mutu Coomaraswamy, *Sutta Nipâta, or Dialogues and Discourses of Gotama Buddha* (London: Trübner, 1874).

6. Hermann Oldenberg, *Buddha; Sein Leben, seine Lehre, seine Gemeinde* (Berlin: W. Hertz, 1881).

7. See André F. M. van der Braak, "Buddhismus," in *Nietzsche-Wörterbuch: Abbreviatur–Einfach*, ed. Paul J. M. van Tongeren, Gerd Schank, and Herman Siemens (Berlin/New York: de Gruyter, 2004), 419–33.

8. Droit, *The Cult of Nothingness.*

9. Originally, AC 20–23 were preceded by the heading "Buddhismus und Christenthum" (KSA, Kommentar zu Band 6, 14, 440). For a detailed analysis of these sections, see Andreas Urs Sommer, *Friedrich Nietzsches 'Der Antichrist.' Ein philosophisch-historischer Kommentar* (Basel: Schwabe, 2000), 203–31.

10. He probably read this quote in Oldenberg, *Buddha*, 299; see also Oldenberg, *Buddha*, 298 for the Buddhist critique of resentment.

11. Sommer, *Friedrich Nietzsches 'Der Antichrist,'* 208. However, the gap between the founding figures (Jesus, Buddha) and the religions established on them is not as great in the case of Buddhism as in Christianity. In Christianity the gap amounts to a complete reversal according to Nietzsche (Skowron, personal communication).

12. Müller, *Über den Buddhismus*, 162–204. See Sommer, *Friedrich Nietzsches 'Der Antichrist,'* 204.

13. Figl, *Nietzsche und die Religionen*, 332.

14. Eberhard Scheiffele, "Questioning One's 'Own' from the Perspective of the Foreign," in *Nietzsche and Asian Thought*, 31–47.

15. Scheiffele, *Questioning One's "Own,"* 32.

16. Figl, *Nietzsche und die Religionen*, 336.

17. Scheiffele, *Questioning One's "Own,"* 41f.

18. Scheiffele gives various examples of Nietzsche's transcultural hermeneutics. His first example is Nietzsche's critique of the Germans. Nietzsche uses the merits and strengths of the French to point out the deficiencies and weaknesses of the Germans (Scheiffele, *Questioning One's "Own,"* 33ff). His second example is Nietzsche's critique of Christianity by contrasting its negative qualities with the positive qualities of Greek religion, as embodied in the mythical figure of Dionysus (Scheiffele, *Questioning One's "Own,"* 37).

19. Figl, *Nietzsche und die Religionen*, 340.

20. For more on Nietzsche's transcultural hermeneutics, see André F. M. van der Braak, "Nietzsche's transcultural hermeneutics: proliferation versus fusion of horizons," in *Nietzsche y la Hermenéutica*, eds. Francisco Arenas-Dolz, Luca Giancristofaro, and Paolo Stellini (Valencia: Nau Llibres, 2007), 79–88.

21. Figl, *Nietzsche und die Religionen*, 329–37.

22. Figl, *Nietzsche und die Religionen*, 337.

23. In an 1885 letter to his sister, Nietzsche writes, "If only I were in better health and had sufficient income, I would, simply in order to attain great serenity, emigrate to Japan" (KGW III 3, 127).

24. Parkes, *Nietzsche and East Asian Thought: Influences, Impacts, and Resonances*, 360.

25. Rolf Elberfeld, "The Middle Voice of Emptiness: Nishida and Nishitani," in *Japanese and Continental Philosophy: Conversations with the Kyoto School*, eds. Bret W. Davis, Brian Schroeder, and Jason M. Wirth, 269–85 (Bloomington & Indianapolis: Indiana University Press, 2011).

Chapter 2

Nietzsche and Zen—Previous Research

This chapter gives a brief overview of the research presented on Nietzsche and (Zen) Buddhism so far and sums up the "ironic affinities" that have been pointed out. This is a complex field due to the wide range of Nietzsche interpretations, the heterogeneity of the Zen tradition, and the range of philosophical traditions from out of which Nietzsche and Zen have been compared (Western, Japanese, and Chinese). I will therefore divide my survey of the comparative literature on Nietzsche and (Zen) Buddhism so far into four categories:

1. Western studies that compare Nietzsche and early Buddhism.
2. Western studies that compare Nietzsche and Mahāyāna Buddhism, and recount the extensive Japanese and Chinese Nietzsche reception.
3. Western and Chinese studies that focus on Nietzsche and Daoism. Whereas Western studies focus on transindividuality, Chinese studies emphasize the individualist and humanist aspects of Nietzsche's thought that make him interesting and valuable for contemporary Chinese thought.
4. Japanese comparative studies on Zen and Nietzsche, which often use Zen Buddhist philosophy as a measuring rod against which Nietzsche's philosophy, although a step in the right direction compared to Western philosophy in general, is ultimately found to be falling short.

WESTERN STUDIES ON NIETZSCHE AND EARLY BUDDHISM

Apart from an abominable early study on Nietzsche and Buddhism by Ladner in 1933 which was mostly out to prove that Nietzsche misunderstood Buddhism, two monographs by Mistry and Morrison, both titled *Nietzsche and Buddhism*, have dominated the field.[1] Both Mistry's and Morrison's comparisons are limited to early Buddhism, the only form of Buddhism that was known well in Europe in Nietzsche's time, and which Nietzsche rejected as a form of nihilism, as we have seen in chapter 1.

Mistry's work highlights many systematic similarities in the philosophies of Nietzsche and Buddhism. Since her findings serve as a basis for further comparison, we will summarize them below.[2] In chapter one (*The Overcoming of Metaphysics and Idealism*), she starts out with Nietzsche's rejection of metaphysical absolutism and truth, as he found those in Indian Vedanta and in Schopenhauer. Although the early Nietzsche followed Schopenhauer in confounding Buddhism and Vedanta, Mistry claims that the later Nietzsche recognized Buddhism to be a revolutionary movement against both the metaphysical absolutism of Vedanta and the resulting skepticism of some other Indian schools:

> In Buddhism's rational confrontation with the prevailing intellectual events that had culminated in a skepticism regarding the concept of deity and attendant metaphysical equivalents, on the other hand, Nietzsche recognized a highly consequential philosophic revolution to which he calls attention with surprising frequency.[3]

Mistry sees a parallel between Theravāda Buddhism's rejection of Upanishadic esotericism and Nietzsche's rejection of the otherworldly spiritualism of Christianity. Nietzsche's death of God corresponds to the godlessness of the Buddha.

In chapter two (*The Analysis of Personality and Universe*), Mistry shows how both Buddhism and Nietzsche reject the notion of a permanent individual self. Nietzsche replaces notions of self and substance by the notion of will to power in which the individual is conceived as a multiplicity of forces and drives. This corresponds to the Buddhist analysis of the personality as made up of five aggregates (*skandhas*). Just as Nietzsche criticizes the Christian soul atomism and essentialist notions of the free will, Buddhism declares the skandha's to be empty of a personal, abiding self (*ātman*). Mistry also compares Nietzsche's perspective on the world as will to power with the Buddhist notion of dependent origination (*pratītya-samutpāda*). Both perspectives reject a substantialist perspective on reality.

In chapter three (*The Experiment with Truth and Reason*) Mistry points out how Nietzsche and Buddhism both reject revealed truth. Although they use reason as a way to self-overcoming, they both stress an experimental, empirical, pragmatic approach.[4] Both are aware of the insufficiencies of dialectical reasoning. According to Nietzsche's perspectivism, there are no facts, only interpretations. Buddhism prefers a perspectival vision on reality as well, away from the extreme perspectives of annihilation and eternalism. Mistry also notes a difference however: Nietzsche insists that all perspectives that make up a world of opposites be admitted in the total affirmation of reality.[5] Early Buddhism, on the other hand, attempts to overcome contradiction altogether: nirvana stands above the world of contradiction. Mistry is right about noting this difference; in the Zen tradition, however, contradiction is not seen as something that could and should be overcome. This is exactly one of the reasons why Zen is a more suitable partner for a dialogue with Nietzsche than early Buddhism.

In chapter four (*On Suffering*), Mistry discusses the attitude toward suffering in Nietzsche and Buddhism. A much heard objection to a comparison between Nietzsche and Buddhism is that they differ widely in their attitude to suffering: Buddhism is about overcoming suffering, whereas Nietzsche aimed at affirming suffering. Nietzsche himself opposed his own practice of active nihilism to what he perceived as the Buddhist passive nihilism, aimed at minimizing suffering. Mistry argues that Nietzsche's criticisms of Buddhist life-denying negative morality should be interpreted as not so much directed against Buddhism per se, but as "negative reactions to the 'cult' of Buddhism as Nietzsche found it fostered by the worldview of a Schopenhauer or a Wagner."[6] Nietzsche's emphasis on a will to suffering and the transfiguration of suffering seems opposed to the Buddhist four noble truths: (1) life is suffering (*duhkha*), (2) caused by greed and desire (*tanhā*); (3) there is a way out of suffering (*nirvana*); (4) this can be realized by the eightfold path. Mistry shows, however, that Nietzsche's interpretation of the Buddhist view of suffering is a misconstruction and that the response to suffering in Nietzsche and Buddhism is much more consonant than Nietzsche would have us believe.[7] Moreover, it is inadequate to translate the term *duhkha* by suffering, misery, or pain[8]; it refers to an experienced sense of life (including all its pleasures and pains) being unsatisfactory.

In chapter five (*The Ethics of the Eternal Recurrence*), Mistry argues that although Nietzsche himself considered his notion of eternal recurrence the reverse of the Indian form of eternal recurrence, in both Nietzsche and Buddhism the notion of eternal recurrence aims at perfect activity in this present existence. Chapter six (*The Transfiguration of Suffering and Nirvana*) argues that both Nietzsche and Buddhism aim at redemption in this world through the creative transformation of suffering. Mistry shows that Nietzsche's misconstruction of the Buddhist nirvana as nihilism, annihilation, and the negation of the will to live was based on Schopenhauer and Köppen[9] and concludes that "Nietzsche's personal philosophy of overcoming is intrinsically affiliated with, not dissociated from Buddhist nirvana."[10] She specifies: "Both philosophies inculcate war against the self for the sake of self-culture; both stress in this process the discovery of a joy that is greater than suffering and therewith perhaps the worthiest acknowledgement of the worth of suffering."[11] Therefore, Mistry concludes, Nietzsche's Dionysian philosophy is commensurate with the Buddhist philosophy of transformation: "The perspective of Dionysian man, necessarily affirmative of suffering as also superior to it, is in essence commensurate with the Buddhist axiom of the necessity of transforming dukkha into nirvana."[12]

Morrison's study focuses on Nietzsche's and Buddhist attempts to overcome nihilism. He attempts to show that there are ironic, unintended affinities between Nietzsche's philosophy and the Buddhism that he rejected. He focuses on the will to power and the process of self-overcoming in Nietzsche's philosophy. He compares these notions with the Buddhist notions of *tanhā* (greed or desire) and *citta-bhāvanā* (the practice of mental cultivation). He removes their traditional, more limited meaning in order to place these concepts in a more Nietzschean framework. *Tanhā* is usually described as the fundamental impulse of desire that causes suffering, a fundamental obstacle on the spiritual path to be overcome. Morrison however describes *tanhā*, along the lines of the Greek notion of *eros*, as the fundamental set of human drives that can be used in skillful or unskillful ways. He draws a parallel with the will to power that describes the world as a constellation of underlying drives. He describes *citta-bhāvanā* as the sublimation of harmful drives and the cultivation of healthy drives, as a practical elaboration of what Nietzsche himself only alluded to in vague and general terms. Reviewer Graham Parkes is critical of Morrison with regard to this comparison. Their discussion will be addressed in chapters 6 and 7.

WESTERN STUDIES ON NIETZSCHE AND MAHĀYĀNA BUDDHISM

Graham Parkes' seminal collection of essays *Nietzsche and Asian Thought* contains, apart from articles on the reception of Nietzsche's thought in China and Japan and the influence of Indian thought on Nietzsche, several contributions that highlight possible affinities between Nietzsche and Mahāyāna Buddhism. Glen Martin compares Nietzsche's ideas with those of Nāgārjuna (see chapter 4). Ryōgi Ōkōchi articulates Nietzsche's understanding of nature against the background of the Daoist Laozi, the medieval Japanese Buddhism of Shinran, and Nishida and Nishitani. Kōgaku Arifuku compares Nietzsche's ideas about the body with those of Dōgen (see chapter 6). Roger Ames highlights some cosmological aspects of Nietzsche's notion of will to power by comparing it to the Daoist notion of *de* (power or virtuosity). Such a cosmological interpretation of the will to power as a "cosmic body," which is suggested by the articles of Arifuku and Ames, will be further worked out in chapter 7. Muneto Sonoda compares Zarathustra's rhetoric of silence with that of the authors of the Mahāyāna Buddhist sutras.[13]

Michael Skowron wrote several articles on Nietzsche and Buddhism that were published together as *Nietzsche, Buddha, Zarathustra: Eine West-Ost Konfiguration*.[14] Manu Bazzano published *Buddha is Dead: Nietzsche and the Dawn of a European Zen*, an aphoristic work on Nietzsche and Zen in which he sees Nietzsche's thought as a helpful contribution toward the development of a European Zen.[15] Bazzano makes it clear, however, that his book is not intended per se as an academic study. Another recent non-academic study on Nietzsche and Zen is the French *Nietzsche l'Eveillé* (Nietzsche, the Awakened One) in which Nietzsche's thought is compared to that of Dōgen, however without much reference to secondary literature.[16]

WESTERN AND CHINESE STUDIES ON NIETZSCHE AND DAOISM

As the contributions to *Nietzsche and Asian Thought* attest to, Nietzsche has been extensively studied not only in the West but also in Asia, particularly in China and Japan. Hans-Georg Moeller has given an overview of the comparative studies on Nietzsche and Chinese thought, which often take the form of comparing Nietzsche to early Daoism, particularly the Daoist thinker Zhuangzi (ca. 4th century BCE).[17] His work, also called the *Zhuangzi*, was highly regarded by Chinese Buddhist thinkers, especially those of the Chan School, and also became very important for the development of Japanese Zen. As Parkes notes, the *Zhuangzi* resonates profoundly with Nietzsche's styles and ideas, a resonance that he further explored in two comparative studies.[18] Other comparative studies on Nietzsche and Zhuangzi have been undertaken by Ames, Chen, and more recently, Shang.[19]

Moeller points out an interesting dichotomy between Chinese and Western types of "Sino-Nietzscheanism." Although both claim to discover affinities between Nietzschean and Daoist thought, these affinities are of a very different nature. Chinese interpreters of Nietzsche (Moeller takes the eminent Chinese Daoist thinker and Nietzsche scholar Guying Chen as an example) tend to read Nietzsche as an "individualist," in line with earlier Western existentialist and humanist Nietzsche interpretations (e.g. Walter Kaufmann's influential interpretation): "The 'individualist' Nietzsche was quite compatible with the search for an 'icon' of modern individualism that might provide some orientation within the quest of modernizing and strengthening the Chinese nation and culture."[20]

Such an individualist reading of Nietzsche allows Chen to read Zhuangzi as an individualist as well. Western Nietzsche interpreters, however, no longer read Nietzsche primarily as an existentialist, but more as a predecessor of postmodern thought—a "pre-postmodernist." Western Nietzscheans with an interest in Daoism therefore use Nietzsche's negation of individuality to come to non-individualist readings of early Daoism.[21] Günter Wohlfart, for example, points out interesting parallels between Nietzsche's criticism of the subject and early Daoist criticism of the "I"—parallels that also apply to a comparison between Nietzsche and Zen. He compares Nietzsche's critique of the individual with Daoist notions such as "no I" [*wu shen*] in the Laozi and "no self" [*wu ji*] and the "forgetting of the ego" [*sang wo*] in the Zhuangzi.[22] Such Daoist notions of no-self obviously went together well with the Buddhist notion of *anātman* and were taken up by Zen.

Graham Parkes also believes that Nietzsche and Zhuangzi share a multi-perspectivism that transcends the unity of the individual and overcomes an anthropocentric worldview. As Western "Sino-Nietzscheans," Wohlfart and Parkes are particularly interested in how both Nietzsche and early Daoism overcome subjectivism, individualism, anthropocentrism, and humanism. For them, especially such "negative" parallels make Nietzsche and Zhuangzi so interesting for today's philosophical discourse.

So, whereas the Chinese Sino-Nietzscheans detect a strong individualism and existentialism in both Nietzsche and early Daoism, for Western Sino-Nietzscheans it is exactly the overcoming of an individualist psychology and an anthropocentric worldview that makes a comparison between Nietzsche and Zhuangzi so interesting. Moeller explains this difference in cultural terms:

> From a Chinese perspective, notions of individuality appear more "provocative," "novel," and "exotic" than from a Western one. [. . .] Thus, some Chinese philosophers tended to be particularly interested in such "modern" aspects as "individualism" when they read Western philosophers. From this perspective, a thinker such as Nietzsche becomes all the more interesting the more "individualist" he is supposed to be. [. . .] For [Western Sino-Nietzscheans], a thinker like Nietzsche is not so much "revolutionary" because of his modern features, but because of those features that promise to overcome modernity [. . .] the anti-individualist elements of Nietzschean thought become more attractive and are perceived as more advanced than the "individualist" ones. [. . .] While for a Chinese "Sino-Nietzscheanist" Nietzsche's "exotic" quality may be his "individualism," a Western "Sino-Nietzschean" will find Nietzsche's anti-individualism to be "exotic."[23]

Moeller concludes that both Chinese and Western Sino-Nietzscheanism may be relevant since Nietzsche, as a multi-perspectivist, may well allow for many different and even opposing and contradicting perspectives on his thought.

NIETZSCHE, THE KYOTO SCHOOL AND ZEN

Nietzsche's thought has been extensively studied and interpreted in Japan. The Meiji restoration of 1868 led to an import of Western culture in Japan, including Western philosophy, which mostly meant German philosophy. Japanese intellectuals attempted to bring about a synthesis between East and West based on a loyalty to their own traditions and a committed openness to Western traditions.

In the departments of philosophy and religion at the State University of Kyoto, a group of Japanese philosophers tried to express Zen Buddhist thought in Western philosophical concepts. The initial inspiration of this new movement, which came to be known as the Kyoto School, was Kitarō Nishida, widely acknowledged as the foremost modern philosopher of Japan, who took his inspiration from phenomenology and William James. Nishida's student Keiji Nishitani was very well read in Nietzsche. Nishitani's Nietzsche interpretation has been very influential in comparative studies on Nietzsche and Zen and will be discussed in chapter 10. Other Japanese philosophers that have published on Nietzsche are Abe, Arifuku, and Ōkōchi.[24] The American philosopher and sympathizer with the Kyoto School Bret Davis has followed on from Nishitani in his article *Zen after Zarathustra* (see chapter 10).[25]

It was especially Nishitani who engaged with Nietzsche's project of overcoming decadence and nihilism. Nishitani sought throughout his work a resolution to the problem of self-overcoming. The Western formulation of the problem was flawed, he argued, because the search for self-overcoming remained strictly within the realm of the cognitive, the logocentric, and the rational. Zen could enrich the search because the breakthrough sought through Zen meditation was one that involved the total person and yielded truths about the nature of the self that went beyond the cognitive to produce a total experiential realization of the self.[26]

Generally speaking, the motivation of the Japanese thinkers of the Kyoto school was to make Zen Buddhist philosophy more accessible to the West, or even to present an apology for Zen. However, their suggestion that Zen philosophy is uniquely suited to facilitate a meeting of East and West and can serve as a remedy for Western nihilism has been criticized as a form of reverse Orientalism. Others have objected that the Kyoto School uses a too schematic opposition of East and West. Jim Heisig, for example, has complained that the East, which the Kyoto School sets up against the West, has been a construction: "At best, it is one constellation of a heritage too long and too plural to be represented fairly by Japan."[27]

The current study on Nietzsche and Zen can be firmly placed in the Western Sino-Nietzschean camp: the parallels between Nietzsche and Zen that will be investigated are especially about a non-anthropocentric, non-essentialist, and non-teleological perspective on the process of self-overcoming. However, I will argue that Nietzsche is more than only a pre-postmodernist; he is also a "post-premodernist" who envisions a revaluation of all values as a return to a pre-Christian value system. Moreover, as this overview has shown, Nietzsche has often been used by Buddhist interpreters in order to prove the superiority of Buddhist thought. This study wants to do justice to both Nietzsche and Zen in the complexity, plurality, and differentiality of their thought.

NOTES

1. Max Ladner, *Nietzsche und der Buddhismus. Kritische Betrachtungen eines Buddhisten* (Zürich: Juchli-Beck, 1933); Mistry, *Nietzsche and Buddhism*; Morrison, *Nietzsche and Buddhism.*

2. Reviewer Graham Parkes considers Mistry's work indeed a useful prolegomenon to further study: "Mistry's contention that the affinities between the Buddhist and Nietzschean paths to self-overcoming are surprisingly numerous and by no means merely superficial is convincingly argued, and her book therefore constitutes—as its subtitle suggests it is intended to—a powerful stimulus for further comparative studies" (Graham Parkes, "Nietzsche and Early Buddhism," *Philosophy East and West* 50/2 (2000), 257).

3. Mistry, *Nietzsche and Buddhism*, 35.

4. Mistry, *Nietzsche and Buddhism*, 92.

5. Mistry, *Nietzsche and Buddhism*, 103.

6. Mistry, *Nietzsche and Buddhism*, 115.

7. Mistry, *Nietzsche and Buddhism*, 116.

8. Mistry, *Nietzsche and Buddhism*, 121.

9. Mistry, *Nietzsche and Buddhism*, 178f.

10. Mistry, *Nietzsche and Buddhism*, 188.

11. Mistry, *Nietzsche and Buddhism*, 194.

12. Mistry, *Nietzsche and Buddhism*, 194f.

13. Martin, Ōkōchi, Arifuku, Ames, and Sonoda all appear in Parkes, *Nietzsche and Asian Thought.*

14. Michael Skowron, "Nietzsches Weltliche Religiosität und ihre Paradoxien," *Nietzsche-Studien* 31 (2002): 1–39; Michael Skowron, *Nietzsche, Buddha, Zarathustra: Eine West-Ost Konfiguration* (Daegu: Kyungpook National University Press, 2006).

15. Manu Bazzano, *Buddha Is Dead: Nietzsche and the Dawn of European Zen* (Brighton/Portland: Sussex Academic Press, 2006).

16. Yannis Constantinidès and Damien MacDonald, *Nietzsche l'Éveillé* (Paris: Ollendorff & Desseins, 2009).

17. Hans-Georg Moeller, "The "Exotic" Nietzsche—East and West," *Journal of Nietzsche Studies* 28 (2004): 57–69.

18. Parkes, *Nietzsche and East Asian Thought: Influences, Impacts, and Resonances*, 376; Graham Parkes, "The Wandering Dance: Chuang-Tzu and Zarathustra," *Philosophy East and West* 29/3 (1983): 235–50.

19. Ames, *Nietzsche's "Will to Power" and Chinese "Virtuality"*; Guying Chen, "Zhuang Zi and Nietzsche: Plays of Perspectives," in *Nietzsche and Asian Thought*, 115–29; Ge Ling Shang, *Liberation as Affirmation: The Religiosity of Zhuangzi and Nietzsche* (Albany: State University of New York Press, 2006). For a review of Shang, *Liberation as Affirmation*, see Michael Skowron, *Rezensionen*.

20. Moeller, *The "Exotic" Nietzsche*, 61f.

21. Moeller, *The "Exotic" Nietzsche*, 63.

22. Günter Wohlfart, "The Death of the Ego: An Analysis of the "I" in Nietzsche's Unpublished Fragments," *Journal of Chinese Philosophy* 26:3 (September 1999), 332.

23. Moeller, *The "Exotic" Nietzsche*, 65.

24. Ryogi Ōkōchi, "Nietzsches *amor fati* im Lichte von Karma des Buddhismus," *Nietzsche-Studien* 1 (1972): 36–94; Ryogi Ōkōchi, *Wie man wird, was man ist. Gedanken zu Nietzsche aus östlicher Sicht* (Darmstadt: Wissenschaftliche Buchgesellschaft, 1985); Masao Abe, *Zen and Western Thought* (Honolulu: University of Hawai'i Press, 1985).

25. Bret W. Davis, "Zen after Zarathustra: The Problem of the Will in the Confrontation between Nietzsche and Buddhism," *Journal of Nietzsche Studies* 28 (2004): 89–138.

26. As Bret Davis notes, even though Nishitani described his own work as coming from "the standpoint of Zen," he can only be considered a Zen Buddhist thinker in the sense of having critically and creatively developed the Zen tradition in philosophical dialogue with Western thought. Bret W. Davis, "The Kyoto School" in *The Stanford Encyclopedia of Philosophy (Summer 2010 Edition)*, ed. Edward N. Zalta (http://plato.stanford.edu/archives/sum2010/entries/kyoto-school).

27. James W. Heisig, *Philosophers of Nothingness: An Essay on the Kyoto School* (Honolulu: University of Hawai'i Press, 2001), 271–72.

Chapter 3

Nietzsche and Zen as Philosophies of Self-overcoming

Both Nietzsche and the various dialogue partners from the Zen tradition employed in this study can be said to advocate a practice of self-overcoming that can be described as a philosophical *áskēsis*. In Nietzsche's case, such an *áskēsis*, which he speaks about as a special self-discipline, a self-overcoming and self-denial, consists of a no-saying part and a yes-saying part. The no-saying part has him take sides against everything sick in him. The yes-saying part, that teaches him to say Yes and Amen, has him cultivate his creative vitality, and attune his instincts back to the earth. The no-saying part of Nietzsche's *áskēsis* also turns against this *áskēsis* itself: Nietzsche's practice of self-overcoming continuously problematizes itself and its goals, and therefore also continually overcomes itself. It is especially this self-problematizing aspect of Nietzsche's *áskēsis* that can be fruitfully elucidated in a dialogue with Zen, with its iconoclasm and continual self-deconstruction. I do not focus on specific ascetic practices of Nietzsche and Zen's *áskēsis* (although I will discuss the sitting practice of zazen), but rather aim to uncover and elucidate the principles behind such an *áskēsis*, as well as its problematic and self-contradictory aspects.[1]

Nietzsche's *áskēsis* needs to be distinguished from the ascetic ideal that he condemns in *On the Genealogy of Morality* (see chapter 4). Nietzsche's texts offer resources for rethinking asceticism in a more constructive fashion. As Tyler Roberts puts it: "the self-cultivation Nietzsche develops in (and through) his writing is closely related to traditional forms of religious ascetic practice."[2] Contrary to what is often assumed, Nietzsche does not reject asceticism, only the ascetic ideal. For Nietzsche, the ascetic ideal is other-worldly and self-deceptive, whereas *áskēsis* is this-worldly and not self-deceptive. Nietzsche's *áskēsis* is an *áskēsis* in the service of life that affirms life: "I want to make asceticism natural once again: in place of the aim of denial, the aim of strengthening; a gymnastics of the will; abstinence and periods of fasting of all kinds, in the most spiritual realm, too" (KSA 12, 9 [93]).

There are versions of *áskēsis* that are not necessarily otherworldly: the Zen *áskēsis* for example. The role of *áskēsis* has been underemphasized in Western interpretations of Zen, especially in the intellectual Zen of the Beat Generation and Alan Watts. Zen is all about practice, not only meditation practice but all kinds of *áskēsis*. Both Nietzsche and Zen radically rethink and reorient asceticism.

NIETZSCHE'S WAY TO WISDOM AND THE ZEN WAY TO ENLIGHTENMENT

Among Nietzsche's notebook fragments of 1884, we find a brief outline for a book with the title *The Way to Wisdom—Hints for an Overcoming of Morality*. In this fragment, Nietzsche distinguishes three stages as part of the process of overcoming morality:

> *The first stage.* To honor (and obey and *learn*) better than anyone. To gather all that is honorable in oneself, and let it conflict with oneself. To bear all that is heavy. Asceticism of the spirit—bravery, time of community.
>
> *The second stage.* To break the adoring heart (when one is *captivated most*). The free spirit. Independence. Time of the desert. Criticism of all that is honored (idealization of the non-honored), attempt at inverted valuations.
>
> *The third stage.* Great decision, whether one is capable of a positive attitude, of affirmation. No longer any God, any man *above* me! The instinct of the creator who knows *what* he is creating. The great responsibility and the innocence. In order to enjoy a single thing, one has to affirm [*gutheißen*] *everything*. Give oneself the right to act. (KSA 11, 26 [47])[3]

In the fragment following this one, Nietzsche elaborates on these three stages. He associates the first stage with overcoming the little evil inclinations, the second stage with overcoming the good inclinations as well, and the third stage with being beyond good and evil. He adds that the third stage is for the very few; most people perish in the second stage (KSA 11, 26 [48]).

These three stages can be seen as three perspectives or modes of experiencing that can be distinguished in Nietzsche's work. In the first stage, one obeys respected authorities and learns from educators, teachers, and examples. One's perspective is heteronomous or other-oriented. The free spirit of the second stage has gained independence from others by liberating itself from his adoration of authorities and examples. This perspective can be called autonomous or self-oriented. The third stage of unconditional affirmation goes beyond such a self-oriented perspective to a cosmic or world-oriented perspective.

As Nietzsche remarks: "We have to *learn to think differently*—in order at last, perhaps very late on, to attain even more: *to feel differently*" (D 103). The transformation from one perspective to another might be interpreted as learning to think differently, as a relative transformation, an emancipation and liberation within the same field of reference. However, these transformations do not only involve a change in cognitive outlook (seeing the world differently) but also a process of letting these different ways of thinking sink in and allow them to change us at the very core of our being (experiencing the world differently). They involve learning to both think and feel differently.

The transformations between these perspectives are expressed famously as the three transformations of the spirit in the first speech of part I of *Thus Spoke Zarathustra*, delivered while in the town of the Motley Cow, the town that the Buddha used to deliver his sermons, as Nietzsche was probably aware of.[4] On its way to wisdom, the spirit first transforms into a camel, a strong, weight-bearing spirit, in which reverence dwells. The camel seeks out challenges; it kneels down to be weighed down with the heaviest burden. In the desert, the camel transforms into a lion, who is able to defeat the dragon of the "thou shalt" by saying "I will" (TSZ I, 1). The spirit that as a camel loved and revered everything that it held sacred now must, as a lion, find delusion and caprice even in the most sacred. It discovers that the will to truth, that drove the camel, is actually an illusion.

But even the lion is not capable of creating new values because it is too identified with its newfound autonomy of "I will." It must realize that both "I" and "will" are illusory notions. The autonomous self with a sovereign free will is a fiction. Therefore the lion voluntarily lets go of its newfound autonomy, and, as Nietzsche puts it, "goes under." It literally overcomes itself and is transformed into a child: "innocence is the child and forgetting, a beginning anew, a play, a self-propelling wheel, a first movement, a sacred Yea-saying" (TSZ I, 1).

Although Nietzsche's images of camel, lion, and child have received much attention from Nietzsche interpreters, they are only one way that Nietzsche speaks about his way to wisdom. Since they occur together only once in Nietzsche's entire work (the passage in *Thus Spoke Zarathustra*), I will only occasionally refer to them in this study. My main hermeneutical schema will be that of the other-oriented, self-oriented, and world-oriented perspectives.

Although these perspectives are roughly isomorphic with the camel, lion, and child figures, they do not completely overlap.

Also in the Zen tradition several hermeneutical schemas have been used in order to describe the way to enlightenment. A famous one is the three stage schema of mountains and rivers, as expressed for example by Zen master Qingyuan (c. 660–740):

> Thirty years ago, before I practiced Zen, I saw that mountains are mountains and rivers are rivers. However, after having achieved intimate knowledge and having gotten a way in, I saw that mountains are not mountains and rivers are not rivers. But now that I have found rest, as before I see mountains are mountains and rivers are rivers.[5]

The insight that mountains are not mountains can be interpreted as the realization of emptiness (*śūnyatā*)[6]: there is no essence to be found anywhere, things are not what they seem to be, all "truths" are exposed as merely conventional designations. All searching for truth needs to be left behind; there is no truth (see chapter 4). The insight that mountains are really mountains refers to the emptiness of emptiness, the end of any attachment to the liberating insight of emptiness. This results in a restoration of innocence and an affirmation of the world as it is. The result of the first self-overcoming, the negation of truth, needs to be overcome as well in a second negation.

These two conceptualizations of the way to wisdom in Nietzsche and Zen have a common structure. Both start with an other-directed perspective: Nietzsche's camel and the seeker after enlightenment initially pursue a way to wisdom by following the teachings and instructions from their respective traditions. For the camel, this is the "thou shalt" that its culture imposes on it. For the Buddhist seeker, it is the Buddhist path toward enlightenment (practicing meditation, studying texts). Both need to emancipate themselves from such an other-oriented perspective. Nietzsche's camel needs to transform into a lion in order to emancipate itself from the dragon of the "thou shalt," the Buddhist practitioner needs to realize the emptiness of all Buddhist conceptions and let go of enlightenment as a goal that can be realized by seeking anything outside himself.

However, for both Nietzsche and Zen this first crisis is followed by a second one: the newfound autonomy of the self-oriented perspective eventually needs to be left behind as well in order to realize a world-oriented perspective. Zarathustra declares that the lion needs to "go under" in order to transform into a child. The lion's emancipation from the camel's heteronomy needs to be followed by an "emancipation from the emancipation," as Nietzsche put it in a letter to Lou Salome (KSB 6:247–8). Similarly, the

Zen practitioner needs to let go of his hard-won realization of emptiness and awaken to the emptiness of emptiness. A second conceptualization of the Zen path, the ten ox-herding pictures, makes this even clearer. After searching for the ox, capturing it, taming it, and riding it home (a metaphor for realizing enlightenment), the ox disappears. And finally, in the tenth picture, the path culminates in returning to the marketplace and effortlessly and unselfconsciously manifesting enlightened activity. From such a world-oriented perspective, any preoccupation with one's own condition of enlightenment has evaporated. Any signs of enlightenment, of being anything special, have gone. One is simply available, ready to respond as needed to the vicissitudes of life, and be of service to life itself.[7]

However, in spite of such structural similarities that can be pointed out, a word of caution is in order. Both in Nietzsche's work and in the Zen tradition, there is a tension between such systematic and linear descriptions of a way to wisdom, and an ongoing deconstruction of such systems. Nietzsche writes in a late notebook fragment, "I distrust all systems and systematizers and avoid them: perhaps someone will discover behind this book the system that I have *avoided* . . ." (KSA 12, 9 [188]). The Zen masters continually frustrate any attempts to fix the Zen teachings into a coherent system, as is clear from the koan collections that contain interactions between Zen masters and their disciples. In a sense, just like Nietzsche's attempts to undermine the Western philosophical tradition with his aphoristic style, the Zen tradition rejects the sutra canon of the established Buddhist traditions and replaces it with several aphoristic koan collections.

NIETZSCHE AND ZEN AS PHILOSOPHIES OF SELF-OVERCOMING

Nietzsche and Zen can be considered philosophies of self-overcoming in at least four different respects:

(1) In a *theoretical* sense: self-overcoming is one of the most important notions in Nietzsche's philosophy. For Nietzsche, life, conceived as will to power, is that which continually overcomes itself. Also as an individual, it is in one's very nature as a creature of will to power that one must continually overcome oneself. Self-overcoming does not only refer to a process of individual self-enhancement, but also to self-*Aufhebung* in a dialectical sense. Nietzsche speaks about the self-overcoming of life, morality, and Christianity.

Also the Zen tradition stresses, like Buddhism in general, the importance of self-overcoming in order to reach awakening or enlightenment. But Zen stresses that enlightenment is non-teleological; it vehemently criticizes early Buddhist conceptions of enlightenment as a goal to be reached. For Zen, self-overcoming is also without any self. Like all Buddhist schools, Zen subscribes to the fundamental perspective of non-self (*anātman*): the human personality is merely an amalgamation of impersonal processes in which no fixed, unchangeable essence (*ātman*) can be found.

(2) In a *performative* sense; Nietzsche's philosophy is not merely abstract or theoretical, but aims at such a self-overcoming in the reader. It is a prime example of what Rorty calls "edifying philosophy." Nietzsche sees himself as an educator who inspires his readers to overcome themselves. In Nietzsche's philosophy, the separation between theory and practice is overcome.

As all Buddhist schools, Zen philosophy is not merely theoretical; the aim of any Zen text is always to stimulate self-overcoming in the student. Zen criticizes other Buddhist schools for being too theoretical and metaphysical. Buddhism has consistently declared itself to be, above all else, a soteriology, rather than a creed. It judges its own doctrines primarily for their transformative power: the truth of a proposition consists in its practical utility rather than its descriptive power. Also for Nietzsche, his writings after Zarathustra are intended as fish hooks in order to transform his readers so they will be capable of assimilating *Thus Spoke Zarathustra*.

Throughout the Buddhist tradition, the Buddha is referred to as a physician or a therapist, rather than a philosopher or a theorist. Also Nietzsche refers to himself as a physician whose task it is to lead himself and those rare others that are capable of it to "the great health" (or at least prepare the way for the philosophers of the future who will be capable of it). Nietzsche refers to the Buddha as "that profound physiologist" (EH I, 6). Although, as we have seen in chapter 1, Nietzsche thinks that he himself would be the opposite of the Indian Buddha, his therapy in fact comes close to Zen therapy.

(3) In a *self-referential* sense: Nietzsche's philosophy practices what it preaches: it continually overcomes itself. His experimental philosophy continually contradicts and leaves behind earlier positions and perspectives, and goes to great lengths to avoid being frozen into a system. Also his views on self-overcoming are continually overcome. For Nietzsche all perspectives are equally expressions of will to power, necessary preconditions for life. Interpretation, for Nietzsche, is the continual mutual confrontation of perspectives, an agonal activity not aimed at agreement, but at a continual self-overcoming. Perspectives are continually superseded by new ones.

In Zen, not only Buddhism but also Zen itself is continually overcome. Even the Buddha himself needs to be left behind. As the popular Zen saying goes, "if you meet the Buddha on the road, kill him." Zen engages in guerilla warfare against any reification of concepts, especially Buddhist ones.

(4) In a *self-expressive* sense: Nietzsche's affirmative, Dionysian philosophy can be viewed as a celebration and expression of self-overcoming. It is a philosophy of laughter and play, what Roberts calls "ecstatic philosophy."[8] Also Zen is a philosophy of laughter and play that considers the embodiment of self-overcoming as a way toward openness and making room for otherness.

HERMENEUTICAL STRATEGIES

A dialogue between Nietzsche and Zen, therefore, should not only involve "ironic affinities" between their doctrines, but also parallels in the way they both *practice* their philosophical *áskēsis.* This study will therefore not only compare views but also hermeneutical strategies. Nietzsche's perspectivism is connected to an order of rank: not all perspectives are equal. In a notebook fragment, Nietzsche writes about the joy of discovering three souls in Socrates:

> It is delightful to watch such a true thinker. But it is even more pleasant to discover that this is all foreground, and that at bottom he wants something else—and in a venturous way. I believe that this was the magic of Socrates: he had one soul, and behind that another one and behind that another one. In the first one, Xenophon laid himself to rest, in the second one Plato, and in the third one Plato again, but with his own second soul. Plato himself is a man with many caves and foregrounds. (KSA 11, 34 [66])

And, we might add, Nietzsche considers himself to be such a man as well. Nietzsche interpretations may lay themselves to rest in his first, second, or third soul. First-soul interpretations would read a new "thou shalt" into it. Examples are the many Nietzsche cults around 1900 or interpretations that read him in accordance with Christian morality. Second-soul interpretations would be Derridean and existentialist interpretations that stop at the deconstructive and no-saying part of Nietzsche's revaluation of values—comparable with interpretations of Buddhism as a passive nihilism. Third-soul interpretations of Nietzsche would include the yes-saying part of his revaluation of all values.

Nietzsche himself often complains about being misinterpreted: "Those were steps for me and I have climbed over them—to that end I had to pass over them. Yet they thought that I wanted to retire on them" (TI 1, 42). Such misunderstanding, however, is inevitable. This is why Nietzsche wears a constantly changing series of masks, which he considers the sign of a true philosopher: "Around every profound spirit a mask is growing continually, owing to the constantly false, namely *shallow*, interpretation of every word, every step, every sign of life he gives" (BGE 40). Also the collection of Zen koans, with their seemingly nonsensical exchanges between masters and disciples, can be viewed as a constantly changing series of masks.

For both Nietzsche and Zen, the various stages of the way to wisdom each come with their own perspective on the very process of self-overcoming itself. Self-overcoming means different things at various stages. In Nietzsche's early work (for example, *Schopenhauer as Educator*) it refers to self-cultivation in the sense of *Bildung:* realizing one's higher self with the help of a teacher. From such an other-oriented perspective, there are stages of self-overcoming. Self-cultivation takes place under the guidance of external authorities, in the context of the ascetic ideal and the will to truth. It involves using the ascetic will to repress and annihilate one's passions.

However, once this first stage has culminated in the self-overcoming of the will to truth and the ascetic ideal, the other-directed perspective changes into a self-oriented perspective. Self-overcoming now aims at becoming able to incorporate more and higher perspectives, not in order to know the truth, but in order to become an embodiment of it. From such a perspective, there are no stages of self-overcoming, only the continual effort at self-overcoming. By cultivating one's bodily drives, incorporating previously repressed passions and instincts, one creates a new self, resurrecting the passions in a newly integrated body, in the context of accumulation, self-augmentation, and growth of strength and order.

For Nietzsche, as eventually both "I" and "will" are recognized as illusions, self-overcoming ultimately has to do without a self. (Obviously, in Buddhism self-overcoming has to do without a self from the very beginning). The gardener metaphor gives way to the notion of the drives educating themselves and continually overcoming themselves and each other. In *Ecce Homo,* Nietzsche even stresses the importance of forgetting oneself: any intentional effort at self-overcoming actually seems to obstruct this process. Nietzsche uses passive metaphors such as those of pregnancy (see chapter 7). In *Thus Spoke Zarathustra*, self-overcoming seems to lead to a positive form of redemption, the opposite of Christian, Wagnerian, or Schopenhauerian redemption. But ultimately, in Nietzsche's Dionysian philosophy of amor fati, self-overcoming seems to turn into an anti-soteriology. For Nietzsche, self-overcoming is non-teleological and non-essentialist: there is no fixed final goal or state of liberation that should be reached. One must become what one is.

From such a world-oriented perspective, there is only a continual effortless self-overcoming, surrendering, opening up the self to life and its "spendthrift economy"[9] governed by an imperative to squander life's energies. Change, destruction, and loss are as essential to this economy as growth and amassing ever larger quantities of power. Life overcomes itself when it sacrifices itself and goes under. Whereas the other-oriented and the self-oriented perspectives can be described for a larger readership, the world-oriented perspective cannot be described but can only be hinted at and must be directly experienced from an "overabundance of light." Nietzsche claims to have experienced such elevated states himself:

> My privilege, that which puts me *ahead* of people, is that I have experienced a fullness of highest and newest states, with respect to which it would be cynical to distinguish between spirit [*Geist*] and soul [*Seele*]. Undoubtedly one has to be a philosopher, profound until [—], to step out of such an overabundance of light. (KSA 13, 22 [29])

Also in Zen, we could distinguish between various perspectives on self-overcoming. The way to enlightenment cannot only be interpreted as a series of developmental stages, but also as the various transformations of the very perspective on self-overcoming and enlightenment itself. From an other-oriented perspective, self-overcoming means seeking for enlightenment with the help of the Buddha as a teacher, as described in the Pali Canon of early Buddhism. The path to enlightenment is conceived as a series of developmental stages in a path. From a self-oriented perspective, self-overcoming is about realizing emptiness: the other-oriented pursuit of a state of enlightenment by following the instructions of the Buddha is seen through as empty. The Buddha as a revered example must be killed. The third, world-oriented perspective refers to the realization of the emptiness of emptiness. Eventually, mountains are mountains again.

Part II of this study will focus on the philosophical practices of self-overcoming that are part of a Nietzschean and Zen *áskēsis*. It is concerned with truth, its nature, and the role that it plays in a philosophical *áskēsis*. Chapter 4 shows that for both Nietzsche and Nāgārjuna, the will to truth that characterizes the ascetic ideal, with its connotations of essentialism and teleology, needs to be overcome. Paradoxically enough, the first part of any true philosophical *áskēsis* is to overcome the ascetic ideal. Chapter 5 argues that the notion of truth is not outdated but needs to be used in a new way: truth is not the goal of philosophical investigation, but philosophy is about becoming more truthful. Philosophy becomes a truth practice in the sense of coming to embody truth personally and letting go of the obsession with seeking an impersonal, objective truth. Linji is a good example of the way this is practiced in the Zen tradition. Chapter 6 elaborates such a practice. For both Nietzsche and Dōgen, such a truth practice amounts to a self-cultivation of the body. Chapter 7 argues that, after essentialism and teleology, also anthropocentrism needs to be left behind in the philosophical *áskēsis* that is employed by Nietzsche and Zen.

NOTES

1. Hutter, *Shaping the Future* describes several of Nietzsche's ascetic practices such as solitude and friendship. Heinrich Schipperges, *Am Leitfaden des Leibes: Zur Anthropologik und Therapeutik Friedrich Nietzsches* (Stuttgart: Ernst Klett Verlag, 1975) describes Nietzsche's philosophy "am Leitfaden des Leibes."

2. Roberts, *Contesting Spirit*, 78.

3. See also KSA 11, 25 [490].

4. The Motley Cow (die Bunte Kuh) is a translation of a name of a town, Kalmasadalmya, which the Buddha visited on his wanderings. See Mistry, *Nietzsche and Buddhism*, 17.

5. This aphorism occurs in many variants in the Zen literature, but was first attributed to Master Qingyuan in the *Compendium of the Five Lamps* [Wudeng Huiyuan], 335a9 ff. See also: Jay L. Garfield and Graham Priest, "Mountains Are Just Mountains," in *Pointing at the Moon. Buddhism, Logic, Analytic Philosophy*, ed. Mario d'Amato, Jay L. Garfield, and Tom J. F. Tillemans (Oxford: Oxford University Press, 2009), 71–82.

6. Although *śūyatā* is mostly translated as "emptiness," another possible translation may be "openness."

7. Garfield and Priest, *Mountains Are Just Mountains*, 74.

8. Roberts, *Contesting Spirit*.

9. The term is from Henry Staten.

Part II

Practices of Self-overcoming

Chapter 4

Nietzsche and Nāgārjuna on the Self-overcoming of the Will to Truth

The burdens that Zarathustra's camel is willing to take upon itself include "feeding on the acorns and grass of understanding and for the sake of truth hunger of the soul" and "stepping into filthy waters, as long as they are the waters of truth" (TSZ I, 1). Such a dedication to truth is characteristic for the camel's perspective on self-overcoming. The camel is willing to conform to the "thou shalt" of external authorities: it operates from an other-oriented perspective. However, its will to truth turns out to be problematic.

NIETZSCHE'S SKEPTICISM: QUESTIONING THE WILL TO TRUTH AND THE ASCETIC IDEAL

Nietzsche is well-known for his skepticism. Initially this skepticism appears within a representational model of knowledge. Can we gain knowledge of things in themselves, or is it impossible for us to know reality as it is in itself (epistemological skepticism)? In an unpublished essay from 1873, *On Truth and Lies in an Extramoral Sense*, Nietzsche seems to suggest that although a true world does exist, we are not able to know it. In his later work, however, he argues that we can never know whether a reality outside language exists, some kind of being to which our ideas ultimately correspond. Nietzsche goes as far as to doubt the very notion of a reality in itself (ontological skepticism). If things in themselves don't even exist, our metaphysical ideas don't represent a fundamental truth, but only the dynamics of the constructive process by which we generate a conceptual world within which we can live. According to the ontological skeptic, the world apart from our condition of living in it doesn't exist as a world in itself.

Therefore, the search for truth within a representational model of knowledge ultimately leads to a skeptical rejection of this very representational model itself and its related notion of a "true world." The true and apparent world give way to the world as interpretation. Epistemological truth claims give way to perspectivism. At this point, Nietzsche's skepticism deepens and becomes psychological and existential: why do we want truth and not untruth? The will to truth is a will to discover truth as an object within a representational model of knowledge. Such a truth, however, might not exist. The question "where does this will to truth come from?" points to a genealogical investigation into the *origin* of the will to truth. The question "why do we will truth and not untruth?" is the question of the *value* of the will to truth.

The genealogical investigation into the *origin* of the will to truth reveals that it is symptomatic of what Nietzsche calls "the ascetic ideal," that

> hatred of the human, and even more of the animal, and more still of the material, this horror of the senses, of reason itself, this fear of happiness and beauty, this longing to get away from all appearance, change, becoming, death, wishing, from longing itself—all this means—let us dare to grasp it—a *will to nothingness*. (GM III, 28)

The ascetic ideal starts with the conviction that there is a true world out there. Not only is it possible to know the truth about this world, but knowing this truth is considered the highest, ultimate value (JS 344). As soon as the will to truth subverts its belief in God, it prompts itself to reject the view that truth has the highest value because it is divine: "From the moment faith in the God of the ascetic ideal is denied, a new problem arises: that of the *value* of truth" (GM III, 20). The question of the *value* of truth has never been posed before, Nietzsche claims. The problem with the idea of truth as correspondence is that it gives no account of why we should value the truth, why it is preferable to error.

A possible answer would be that truth is valuable for the pragmatic reason that it is effective. Nietzsche describes such a line of reasoning: "One does not want to allow oneself to be deceived because one assumes that it is harmful, dangerous, calamitous to be deceived. In this sense, science would be a long-range prudence, a caution, a utility" (JS 344). But Nietzsche argues that it is not always harmful to allow oneself to be deceived. The opposite of the will to truth, the will to ignorance, can be equally beneficial for life. We strategically, often unconsciously, overlook and forget features of the world that are not relevant to our purposes and values. Errors are often more valuable than truths.

> We have arranged for ourselves a world in which we can live—by positing bodies, lines, planes, causes and effects, motion and rest, form and content: without

these articles of faith nobody could now endure life. But that does not prove them. Life is no argument; the conditions of life might include error. (JS 121)

Nietzsche speaks repeatedly about the battle between life-sustaining errors and illusions that "work" and more truthful perspectives that may threaten one's health. He seems to acknowledge some moral obligation to face up to such dangerous truths, rather than remain content with errors that "work."

The will to truth cannot be justified, therefore, on pragmatic grounds; it is based on moral grounds—the moral prescription not to deceive, not even oneself ("Thou shalt not lie"). The conviction of science that a "real" and "true" world exists to be discovered is simply a metaphysical faith. The conviction that there is some absolute foundation, some way the world really is, is nothing but a need that has been transformed into a faith. Science, in its conviction that truth can be found, that the true world is there somewhere awaiting adequate representation by thought or language, represents the latest incarnation and the kernel of the ascetic ideal (GM III).

In our times the will to truth demands its own self-overcoming: a revaluation of truth in the name of truth and truthfulness [*Wahrhaftigkeit*]. The ascetic ideal has been undermined. Both of its presuppositions (that there is a true world and that knowing the truth about that world is the ultimate value) have been undercut. The representational model of knowledge has been overcome. This is not only a theoretical discovery, but it also spells the end of the ascetic ideal as a *moral* imperative. The will to truth is no longer the highest value.

Nietzsche is not arguing, however, for a rejection of truth in favor of deception. Both the will to truth (the desire accurately to represent the world as it really is) and the will to ignorance are useful and of value for life. Both extremes need to be avoided. Both are only justified by Nietzsche insofar as they function in the service of life. The metaphysicians and theologians lie in an objectionable, moral sense. They are not willing to scrutinize their convictions and shield them from the will to truth of science.

NĀGĀRJUNA'S SKEPTICISM: QUESTIONING ABHIDHARMA THROUGH EMPTINESS

Nietzsche's struggle with the Platonic-Christian metaphysical tradition is mirrored by Nāgārjuna's battle with the metaphysical schools of early Buddhism. According to the Buddhist Pali Canon, the historical Buddha himself had refused to answer questions on metaphysical topics such as life after death. He felt that such philosophical speculation was not conducive to liberation from clinging and ignorance. But in the centuries after the Buddha's death, his sermons were collected, memorized, and eventually written down in sutra collections. Over time, his teachings were canonized and systematized. As the commentaries and interpretations grew more voluminous, different schools arose. According to research findings, there were up to eighteen different Buddhist schools, each with their own Buddhist canon, consisting of sutras, monastic regulations, and Abhidharma writings (generalizations and reorganizations of the doctrines presented piecemeal in the narrative sutra traditions).[1]

The Buddha had taught that everything is unsatisfactory (*duhkha*), impermanent (*anitya*), and non-self (*anātman*). Some of the Abhidharma schools that arose after his death systematized these teachings into elaborate metaphysical philosophical systems containing ontological speculations regarding the ultimate constituents of reality, called *dharmas*: insubstantial, momentary, "constituent factors" of human experience and of the entire mental and material world.[2] These *dharmas* were the only type of entity that truly existed, they claimed. Reality was conceived as an ontology of becoming, a flux of ever-changing configurations and constellations of *dharmas*. The Abhidharma writers constructed brilliant models of the mind and of reality, but as time went by, these models were increasingly seen as true descriptions of reality, only accessible to the refined perception of experienced meditators.

Nāgārjuna takes on the dogmatic scholasticism of the early Buddhist Abhidharma schools, with their associated renunciate morality aimed at a purification of the person by battling the unwholesome drives of ignorance, aggression, and desire. Their approach in some respects mirrors Plato's introduction of the intelligible world as ultimate reality and the *adequatio* conception of truth that goes with it (the representational model of knowledge).[3] In Nietzschean terms, one could say that Nāgārjuna criticizes the Abhidharmists for their will to truth, their conviction that truth is possible, that a system can be devised to describe ultimate reality. Nāgārjuna shows that such attempts necessarily must fail.

For Nāgārjuna, the will to truth would be an epistemological variation of *tanhā*: a clinging to certain thought constructions that are regarded as representations of a real multiplicity of substantial things in the world. It is such clinging that generates the suffering that Buddhism describes, connected with greed, desire, and all forms of attachment. Liberation from such clinging to wrong views is the way to end suffering. Once liberated, according to the Buddhist view, one is able to perceive reality and function freely in the world without compulsively needing to take refuge in limiting perspectival stances.

Nāgārjuna elaborates on the *Prajñāpāramitā* sutras that claim that all phenomena are *śūnyatā*, that is, empty of any essence. To have an essence would mean to exist in virtue of intrinsic properties. All phenomena, however, exist only in virtue of extrinsic relations. While the emptiness of all phenomena is simply stated in the *Prajñāpāramitā* sutras, Nāgārjuna attempts to transpose emptiness into a philosophical key. He stresses that emptiness does not mean nonexistence. As Garfield puts it, "To be empty of essence is not to be empty of existence. Instead, to exist is to be empty."[4]

Jan Westerhoff points out that, within the Indian Buddhist context, emptiness means "empty of *svabhāva*." This complex term is used by Nāgārjuna in various contexts and can carry the meaning of "essence," "substance," or "true nature." It has not only an ontological meaning, but also a cognitive: because of a "*svabhāva* projection," we continually project a sense of permanence onto our experience. One of the functions of the notion of *śūnyatā* is precisely to break through such a *svabhāva* projection.[5]

In his main work, the *Mūlamadhyamakakārikā* (Fundamental verses on the Middle Way) Nāgārjuna systematically deconstructs the Abhidharma views. Nāgārjuna negates the separate existence of *dharmas*. He shows that concepts such as causality, time, dharma, and substance are inconsistent and contradictory when subjected to thorough philosophical scrutiny. His method involves the dialectical deconstruction of the central categories by which language seduces us into accepting its thought constructions as realities. Nāgārjuna uses the Buddhist logical form of the tetralemma: A, not-A, both A and not-A, neither A nor not-A. Through a method of *reductio ad absurdum* he proves that all four horns of the tetralemma lead to incoherent conclusions. In this way, Nāgārjuna not only negates every possible positive assertion, he also negates the negation of that assertion.

In the twenty-seven chapters of the *Mūlamadhyamakakārikā*, Nāgārjuna examines twenty-seven different thought categories. In every case he examines the dichotomies by which we characterize our world (such as origination and extinction, permanence and impermanence, identity and difference, enlightenment and unenlightenment) and shows that we cannot logically accept either category. One of the categories that Nāgārjuna deconstructs, for example, is that of "existence." To say that things exist is an eternalist, substantial view. To say that they don't exist is a nihilistic view. Ultimately things neither exist, not do they not exist. But also that view turns out to be logically incoherent.

Nāgārjuna also revises Abhidharma soteriology. Early Buddhism had conceived of liberation as finding a way out of conditioned existence (samsara) in order to reach liberation (nirvana). Gradually nirvana (which literally means "extinction") acquired a metaphysical meaning. It became hypostasized as "nothingness." The way to nirvana meant extinguishing the flames of craving and clinging until the state of nothingness was attained. This final state of enlightenment was considered to be very different from ordinary consciousness. In general, this has been the kind of nirvana as *unio mystica* that has been transmitted to its Western interpreters.[6]

In *Mūlamadhyamakakārikā* chapter 25, Nāgārjuna states that there is not the slightest difference between samsara and nirvana. The Buddhist path is not about escaping the world in order to dissolve into nothingness, but rather about finding a new perspective on it, free from craving and clinging to fixed views and concepts. Nirvana doesn't refer to escaping or overcoming samsara in order to reach a state of everlasting bliss, but to the realization of a liberating perspective: that there is no difference between samsara and nirvana. As Jay Garfield puts it, this is "a nirvana not found in an escape from the world but in an enlightened and awakened engagement with it."[7] Nirvana implies a different way of being in *this* world. The early Buddhist notion of nirvana as a liberation from samsara is not considered wrong or untrue but is seen as a preliminary perspective for those starting out on the Buddhist path. Once one has progressed on the path, one is ready for the more advanced nondual perspective that nirvana and samsara are the same.

PASSIVE AND ACTIVE NIHILISM

Both Nietzsche and Nāgārjuna can be seen as skeptical, iconoclastic philosophers for whom self-overcoming involves overcoming the ascetic ideal that sets up a static goal of self-overcoming. Both criticize a representational model of knowledge (reality/appearance), and both criticize metaphysical opposites. They both battle the various dogmatic schools in their own philosophical tradition. Whereas Nietzsche fights the metaphysical views of Plato, Christianity, and Idealism, which all set up a Beyond that could be intuited in a redemptive experience, Nāgārjuna battles the metaphysical Buddhist philosophical schools. Both show that "true reality" and "true knowledge" are fictions, that there are no facts but only interpretations, and bring thought to an *aporia*.

Nihilism now looms large: if there is no truth, there is no ultimate value, no goal, and nothing to pursue. The only thing that seems to be left is a will to nothingness: man would rather will nothingness than not will at all. For Nietzsche, such a will to nothingness can be found in Schopenhauer and in the Buddhist nirvana. This is what he calls "passive nihilism." As a remedy, Nietzsche advocates a practice of active nihilism: an effort to push oneself and others more deeply into nihilism, ruthlessly confronting and exposing any hidden need for security, any grasping at metaphysical concepts, any clinging to a fixed perspective. Active nihilism means pushing nihilism to its limits, toward the self-overcoming of nihilism (see chapter 10 about Nishitani). Active nihilism implies the further deconstruction of the essentialist notion of truth as a "thing," as a particular insight into the true nature of reality. It also refers to the further deconstruction of teleology: there is no goal, no ultimate value.

According to Nāgārjuna, Nietzsche may be right in considering early Buddhism a form of passive nihilism. But for Nāgārjuna, the label of nihilism only applies to a Buddhist philosophical dogmatism, not to the teachings of the Buddha himself. Incidentally, Nāgārjuna himself anticipated that he might be accused of being exactly such a passive nihilist: if everything is empty, there is no way to realize liberation, and we might as well give up.

In chapter 24 of his *Mūlamadhyamakakārikā*, Nāgārjuna enters into a dialogue with an imaginary Buddhist opponent. This opponent objects that if everything is empty, as Nāgārjuna claims, there can be no such thing as the four Buddhist noble truths: no such thing as *duhkha*, or *tanhā*, or *nirvana*, or a Buddhist path. Then Buddhism as a whole becomes irrelevant. Therefore, Nāgārjuna is a nihilist. In his response, Nāgārjuna shows that it is his opponent who is the nihilist. By insisting on fixed Buddhist concepts and becoming immolated in Buddhist dogma, liberation becomes impossible. On the other hand, everything is possible for those who know emptiness.

CONVENTIONAL AND ULTIMATE TRUTH

In refuting his opponent who accuses him of nihilism, Nāgārjuna argues that his opponent has a limited notion of truth: "The various buddhas' teaching of the Dharma relies upon two truths: the conventional truth of the world (*lokasamvrtisatya*) and what is true from the ultimate perspective (*paramārthatah*)."[8] Nāgārjuna refers here to the Buddhist notion of two truths (*satyadvaya*): conventional truth, which is based on intersubjective agreement between participants in a language game, and ultimate truth, which is based on awakening. This notion originally served as a hermeneutical device to reconcile apparently contradictory statements in Buddhist scripture. Nāgārjuna argues that his opponent confuses the conventional truth of our everyday perspectives with the ultimate truth of awakening. We can only speak about such ultimate truth through conventional truth. The notion of emptiness is itself also merely a conventional truth, but it can serve as a liberating perspective that creates room for awakening.

What would Nietzsche have said about the two truths? He would have rejected the notion of ultimate truth if it would refer to "the world as it really is." There are some Nāgārjuna interpretations that claim that ultimate truth refers to the ineffability and unknowability of the world. It is tempting to take conventional truth to refer to things as they seem to be, and ultimate truth to things as they truly are. Conventional and ultimate truth would then stand to one another as appearance and reality.

Westerhoff rejects such an interpretation: if we regard the true nature of things as ineffable, we still assume that they have a mind-independent intrinsic nature.[9] All we have is conventional truth, a collection of various perspectives, of which some are more useful than others. Ultimate truth doesn't amount to some kind of mystical insight or *unio mystica*, but to the realization that there is no final way that the world really is:

> According to the Madhyamaka view of truth, there can be no such thing as ultimate truth, a theory describing how things really are, independent of our interests and conceptual resources employed in describing it. All one is left with is conventional truth, truth that consists in agreement with commonly accepted practices and conventions.[10]

Śūnyatā is not a philosophical, an ontological, or an empirical concept; neither, indeed, is it a concept at all. It can only be known through direct realization. Emptiness neither refers to a direct intuition of a noumenal realm, nor is it just an empirical and pragmatic notion. It points to the "inexpressible," to nondual awareness. Ultimate truth does not refer to a self-existent dimension of reality beyond the everyday. Rather, it is everyday reality viewed from a radically different perspective. The only difference between an awakened and an ignorant person is this realization of emptiness.

For Nāgārjuna, it's not that the Abhidharmists are to be blamed for uttering untruthful assertions, not even that they use the wrong set of criteria for truth: there is no fixed set of criteria for (ultimate) truth, only contingent criteria for conventional truth. For Nāgārjuna, the conception of things in themselves is logically inconsistent. There is no such thing as "ultimate nature," no appearance-reality distinction. As Garfield points out,

> emptiness is not a deeper truth hidden behind a veil of illusion. The emptiness of any phenomenon is dependent on the existence of that phenomenon, and on its dependence, which is that in which its essencelessness consists. Emptiness is itself dependent, and hence empty. This doctrine of the emptiness of emptiness, and of the identity of interdependence, or conventional truth, and emptiness, or ultimate truth, is Nāgārjuna's deepest philosophical achievement.[11]

Therefore, apart from the realization of emptiness, Nāgārjuna recognizes a second transformation: the realization of the emptiness of emptiness. This second transformation does not refer to the discovery of some kind of ultimate truth beyond conventional truth, but to the realization of the very identity of conventional and ultimate truth:

> It might appear that the distinction between conventional and ultimate reality is tantamount to the distinction between appearance and reality, and that Nāgārjuna holds that the conventional truth is merely illusion, in virtue of being

empty, while the ultimate truth—emptiness—is what is real. But Nāgārjuna argues that emptiness is also empty, that it is essenceless, and exists only conventionally as well. The conventional truth is hence no less real than the ultimate, the ultimate no more real than the conventional.[12]

FROM DECONSTRUCTION TO AFFIRMATION: STRONG SKEPTICISM

Glen Martin has pointed out that both Nietzsche and Nāgārjuna engage in a critical deconstruction of their respective philosophical traditions, not as a goal in itself but in order to find a breakthrough to a new mode of affirmation. Nietzsche's radical skepticism, culminating in the death of God, is the doorway to a new feeling of liberation: "all the daring of the lover of knowledge is permitted again; the sea, *our* sea, lies open again; perhaps there has never been such an 'open sea'" (JS 343). For both Nāgārjuna and Nietzsche, liberation means living in the ordinary world in a transformed way. Nāgārjuna expresses this in his equation of samsara with nirvana (liberation). Nietzsche expresses this as the ecstatic affirmation of the thought that every moment of our life will return eternally.[13]

Nāgārjuna's philosophical activity may be regarded, in a Nietzschean sense, as a form of active nihilism. By using the teaching of emptiness to undermine all cherished Buddhist concepts, he attempts to create a sense of impasse and *aporia*, out of which a liberating breakthrough to an affirmative relationship to life is possible. Seen from this perspective, Nāgārjuna undertakes a Buddhist kind of revaluation of all values.

In Mahāyāna Buddhism, the relationship between no-saying skepticism and yes-saying breakthrough to affirmation is clarified by the notion of *upāya* (skillful means). There are several passages in Nietzsche's work that we can interpret as a description of a strategy of *upāya*. In *The Antichrist* 54, for example, Nietzsche first stresses the importance of skepticism: "Great spirits are skeptics. Zarathustra is a skeptic [. . .] A mind that aspires to great things, and that wills the means thereto, is necessarily skeptical. Freedom from any sort of conviction belongs to strength, and to an independent point of view" (AC 54). Then he goes on to describe making use of convictions as *upāya*: "Conviction as a means: one may achieve a good deal by means of a conviction. A grand passion makes use of and uses up convictions; it does not yield to them—it knows itself to be sovereign" (AC 54).

For both Nāgārjuna and Nietzsche, active nihilism is not a goal in and of itself, but only a means to an end. Nāgārjuna is, just like the Buddha, a physician who diagnoses his opponents as being poisoned with philosophical dogmatism. The pill is skeptical inquiry. But when the poison is purged, the inquiry is no longer necessary. In the same way Nietzsche makes use of convictions and perspectives, not as a goal in itself, but in a performative sense. The point of skepticism is not just to fight dogmatic convictions. The goal is to create as much doubt as possible in the values that have up until now been seen as true (the will to truth and the ascetic ideal) in order to make room for new values.

Such a skepticism is different from ordinary skepticism. Nietzsche diagnoses the skeptical, scientific spirit of his times as motivated by a weakness in willing, a nihilistic inability to affirm existence. Such a skepticism doesn't dig deeply enough, since it still leaves the psychological need for metaphysical illusions intact. In the end, such a skepticism leads to passive nihilism. But for those who are strong enough to face into their hidden metaphysical needs, Nietzsche opposes such a skepticism with "another and stronger kind of skepticism," "the skepticism of daring manliness." "This skepticism despises and nevertheless grasps; it undermines and takes possession; it does not believe, but it does not thereby lose itself; it gives the spirit a dangerous liberty, but it keeps strict guard over the heart" (BGE 209). In his notebook fragments, Nietzsche differentiates between a "skepticism of weakness and one of courage" (KSA 10, 24 [30]), a weak and a strong skepticism.[14] He speaks about "overcoming the weak skeptics" (KSA 11, 26 [241]).

Weak skepticism means accepting that truth as correspondence is no longer possible, and therefore settling for other standards of truth, such as intersubjective agreement. The weak skeptic accepts, for example, a pragmatic theory of truth. Or he redefines philosophy as merely a play with perspectives without goal or aim (postmodernism), or a literary genre (Rorty). In terms of Nāgārjuna, the weak skeptic resigns himself to the fact that all we have is conventional truth.

Strong skepticism, on the other hand, is practiced by Nietzsche's philosophers of the future, for whom philosophy is no longer a theoretical or speculative exercise, but an ongoing experiment in revaluation of values, based on an order of rank in people and perspectives. The philosopher of the future is a skeptic who is able to play with perspectives and convictions out of a great passion. The point of such skepticism is not merely to do battle with dogmatism, but more generally to cause maximal doubt about existing truth practices based on a representational model of knowledge, in order to make room for a new truth practice.

DISCUSSION

Nāgārjuna's contribution to an understanding of Nietzsche's thought is twofold. First, the way that he deconstructs Abhidharma soteriology using *śūnyatā* as a philosophical tool to overcome essentialism and teleology can elucidate how Nietzsche tries to come to a non-essentialist and non-teleological understanding of truth and of philosophical *áskēsis* in general. And second, his two truths theory gives us a hermeneutic of *upāya*, which can be helpful to understand how Nietzsche's strong skepticism is not just part of a philosophy that is a theoretical enterprise, but gives rise to a radically altered vision of philosophy as a revaluation of all values. Philosophy thus gains an existential dimension and turns into an epistemological *áskēsis* aimed at a liberation of the individual, enabling him or her to live in the world without being hypnotized by conceptual essences such as "truth" and "being."

Whether Nāgārjuna also puts forward such an alternative conception of philosophy is a topic of debate within the Mahāyāna Buddhist tradition. Nāgārjuna's text is unusually susceptible to interpretation, as it is expressed almost wholly as a series of often cryptic refutations. According to the influential Prāsangika school, led by his disciple Candrakīrti (600–c. 650), for Nāgārjuna, philosophy goes no further than a no-saying active nihilism. Nāgārjuna himself held no views. Everything he wrote served as *upāya*. Philosophical perspectives only serve to bring the reader beyond thought constructions to liberation. According to the Svātantrika school (led by his disciple Bhāvaviveka, c. 500–c. 578), Nāgārjuna did put forward his own alternative view, that is, that all things are empty. Mahāyāna schools such as the Yogācāra in India or the Huayan in China have regarded Nāgārjuna's philosophy as the basis for their metaphysics.[15]

Although much comparative research has already been done on Nāgārjuna and Western philosophers, there is no clear agreement on the interpretation of his thought (any more than there is agreement on the interpretation of Nietzsche's thought). Andrew Tuck has shown that the Nāgārjuna reception in the West has been strongly influenced by the philosophical vogues of the time. There have been many Nāgārjunas: the Neokantian, the logical empiricist, and the Wittgensteinian theorist of language. Since Tuck's study appeared in 1990, perhaps the Derridean deconstructivist Nāgārjuna can be added to the list.[16]

Garfield and Dreyfus have attempted recently to frame the debate on the interpretation of Nāgārjuna in terms of ancient Greek skepticism.[17] They liken the Svātantrika interpretation to Academic skepticism: even though there is no truth in the sense of a true description of reality, they still aim at providing the most justifiable and least misleading way of thinking about reality.[18] Such conventional truths can lead others to understand the ultimate truth that is beyond language and thought. The Prāsangika school, on the other hand, can be seen as a kind of Pyrrhonism: Nāgārjuna's arguments are not aiming at the realization of some higher truth, but aim to get us out of the very game of truth and falsity altogether, without committing to any standpoint, positive or negative.[19]

The similarity between the Madhyamaka school and Pyrrhonism has been extensively explored by Kuzminski, who even speculates that Greek Pyrrhonism may have originated from contacts between Pyrrho and Indian sages.[20] However, there are also substantial differences between Nāgārjuna and Pyrrhonism, and such differences may come to light more clearly by focusing on how Nāgārjuna's skepticism, like Nietzsche's strong skepticism, differs from Pyrrhonism: its goal is not *ataraxia* but a revaluation of all values.

Daniel Conway and Julie Ward argue that Nietzsche uses the Pyrrhonist therapeutic methods of Sextus Empiricus, but to very different ends. As a skeptical rhetorical strategy, Nietzsche relies on the very paradigm he seeks to discredit. They give an example out of *Beyond Good and Evil*, where Nietzsche temporarily inhabits the dogmatist's paradigm. From within the representational model of knowledge, he argues that "untruth is a precondition of life," "the falsest judgments are the most indispensable for us [. . .] without a constant falsification of the world, man could not live. Renouncing false judgments means renouncing life" (BGE 4). Nietzsche seeks to lessen confidence in the dogmatist's paradigm. But it is only from within the representational model of knowledge, that truthful representations and falsifications are opposites. As Conway and Ward note, "Nietzsche adopts the assertorial mode of dogmatism only in order to reveal its limitations. His own 'position,' which he elsewhere articulates, expresses his skepticism about our capacity to judge whether or not our judgments correspond in any intelligible sense to the 'real' world."[21]

Whereas theoretical philosophy as the pursuit of truth within the ascetic ideal has its place on the way to wisdom, philosophy becomes a truth *áskēsis* for those who have overcome the will to truth in themselves and are willing to follow Nietzsche in a revaluation of truth. Nietzsche calls them "new philosophers," "free spirits," "philosophers of the future." In chapter 5, I will investigate what such a revaluation of truth would look like, with the help of some examples from the Zen tradition.

NOTES

1. See Johannes Bronkhorst, *Buddhist Teaching in India* (Boston: Wisdom Publications, 2009).

2. Bronkhorst argues that especially the Sarvāstivāda missionary school in North-West India became quite scholastic (Bronkhorst, *Buddhist Teaching in India*,

109–14). Perhaps as a consequence of contact with post-Alexander the Great Greek colonists, Buddhist monks may have felt the need to answer their Greek opponents with philosophical arguments. Alternatively, some of those Indian Greeks may have converted to Buddhism, like the Bactrian king Menander [Milinda], whose discussions with the Buddhist monk Nagasena were recorded in "The Questions of King Milinda."

3. Thomas McEvilley, *The Shape of Ancient Thought: Comparative Studies in Greek and Indian Philosophies* (New York: Allworth Press, 2002), 167–69 further lists the parallels.

4. William Edelglass and Jay L. Garfield, eds., *Buddhist Philosophy: Essential Readings* (Oxford: Oxford University Press, 2009), 27.

5. Jan Westerhoff, *Nāgārjuna's Madhyamaka: A Philosophical Introduction* (Oxford: Oxford University Press, 2009), 12f and 19–52.

6. See G. R. Welbon, *The Buddhist Nirvana and Its Western Interpreters* (Chicago: University of Chicago Press, 1968); Droit, *The Cult of Nothingness*; Volker Zotz, *Auf den glückseligen Inseln: Buddhismus in der deutschen Kultur* (Berlin: Theseus, 2000).

7. Jay L. Garfield, *The Fundamental Wisdom of the Middle Way: Nāgārjuna's Mūlamadhyamakakārikā* (Oxford: Oxford University Press, 1995), 341.

8. Nāgārjuna, *Mūlamadhyamakakārikā* XXIV.8. Quoted in: The Cowherds, *Moonshadows: Conventional Truth in Buddhist Philosophy* (Oxford: Oxford University Press, 2011), 3.

9. Westerhoff, *Nāgārjuna's Madhyamaka,* 206.

10. Westerhoff, *Nāgārjuna's Madhyamaka,* 220.

11. Jay L. Garfield, "Nāgārjuna's *Mūlamadhyamakakārikā* (*Fundamental Verses of the Middle Way*): Chapter 24: Examination of the Four Noble Truths," in *Buddhist Philosophy: Essential Readings,* 27.

12. Garfield, Nāgārjuna's *Mūlamadhyamakakārikā,* 27.

13. Glen T. Martin, "Deconstruction and Breakthrough in Nietzsche and Nāgārjuna," in *Nietzsche and Asian Thought*, 91. Martin points out that Nietzsche also speaks about such a transformation of our relation to the world. He explores Nietzsche's metaphors of the alchemist (who transforms lead into gold), the creative artist, and the playing child.

14. See Paul J. M. van Tongeren, "Nietzsche's Symptomatology of Skepticism," in *Nietzsche, Epistemology, and Philosophy of Science*, eds. Babette Babich and Robert S. Cohen (Dordrecht: Kluwer Academic Publishers, 1999), 66.

15. Modern Theravādins interpret Nāgārjuna's philosophy at best as a mere recapitulation of early Buddhist *anātman* theory. Some contemporary Sri Lankan Theravāda Buddhists plainly state that "Nāgārjuna was wrong."

16. Andrew Tuck, *Comparative Philosophy and the Philosophy of Scholarship* (Oxford/New York: Oxford University Press, 1990).

17. Georges Dreyfus and Jay L. Garfield, "Madhyamaka and Classical Greek Skepticism," in *Moonshadows*, 115–30. See also Georges Dreyfus, "Can a Mādhyamika Be a Skeptic? The Case of Patsab Nyimadrak," in *Moonshadows,* 89–113.

18. Dreyfus and Garfield, *Madhyamaka and Classical Greek Skepticism*, 128.
19. Dreyfus and Garfield, *Madhyamaka and Classical Greek Skepticism*, 118.
20. Adrian Kuzminski, *Pyrrhonism: How the Ancient Greeks Reinvented Buddhism* (Lanham: Lexington, 2008).
21. Daniel W. Conway and Julie K. Ward, "Physicians of the Soul: Peritrope in Sextus Empiricus and Nietzsche," in *Nietzsche und die antike Philosophie*, ed. Daniel W. Conway and Rudolf Rehn (Trier: Wissenschaftlicher Verlag, 1992), 203.

Chapter 5

Nietzsche and Linji on Truth as Embodiment

What to do after the will to truth and the ascetic ideal have been seen through? Nietzsche's epistemological practice of active nihilism reinforces that "the truth" does not exist and cannot be sought out as a goal. The conviction that truth is the ultimate value has been *the* conviction upon which most of Western thought has been based. Overcoming that conviction (the revaluation of truth) is the end of philosophy as epistemology. From then on, philosophizing can no longer be a theoretical enterprise aimed at establishing true views. Outside a representational model of knowledge, what could it possibly mean to "know" something? Is there still any place for a notion of truth? According to some, Nietzsche continues to practice truth in a pragmatic sense: truth is "what works." However, for the pragmatists, truth still remains the highest good. They don't question the value of truth but just claim that its value lies in its efficacy. The pragmatists limit truth to Nāgārjuna's conventional truth.

Christoph Cox notes that every major theory of truth (correspondence, pragmatic, coherence, semantic) has been attributed to Nietzsche by one commentator or another, whereas others have argued that Nietzsche does not provide a theory of truth and is not interested in doing so.[1] According to Cox, all are partially right. In Nietzsche's new conception, he says, "Truth is concerned not with the determination of absolute and ultimate being, but with a specification of the perspectives and interpretations relative to which the world appears as being such and such."[2] Truth is not something given that may be found but must be perpetually constructed and reconstructed.

> Will to truth is a *making*-firm, a *making*-true and -durable. [. . .] Truth is therefore not something there, that might be found or discovered—but something that *is to be created* and that gives a name to a *process*, or rather to a will to

> overcome that has no end—introducing truth, as a *processus in infinitum*, an *active determining—not* a becoming-conscious of something that is "in itself" firm and determined. (KSA 12, 9 [91])

Constructing and reconstructing truth requires a constant weighing and measuring of interpretations against one another. "At every step one has to wrestle for truth" (AC 50). Such a wrestling for truth requires a strong will. Knowledge and objectivity are still possible as long as they are conceived as "the ability to have one's For and Against *under control* and to engage and disengage them, so that one knows how to employ a *variety* of perspectives and affective interpretations in the service of knowledge" (GM III, 12). Cox concludes that "Nietzsche is not interested in providing a theory of truth, then, because truth is not something that admits of final determination by a fixed set of criteria. Truth is the fleeting calm between battles within a war that has no preordained or final victor."[3]

Nietzsche's new epistemological practice is perspectivism. To know something means to inhabit its perspective, to incorporate it, to become it, to become one with it, to interpret it. A dogmatic will to truth maintains that there is only one true perspective. Nietzsche allows for a multiplicity of perspectives, which are continually switched and inverted. There are only interpretations. Therefore, the sense of truth that remains seems to be more like truth as emptiness:

> This bad taste, this will to truth, to "truth at any price," this youthful madness in the love of truth—has lost its charm for us; for that we are too experienced, too serious, too merry, too burned, too profound . . . We no longer believe that truth remains truth when the veils are withdrawn [. . .] Perhaps truth is a woman who has reasons for not letting us see her reasons? Perhaps her name is, to speak Greek, Baubo . . . ? (JS Foreword, 4)

According to Greek mythology, Baubo was an old woman who exposed herself to Demeter. She is also a goddess herself and portrayed as a woman exposing herself. She is, as Tim Freeman has described it,

> perhaps even a personification of the fecundity of the female represented by the exposed vulva. In revealing the woman-truth an abyss opens up. The woman-truth is thus not something present, a presence which could serve as a ground, a solid foundation upon which to build an unshakeable edifice of knowledge. She is instead the very *absence* of ground. She is the abysmally deep ground which undermines every attempt to furnish grounds. She is what might be called the void or *emptiness*.[4]

The truth as the abysmal absence of ground cannot be borne by everyone. This is why when Nietzsche asks "will the philosophers of the future still be friends of truth?," the answer is "yes, but their truths are not for everyone" (BGE 43).

ZEN DECONSTRUCTION

Nietzsche's practice of active nihilism can also be found in the Zen tradition. It rejects any notion of truth that is essentialist and teleological. As we have seen in chapter 4, in early Buddhism, nirvana tends to be interpreted as the cessation of suffering, a state of irreversible liberation from worldly existence (samsara) that can be reached through a practice of self-cultivation and meditation. The Zen masters go to great lengths to prevent their disciples from conceiving of enlightenment as an ultimate truth to be realized, a particular insight or state of consciousness. Zen deconstruction and iconoclasm, a radicalization of Nāgārjuna's skepticism, is already apparent in its founding myth. According to Zen legend, in 527 during the Liang Dynasty, Bodhidharma, the first Zen Patriarch, visited Emperor Wu, a fervent patron of Buddhism. The following brief dialogue ensued:

- What is the first principle of sacred truth?
- Vast emptiness, nothing sacred.
- Who then is facing me?
- Don't know.[5]

The paradigmatic expression of such Zen deconstruction is Linji Yixuan. Although Albert Welter's historical research has shown that the authorship of texts attributed to Linji is in actuality a very complicated question and that many "radical" elements are in fact a later addition, the traditional image of Linji within the Zen tradition is that of an iconoclastic figure and a personal embodiment of truth.[6] The record of Linji's teachings, the *Linji lu*, contains some very strong rhetoric that denies the possibility of finding any kind of ultimate truth and stresses the futility of striving after it:

> Bodhi [awakening] and nirvana are hitching posts for donkeys.[7]
> There's no Buddha, no Dharma, no practice, no enlightenment.[8]
> If you meet the Buddha, kill the Buddha.[9]

Such phrases utterly deconstruct enlightenment as a soteriological goal that can be reached through Buddhist practice or studied via Buddhist sutras. Linji stresses that the very seeking is part of the problem. There is nothing to seek for: "There is no Buddha to be sought, no Way to be carried out, no Dharma to be gained."[10]

Linji has a radical anti-*mārga* rhetoric. He fights the temptation to view emptiness as a final truth and to pursue enlightenment as a telos. Again and again he returns to non-essentialism and non-teleology of the Zen *áskēsis*. Linji is the most radical Zen deconstructivist thinker. Youro Wang holds that "Linji may be the one, among all Zen masters, who uses the clearest language to deconstruct all [. . .] terms that Zen Buddhists have been using, including those used by himself."[11]

TRUTH AS ÁSKĒSIS

However, in spite of Nietzsche's practice of active nihilism, the notion of truth doesn't disappear but remains as a practice, an *áskēsis*. Epistemological truth as representation gives way to the ethical virtue of truthfulness and being true. For Nietzsche, truthfulness does not refer to merely the intention to accurately reflect what is true. "Perhaps no one has been truthful enough about what constitutes truthfulness," he remarks (BGE 177). Nietzsche's view of truthfulness refers to the ethical truthfulness with which the lover of knowledge conducts an experimental life: "I think well of all skepsis to which I may reply: 'let's try it!' [*versuchen wir's*]. But I no longer want to hear anything of all those things and questions which do not permit experiments. This is the limit of my 'truthfulness'; for there courage has lost its rights" (JS 51).

Strong skepticism requires that we find a way to live with the continual realization that our perspectives give us nothing but lies and illusions. In this way the word truth takes on an ethical meaning. A person's strength and courage are revealed by the degree to which he or she can endure the truth that all meanings and all values have disintegrated, along with the notion of "being" and its religious correlate, "God." Strong skepticism refers to a new truth practice, aimed not at discovering static truths about reality, but at becoming a strong, healthy, and truthful person. In this sense this new truth practice has a strong ethical component. Truth must not be understood from an epistemological but an ethical perspective.[12] One's words and deeds stem from one's character. Therefore, there is a virtue-ethical need for self-cultivation, to harmonize the hierarchical multiplicity of one's drives into a unity.

Nietzsche's notion of truth as philosophical *áskēsis* has its antecedents in ancient philosophy, especially in the pre-Socratics, whom Nietzsche greatly admired. Béatrice Han has argued that the ancient notion of truth can be understood as a "magisterial" understanding of truth. She borrows the expression "Master of Truth" from Marcel Detienne in order to describe the pre-Socratic Greek masters who were seen as being able to embody truth. The joint invention of an intelligible world as ultimate reality and truth as *adequatio* with such an ultimate reality replaced such an archaic magisterial understanding of truth. Han argues that Nietzsche seeks, through his existential practice of philosophy, to revive the magisterial understanding of truth of the pre-Socratics: "The truth content of a proposition does not depend on its adequation with an objective referent [. . .] but on its link to the living singularity of its author [. . .] A true claim is one that is asserted by someone truthful (the Master)".[13] Any true philosophical doctrine owes its authenticity to the singularity of its author rather than to its objective content.[14] This leads to a new hermeneutic. The worth of an action depends on who accomplishes it and on whether it stems from the depth or the surface of the individual, that is, on its individuality.

The Master of Truth is the opposite of the scholar, who is not a unity and is alienated from himself. The modern subject is the antithesis of true selfhood. True persons are rare. A Master of Truth is a superior philologist and physician. He is able to "read" the world better than others because he is healthier. He is a superior physician because he is good at stimulating healthy interpretations and battling unhealthy ones, helping others to become more capable of affirmation, to overcome their will to truth and increase their capacity for bearing the absence of metaphysical truth. The will to truth is a sign of weakness and decadence. Weak people need to believe that "the truth is out there." The strong and healthy person, who is able to do without metaphysical truth, can be seen as a Master of Truth.

Nietzsche's new approach to truth as philosophical *áskēsis* is most apparent in his works from 1888, especially *Ecce Homo*. One of the remarkable and even shocking things in *Ecce Homo* is Nietzsche's insistence, already in the Foreword, that such a thing as "truth" *does* exist. Being able to perceive truthfully seems a moral issue for Nietzsche; it has to do with who one is, how tough and sincere one dares to be with oneself. "How much truth can a spirit *stand*, how much truth does it *dare*?—for me that became more and more the real measure of value. Error (belief in the ideal) is not blindness, error is *cowardice* . . ." (EH Foreword, 3). However, on the other hand, how much of reality one can stand simply depends on one's health. The idealist cannot help but recoil from it, whereas the healthy person naturally embraces reality as it is. Later on in *Ecce Homo*, as he discusses *The Birth of Tragedy*, Nietzsche says,

> One comes only so close to truth as one's strength *allows* one's courage to dare advance. Knowledge, saying "yes" to reality, is just as much a necessity for the strong as are, for the weak (inspired by weakness), cowardice and *flight* from reality—the "ideal" . . . They are not free to know: *décadents need* the lie, it is one of the conditions of their preservation. (EH III BT, 2)

Because the healthy do not need to flee from reality, they not only have a wider range of perspectives at their disposal, but they also are capable of certain higher experiences that decadent people are not, Nietzsche claims. Because of this, they are more attuned to reality and are therefore capable of affirmation and of embodying truth. Zarathustra is an example of this: "His teaching and it alone has as its highest virtue truthfulness," he is "more truthful than any other thinker" (EH IV, 3).

Nietzsche's emphasis on truth in *Ecce Homo* cannot be explained away as merely rhetoric or a sign of impending madness. Nietzsche holds the same perspective on truth in *The Antichrist* and *Twilight of the Idols*. Daniel Conway has addressed this "emergent realism" in the works of 1888.[15] In those works, Nietzsche speaks about reality as the Dionysian flux of life that the healthy are able to stand, and the decadent need to be protected from. The healthy dare to look into the abyss, and the decadent shy away from it. In *The Antichrist* 30, he speaks about the decadent priest's "instinctive hatred of reality" that goes with such decadence, a pathological recoil of it. The opposite of that would be a healthy, receptive attunement to reality, which in fact amounts to the realization that there is no such thing as an external, objective "reality."

TRUTH-SEEKERS AND WAY-SEEKERS

The notion of a truth practice may seem foreign to the Western philosophical tradition but fits in very well with the Chinese way of thinking that emphasizes "way seeking" rather than "truth seeking." As comparative philosophers Hall and Ames point out, one of the more provocative questions raised among sinologists is whether the Chinese have any concept or theory of "truth" at all. According to sinologist Angus Graham, they do not. A correspondence theory of truth assumes a strict distinction between theory and practice. Propositions about the world are separated from practical engagement with it. Such a separation is mostly absent among the classical Chinese.[16] Hall and Ames concur that Chinese thought doesn't care very much about a theory of truth.[17] Westerners are Truth-seekers, Chinese are Way-seekers. In China, the most important philosophical question is not "what is the Truth?" but "what is the Way?"

> For the Chinese, knowledge is not abstract, but concrete; it is not representational, but performative and participatory; it is not discursive, but is, as a knowledge of the way, a kind of know-how. [. . .] For the Way-seekers, truth is most importantly a quality of persons, not of propositions. Truth as "Way" refers to the genuineness and integrity of a fully functioning person.[18]

Hall and Ames point out that the dominant Western conception of truth as correspondence has been based on the assumption of a single ordered world (a cosmos) and a reality/appearance distinction. Both of these assumptions (in which we recognize Nietzsche's true and apparent world, and his description of the ascetic ideal) were of no cultural importance in the Chinese tradition.[19] It is especially this absence of a theory of truth that might make for a fruitful comparison with Nietzsche's thinking about truth. Nietzsche's revaluation of truth is difficult to understand from a Western framework. But from a Chinese framework it makes perfect sense: whereas Nietzsche's camel is a Truth-seeker, his lion is a Way-seeker.

A Way-seeker seeks to "know his way around" in reality by being in touch with it. As Francois Jullien has described, Chinese thought doesn't use the Western metaphor of the veil of illusion that needs to be pierced in order to arrive at truth. Instead, it uses Zhuangzi's metaphor of the fishing net: language is a tool. Using a language is about skillfully learning to apply words and concepts in order to catch fish.[20] A Way-seeker learns how to negotiate reality by going with the flow, such as Zhuangzi's swimmer, who becomes one with the water, and cook Ding, who lets his knife find its way through the carcass guided by the *dao*. Therefore, for a Way-seeker, learning to know reality is connected with practices of self-cultivation and self-overcoming. In such self-cultivation, embodiment is of prime importance.

Self-cultivation is conceived of in various ways in Chinese thought.[21] Confucian virtue ethics emphasizes personal self-cultivation by means of studying the classics. For Confucius, ritual conduct (*li*) offers the opportunity to directly embody the wisdom of the ancestors. This wisdom can then be applied to one's own situation. Ritual conduct attunes one to the cosmos, especially when properly executed with *ren* (mostly translated with "true humanity"). A self-cultivated person is like a virtuoso pianist who gives an inspired rendition of a Mozart sonata; others can play that sonata as well, but the virtuoso can bring the music to life and deeply move his audience.

Daoism emphasizes being in harmony with the natural patterning of things (*dao*), not by means of rules and principles, but by letting go of all principles and allowing a natural spontaneity (*ziran*) to manifest itself. One needs no Confucian-style self-cultivation; cultural conditionings are to be let go of so one can give oneself over to "free and easy wandering" (*xiaoyaoyou*), as

Zhuangzi calls it. If the Confucianist can be compared to a virtuoso Mozart interpreter, the Daoist can be compared to a jazz musician who responds improvisationally with his solo to changes in the rhythm section of the combo. The jazz musician possesses a virtuoso flexibility; his performance is an unhindered, adaptive improvisation.

Chinese Buddhism finds a middle way between the Confucian mastery of the *li* and the Daoist spontaneous improvisation with regard to the *dao*: One has to recognize the emptiness in all things (the Confucian standards are empty), but one also has to learn to respond from out of that emptiness to the fullness of one's situation (rather than respond from out of one's karmic conditioning). As the Heart Sutra says, form is emptiness, but emptiness is also form. Whereas Confucianism emphasizes form, and Daoism emptiness, Buddhism emphasizes both.

TRUTH AS EMBODIMENT IN LINJI

Such Chinese notions of self-cultivation have influenced how the Zen tradition has interpreted Nāgārjuna. Whereas conventional truth has pragmatic and intersubjective meaning, ultimate truth can, in the Zen tradition, only be "known" by being one with it. In this way, Zen can be seen as initiating a new truth practice: Buddhist practice is not about attaining an insight into reality as it really is, but about personally embodying truth by becoming one with it.

In the Zen tradition, the Zen master is seen as a living Buddha, the recipient and embodiment of an esoteric dharma transmission, a Master of Truth.[22] Therefore, we could say that Nāgārjuna's attempts to overcome the adequationist conception of truth of the early Buddhist Abhidharma schools have been interpreted in the Zen tradition as a return to a magisterial conception of truth comparable to the pre-Socratic notions of the Masters of Truth.

Such a magisterial conception of truth can be found in Linji. For Linji, this notion of personally embodying truth is connected to being able to embody one's own personal standpoint (*zong*). Unlike teachers from other Buddhist schools, Linji provides no prescriptions for his students. He takes away any external rules, regulations, and prescriptions in order to make room for the spontaneous authenticity of the person itself to emerge:

> Followers of the Way, if you want to get the kind of understanding that accords with the Dharma, never be misled by others. Whether you're facing inward or facing outward, whatever you meet up with, just kill it! If you meet a buddha,

> kill the buddha. If you meet a patriarch, kill the patriarch. If you meet an arhat [enlightened person], kill the arhat. If you meet your parents, kill your parents. If you meet your kinfolk, kill your kinfolk. Then for the first time you will gain emancipation, will not be entangled with things, will pass freely anywhere you wish to go.[23]

Linji calls such a person "an authentic person without rank" (*wuwei chenren*), that is, a person independent of social status and the opinions of others.[24] Nietzsche would agree with Linji that such true persons are very rare: most people satisfy themselves with "phantom selves" (D 105). For Linji, any form of absolute truth that one thinks one must realize is a hitching post for donkeys: almost literally something that keeps camels occupied. Whereas Nāgārjuna overcomes the will to truth (the will to nirvana) and the ascetic ideal on a theoretical level, Linji overcomes it on an existential level: he wants his students to embody truth personally.

According to Béatrice Han, in a magisterial understanding of truth, "the truth value of a discourse will vary with the speaker's identity—it does not depend on gnoseological but on ethical criteria."[25] This is why, in the Zen koans, we see examples where the disciple imitates the master only to be severely castigated. The master is able to embody emptiness because he has become master over himself, just as the pre-Socratics: "The pre-Socratics are still governed by an instinctual hierarchy through which the multiple forces that compose the individual are harmonized."[26] The master is not someone who has discovered truth (not even the truth of emptiness) but who is able to *manifest* truth in his actions. This capacity stems from his *being true*. Peter Hershock describes this ability as a situational virtuosity: not a particular state of consciousness, but the capacity for liberated action and liberating intimacy.[27]

The embodiment of emptiness is not merely coming to an understanding of emptiness but means to fundamentally change one's very perspective toward reality. This also involves liberating oneself from redemptive teleological notions such as "enlightenment" and "nirvana." Enlightenment is not an object or a state that can be reached. Rather, it refers to a process of attunement to life, of improvisational virtuosity, of a liberating intimacy with all things. And, as Peter Hershock puts it, "If all things are truly interdependent and empty, there is no ultimate warrant for talking about "my enlightenment" or "your suffering."[28]

Such a capacity for manifesting truth, whether in Zen or for Nietzsche, is connected with a truth *áskēsis*. Such a truth áskēsis in Nietzsche and Zen is based on the following four characteristics: (1) not seeing truth as an essence to be realized; (2) not seeking truth as a telos (as exemplified in Linji's rhetoric);

(3) not imitating the teacher (this is a practice for camels), but "killing the Buddha"; (4) no longer seeking propositional truth but situational virtuosity (Way-seeking rather than Truth-seeking). This last point refers to the constructive aspects of this truth *áskēsis*: it is connected to an ongoing practice of self-cultivation. But how does one become a personal embodiment of truth? How can one enlarge the capacity to endure truth as embodied emptiness? Chapter 6 examines practices of self-overcoming through a self-cultivation of the body.

NOTES

1. Christoph Cox, *Nietzsche: Naturalism and Interpretation* (Berkeley: University of California Press, 1999), 28f. See his extensive references to the literature in n.16, 17, 18.

2. Cox, *Naturalism and Interpretation,* 32.

3. Cox, *Naturalism and Interpretation,* 61.

4. Timothy J. Freeman, *Zarathustra's Lucid Dream and Asian Philosophy,* unpublished manuscript, 6.

5. Stephen Addiss, Stanley Lombardo, and Judith Roitman, eds. *Zen Sourcebook: Traditional Documents from China, Korea, and Japan* (Indianapolis/Cambridge: Hackett Publishing Company, 2008), 9.

6. Albert Welter, *Monks, Rulers, and Literati: The Political Ascendancy of Chan Buddhism* (Oxford: Oxford University Press, 2006); Albert Welter, *The* Linji lu *and the Creation of Chan Orthodoxy: The Development of Chan's Records of Sayings Literature* (Oxford: Oxford University Press, 2008).

7. *Taishō shinshū daizōkyō* (henceforth "T") 47.497c11; see Watson, *The Zen Teachings of Master Lin-Chi,* 26.

8. T47.500c4; Watson, *The Zen Teachings of Master Lin-Chi,* 53.

9. T47.500b22; Watson, *The Zen Teachings of Master Lin-Chi,* 52.

10. T47.501c24; Watson, *The Zen Teachings of Master Lin-Chi,* 62.

11. Youro Wang, *Linguistic Strategies in Daoist Zhuangzi and Chan Buddhism: The Other Way of Speaking* (London: Routledge, 2003), 79.

12. Béatrice Han, "Nietzsche and the 'Masters of Truth': the pre-Socratics and Christ," in *Nietzsche and the Divine,* ed. John Lippitt and Jim Urpeth (Manchester: Clinamen Press, 2000), 117.

13. Han, *Nietzsche and the "Masters of Truth,"* 117.

14. Han, *Nietzsche and the "Masters of Truth,"* 117f.

15. It seems as if Nietzsche is reviving a two-world theory here, with "the world as it really is" inaccessible to cowards and weak people, but accessible to Nietzsche himself. Conway, however, attempts a charitable reconstruction and defense of this new emergent realism: it is meant as a symptomatology that "reduces all philosophical judgments, *pro* and *contra,* to signs (or symptoms) of an underlying physiological condition. Daniel W. Conway, "Beyond Truth and Appearance: Nietzsche's Emergent

Realism," in *Nietzsche, Epistemology, and Philosophy of Science, Part II*, ed. B. Babich and R. Cohen (Dordrecht: Kluwer, 1999), 111.

16. David L. Hall and Roger T. Ames, *Thinking from the Han: Self, Truth, and Transcendence in Chinese and Western Culture* (Albany: State University of New York Press, 1998), 129.

17. Hall and Ames, *Thinking from the Han*, 106.

18. Hall and Ames, *Thinking from the Han*, 104f.

19. Hall and Ames, *Thinking from the Han*, 110. Hall and Ames point to the Hebrew prophets who viewed truth as the strength to maintain oneself. They can be seen as the Hebrew Masters of Truth.

20. Jullien, *Detour and Access*.

21. This overview is based on Peter D. Hershock, *Chan Buddhism* (Honolulu: University of Hawai'i Press, 2005), 39–45.

22. See Alan Cole, *Fathering Your Father. The Zen of Fabrication in Tang Buddhism* (Berkeley: University of California Press, 2009).

23. T47.500b22; Watson, *The Zen Teachings of Master Lin-Chi*, 52.

24. In true deconstructive fashion, soon after Linji proposes this notion, he adds "What kind of shitty ass-wiper this authentic person without rank is!" (T47.496c10–14; Watson, *The Zen Teachings of Master Lin-Chi*, 13).

25. Han, *Nietzsche and the "Masters of Truth,"* 118.

26. Han, *Nietzsche and the "Masters of Truth,"* 118.

27. Peter D. Hershock, *Liberating Intimacy. Enlightenment and Social Virtuosity in Ch'an Buddhism* (Albany: State University of New York Press, 1995); Hershock, *Chan Buddhism*.

28. Hershock, *Chan Buddhism*, 103.

Chapter 6

Nietzsche and Dōgen on the Self-cultivation of the Body

As we have seen, both Nietzsche's strong skepticism and Linji's deconstruction are not merely a celebratory endless play with perspectives (a theoretical overcoming of skepticism), but also entail an ethical process of self-cultivation and self-overcoming; they aimed at becoming strong enough to become capable of manifesting truth (a practical overcoming of skepticism). For both Nietzsche and Zen, theory and practice are closely connected. As we've seen in chapter 5, in such a process, embodiment is very important. Let us therefore look at how the body is viewed by Nietzsche and another dialogue partner from the Zen tradition, Dōgen.

In this chapter, Nietzsche's views on the body and its cultivation will be further explored and compared with Dōgen's thought on body, mind, and cultivation, which is quite similar to Nietzsche's in its basic assumptions. In an interesting exercise of comparative philosophy, John Maraldo has contrasted the Western approach to the body-mind problem to that of Dōgen.[1] He argues that Dōgen's approach could give fresh impulses to a philosophical articulation of this problem beyond the myopic view of the Western philosophical tradition. Kōgaku Arifuku has pointed out some interesting correspondences between Nietzsche and Dōgen.[2] Both thinkers deny the priority of mind over body; they even deny that the distinction between mind and body is ultimately valid. Both reject the myth of the independent subject and criticize the ego. Dōgen's distinction between the intellectual/spiritual practice of philosophy and the somatic practice of zazen will be used to suggest some possible interpretations of Nietzsche's new philosophy *am Leitfaden des Leibes.*

NIETZSCHE'S OPPOSITION TO MIND-BODY DUALISM

On the one hand, Nietzsche seems to reverse the Platonic-Christian positive valuation of the mind over the body: as a great physiologist, he stresses the importance of the body.[3] On the other hand, Nietzsche attempts more than a simple reversal of the status of mind and body in his work: he wants to overcome the dualistic opposition between body and mind itself.

In the Western philosophy of mind, this dualism occurs in several forms. Some maintain a Cartesian separation between body and mind and consider them two different substances. But if the mind is a spiritual thing and the body a material thing, how do they interact? Some have tried to find solutions by reducing the mind to the body (materialism) or reducing the body to the mind (idealism). Such solutions have been connected with epistemologies of representation. In idealism, the mind comes to represent (or take the place of) the objects in the world. In realism and empiricism, the mind re-presents or reflects objects in the world as a mirror. Others have tried to work with the distinction of body and mind in a less dualistic way. Is the mind a thing, a substance, at all? Is the mind rather only a metaphor for what the brain does? What do words signifying mental events really mean?

Throughout his work, Nietzsche rejects the division of the human totality into a bodily part and a spiritual/mental part (the German word *Geist* can be translated as "spirit" or as "mind"; sometimes the word *Seele* (soul) is also used to indicate the mental part). He attacks the Platonic and Christian myth of the immortal soul in a mortal body as a life-denying, unhealthy perspective. For Nietzsche, the body seems more fundamental than mind or spirit. But it is not so much that the body is higher or more important than the mind: in an important sense, what we usually call "the mind" is simply shorthand for something about the body: "There are only bodily states: the mental ones are consequences and symbolism" (KSA 10, 9 [41]).

The German language has a distinction between *Leib* and *Körper*; the latter is close to the English "body," and the former doesn't exist in English. Nietzsche uses *Körper* (etymologically related to corpus/corpse, invoking associations with the Platonic notion of the body as a mere tomb for the soul) less frequently (150 times) than *Leib* (532 times). When Nietzsche does use *Körper*, he usually refers to the dualistic conception of an immortal soul within a mortal body, as when he refers to "the popular and totally false opposition between soul and body [*Körper*]" (BT 21). Out of a desire to avoid all dualistic ways of thinking and speaking about human nature, Nietzsche prefers to use *Leib* to speak about the whole human being.[4] *Leib* is not a mere biological metaphor; it refers to the body as a unity of body, mind and soul.[5]

In the chapter "On the Despisers of the Body" in *Thus Spoke Zarathustra*, Zarathustra speaks about two possible perspectives on human nature: a childish perspective that distinguishes between body and soul, and the perspective of "the awakened one, the one who knows," for whom the body is all there is: "'Body am I and soul'—thus talks the child. And why should one not talk like children? But the awakened one, the one who knows, says: Body am I through and through, and nothing besides; and soul is merely a word for something about the body"(TSZ I, 4).

Although Nietzsche uses the metaphor of the child elsewhere in *Thus Spoke Zarathustra* to refer to the third and ultimate transformation, here the child's perspective is meant to indicate an immature, unreflective perspective: the dualistic view that sees body and soul as two separate substances. But if the body is not something separate from the mind, then what is it? Zarathustra continues to further describe the "awakened" perspective on the body: "The body is a great reason, a manifold with one sense, a war and a peace, a herd and a herdsman. A tool of the body is your small reason too, my brother, which you call "spirit" [*Geist*], a small tool and toy of your great reason" (TSZ I, 4).

The body, as a great reason, is a multiplicity that contains and rules the conscious mind, the small reason. What we call "spirit" is a mere tool or vehicle for this larger multiplicity. This great reason is what rules us, even when we think we rule ourselves.[6] Zarathustra describes this great reason as a "Self" that lies behind the senses and the mind:

> Tools and toys are senses and spirit: behind them there yet lies the Self. The Self seeks with the eyes of the senses too, it listens with the ears of the spirit too.
>
> Always the Self listens and seeks: it compares, compels, conquers, destroys. It rules and is also the I's ruler. Behind your thoughts and feelings, my brother, stands a mighty commander, an unknown wise man—his name is Self. In your body he dwells, he is your body. (TSZ I, 4)[7]

BODY AND MIND IN THE BUDDHIST TRADITION

In the Buddhist tradition, the body-mind problem is not an issue in the same way as in the West. Although "body" and "mind" are used as conventional terms, they are not conceived as two different substances. The Buddhist view of non-self is radically opposed to the Platonic-Christian myth of an immortal soul in a mortal body. According to Buddhist philosophy, the human person can best be described as made up of five aggregates (*skandhas*): (1) matter or form (*rūpa*), (2) sensations or feelings (*vedanā*), (3) perception (*samjñā*), (4) volitional dispositions (*samskāra*), (5) consciousness (*vijñāna*). These five aggregates are constantly in flux, in an endless variety of changing configurations.

As Mistry and Morrison have shown, this Buddhist idea of the *skandhas* as the five types of processes that make up the individual psycho-physical organism, can be compared to Nietzsche's view of the person as a constellation of bodily drives:

> Nietzsche's perspective of man as a grouping of interfunctional energies "designated" and "organized" by such categorizations as intellect, thought, affections, will, memory and consciousness, bears an unmistakable analogy to the Buddhist analysis of personality. In Buddhism, the aggregates constituting the personality [. . .] *exist* as interdependent and conditioning; they do not incorporate an independent and specific essence.[8]

Nietzsche's view of the world as an ever-changing configuration of drives can be compared to the Buddhist view of the world as a continually shifting arrangement of impermanent formations (*dharmas),* which is expressed in the Buddhist doctrine of dependent origination (*pratītya-samutpāda*).

The Indian Buddhist schools, as is reflected in contemporary Theravāda Buddhism, shared a tendency to assume a somewhat negativistic and ascetic attitude to the body. The impurity of the body was assumed and was seen as something to be overcome through cultivation. As Buddhism moved to China and Japan, however, the body took on more of a positive importance and became a vehicle for transformation. The ninth-century Japanese Buddhist thinker Kūkai (774–835), founder of Shingon (mantra) Buddhism, stressed the role of the body. The crucial point for Kūkai is not only that enlightenment is not a final redemptive state to be achieved over many lifetimes, but also that it is not some other-worldly truth to be grasped via a mystical experience. The central idea in Kūkai's philosophy is to "become a Buddha in this very body" [*sokushin jōbutsu*].[9] Cultivation is therefore not aimed at attaining a mystical experience but at increasing the body's ability to process, to "digest" our ordinary experience, to incorporate the world. In this way, it reverses the way we understand the world in ordinary experience. Kūkai distinguishes his own esoteric Buddhism, which aims at such a reversal of perspective, from exoteric Buddhism, which aims at attaining a mystical enlightenment experience through self-cultivation (interpreted as a purification of body and mind).

Dōgen inherited from Kūkai the tradition of giving precedence to the body over the mind. He maintained that in cultivation, the body plays the most important role. As Kim notes

> The human body, in Dōgen's view, was not a hindrance to the realization of enlightenment, but the very vehicle through which enlightenment was realized [. . .] Dōgen claimed that we search with the body, practice with the body, attain enlightenment with the body, and understand with the body.[10]

Although in Japanese Buddhism the body seems to be more important than the mind, in reality the distinction between body and mind is only provisional. According to the contemporary Japanese philosopher Yuasa, Japanese thought tends to view the mind-body as a single evolving system that can be further developed, integrated, and enhanced, leading up to an exemplary, evolved human existence: the accomplished artist, the theoretical genius, the enlightened religious master.[11]

Cartesian dualism differs in at least two respects from Japanese notions of body and mind. Firstly, although mind and body may be conceptually distinguishable from some perspectives, they are not seen as ontologically distinct.[12] Secondly, Japanese thought—and Eastern philosophies generally—treat mind-body unity as an achievement attained by a disciplined practice, rather than as an essential relation. This undercuts the Western dichotomy between theory and practice.[13]

In Japanese thought, the notion of *shinjin ichinyō* (oneness of body and mind) has been developed in order to overcome a dualistic approach to body and mind. It is used in Zen, No drama, and martial arts (judo, kendo), and it is an ideal for inward meditation as well as for outward activities. *Shinjin* (body-mind) is a Japanese neologism; it is rarely found as a phrase in Chinese.[14] Although a provisional distinction can be made between the body and the mind (corresponding to the distinction between the *rūpa*-aggregate and the remaining four "mental" aggregates), body-mind is conceptually seen as a unity. Such a unity between body and mind is also expressed in Dōgen's work: "Because the body necessarily fills the mind and the mind necessarily fills the body, we call this the permeation of body and mind."[15]

Dōgen criticizes the so-called "Seneki heresy," a view that maintained that the mind does not perish after bodily death (a dualism similar to that of Descartes):

> You should consider carefully that the Buddha-dharma has always maintained the thesis of the nondual oneness of body and mind. And yet, how can it be possible that while this body is born and dissolves, mind alone departs from the body and escapes from arising and perishing? If there is a time when they are one and another time when they are not, the Buddha's teaching must be false indeed.[16]

This primordial unity of body and mind, which plays an essential part in the philosophies of both Kūkai and Dōgen, has been contrasted by Shaner to Platonic and Cartesian philosophy, in which body and mind are by definition ontologically distinct.[17]

BODY-MIND AS WILL TO POWER

Nietzsche would agree with such a Japanese Buddhist notion of the primordial unity of body-mind. Throughout his work, Nietzsche stresses that body-mind dualism itself is an unhealthy, life-negating perspective that must be overcome and replaced by a more healthy and even "higher" perspective: both body and mind, as well as nature as a whole, are to be interpreted as will to power. This amounts to a naturalism that is not a reductionism.[18] Whenever Nietzsche speaks about the body, it is not just the physiological body, but the body as will to power that he refers to. The body is for Nietzsche something much higher and complex than we usually assume (KSA 10, 7 [133]); it contains the mental functions as well. All conscious processes of thinking and knowing are a result of underlying physiological drives. Therefore, in order to overcome the unhealthy perspective of body-mind dualism and become capable of holding the "higher" and healthier perspective of body and mind as will to power, Nietzsche stresses that one must engage in a process of cultivation of the body.

In *Beyond Good and Evil* 36, Nietzsche describes the world as will to power. On the basis of the assumption that "nothing else were 'given' as real except our world of desires and passions, and we could not get down, or up, to any other 'reality' besides the reality of our drives," Nietzsche describes this reality as "a kind of instinctive life in which all organic functions are still synthetically intertwined along with self-regulation, assimilation, nourishment, excretion, and metabolism." This is the reality that Nietzsche proposes to designate as will to power.

Will to power is Nietzsche's new conception of nature without the dualistic oppositions of subject and object, knower and known, epistemology and ontology. Instead, will to power conceives all of nature as engaged in an active interpretation. It is a rigorously antimetaphysical naturalistic attempt to account for the multiplicity and perpetual becoming of the natural world. The spiritual, the mental, and the divine no longer occupy a world apart. Nature has no ontological hierarchy. Nietzsche replaces a hierarchy of being with a hierarchy of power and relative value. The result is a substance-less, subject-less, non-essentialist worldview, an a-metaphysical metaphysics.

Nietzsche looks for a criterion to judge nature that is immanent in nature itself. Nature, seen as will to power, as a "great reason," is alive and has self-consciousness, and judges itself, according to immanent criteria, in terms of sickness and health. For Nietzsche, the will to power is the most suitable perspective from which to view the process of struggle and incorporation that makes up life: "Life itself is *essentially* appropriation, injury, overpowering of what is alien and weaker; suppression, hardness, imposition of one's own forms, incorporation and at least, at its mildest, exploitation [. . .] because life itself is will to power" (BGE 259). Nietzsche's interpretation of life as will to power is part of his project of "the dehumanization of nature and then the naturalization of humanity, after it has attained the pure concept of 'nature'" (KSA 9, 11 [211]). The dehumanization of nature refers to taking back our anthropomorphic projections on what we perceive as nature "out there."

Let us return to Zarathustra's two perspectives on human nature, the childish one and the awakened one. For Nietzsche, the awakened perspective refers to experiencing oneself not as a combination of two substances, body and soul, but as the multiplicity of will to power. The "one who knows" is capable of a perspective from a higher vantage point, a perspective "from above." Could this be the Hyperborean perspective that Nietzsche himself claims to inhabit and from which he claims to be able to criticize other perspectives?[19] In several places in his work, Nietzsche alludes to such a perspectival order of rank, most notably in *Beyond Good and Evil* 30. I will go into this further in chapter 11.

If there is a Cartesian perspective "from below," where one experiences oneself as body and soul, and a Nietzschean perspective "from above," where one experiences oneself (and the world) as will to power, is there any way to ascend or aspire to this higher perspective? From a Cartesian perspective, the mind is seen as a knowing subject, whereas the body is considered part of a world of matter. The way to ascend to a higher perspective would be through gaining understanding and insight, that is, through mental cultivation. In such a way, one can gain more accurate mental representations of the world.

From the perspective of will to power, however, the process of knowing is not a mirroring or representing of the world by means of the mind. Rather, our bodily drives interpret the world, or even, they digest the world. Nietzsche uses the metaphors of nutrition [*Ernährung*] and incorporation [*Einverleibung*]. Thought, judgment and perception are based on a making equal that is similar to the way the amoeba incorporates matter (KSA 12, 5 [65]). Knowledge is just a form of assimilation, a means of nutrition. It does not start with sense impressions (only the superficial speak of "impressions," Nietzsche says), but with an active creation of forms, that make up what we then call "reality:"

> This is how our world, our whole world, arises: and this whole world, that belongs to us alone and is created by us, doesn't correspond to any so-called "true reality," no "in itself:" but it is our only reality, and "knowledge" turns out to be, from this perspective, only a means of nutrition (KSA 11, 38 [10]).

In Nietzsche's philosophy, what is called *Wirklichkeit* [reality] is indeed something that works: *Wirklichkeit* refers to the *energeia* of nature, understood as will to power.

Our thoughts, convictions, and judgments result from constellations of bodily drives that not only interpret, but even create our world. Perception is simplification, according to what can be incorporated into the body. "There is nothing 'objective' in that: but a kind of incorporation and adjustment, for the sake of nutrition" (KSA 11, 26 [448]). Therefore, the kind of beliefs and views that we hold is not determined by some kind of correspondence with reality, but by their usefulness for our bodily drives, and by our capacity to digest those views.

The distinction between body and mind, that we continue to experience even if we know this to be false, is only one of the fundamental illusions that we cannot shake off. According to Nietzsche, we experience a world that is characterized by continuity, stability, substance, a self, a free will, irrespective of whether this is actually the case. The reason for this is that these illusions have proven to be of evolutionary benefit, and they have become second nature to us. Certain ways of perceiving and experiencing reality become incorporated over time, when they acquire, through repetition, a kind of solidity and power over us. They become instinctual. "I speak of instinct, when a *judgment* [. . .] has become incorporated, so that it now spontaneously manifests itself, and doesn't have to wait for stimuli anymore" (KSA 9, 11 [164]). We are able to live successfully due to such completely certain beliefs that we willingly accept without question, for example, that external objects exist, or that we possess free will. We have "incorporated opinions about certain causes and effects, about a mechanism, about our 'I,' and so on. It's all false however" (KSA 9, 11 [323]).

The will to power is on the one hand both an epistemological and an ontological doctrine: it offers an account of knowing and of being. On the other hand, it is neither, because it collapses the oppositions of subject and object, knower and known, upon which epistemology and ontology are traditionally founded.[20] It seems to inescapably lead to ontological skepticism (there can be no such thing as "ultimate reality" or "reality in itself, apart from all interpretation") and to epistemological skepticism (it is impossible to determine whether some perspectives are more "true" than others).

And yet, as we have seen in chapter 5, Nietzsche conceives of a new truth practice based on perspectivism and will to power, which is connected to becoming an optimally functioning, active, healthy, continually changing set of configurations and constellations of will to power. Such an optimally functioning organism would be able to incorporate truth, not in the sense of adequately reflecting reality [*Wirklichkeit*], but in the sense of maximally participating in the ongoing process of reality (the *Wirkung* of *Wirklichkeit*) seen as the *energeia* of will to power. Such a practice of self-cultivation involves leaving behind incorporated illusory and life-denying perspectives (such as the unhealthy Platonic-Christian myth of the mind incarcerated in the body) and incorporating more "truthful" and affirmative perspectives on life (such as the perspective on body and mind as will to power). "Truth" should be seen here not as something to be discovered, but as something being created in the ongoing digestion and interpretation of experience.

This means that not everyone is capable of knowledge to the same extent. Just as it takes a strong digestion to be able to consume certain food, one's state of bodily health determines what one is able to know. One's constellation of bodily drives determines which types of experience one is able to digest and which perspectives one is able to inhabit. Nietzsche distinguishes an order of rank in perspectives. Certain elevated perspectives can only be inhabited by those of strong health. Only a Master of Truth is able to incorporate certain "higher" and "truer" perspectives. Incorporating truth does not mean "viewing the world in a more truthful way," in the sense of forming more truthful representations of an objective world, but in the sense of being able to engage with the world from an epistemic paradigm that is beyond representational thinking. Again, the constellation of one's physiological drives determines how one views the world and to what extent one is able to refrain from not only distorting one's perception, but to step outside the very representational model of knowledge itself.

TO WHAT EXTENT DOES TRUTH BEAR INCORPORATION?

In part III of *The Joyous Science*, Nietzsche starts with a few aphorisms that all stress the need for a radical change in perspective. In *The Joyous Science* 108, entitled "New Battles," Nietzsche mentions the story that after Buddha's death, his shadow was seen for centuries in caves. In a similar way, it is necessary for free spirits to fight the shadows of God after his death. In *The Joyous Science* 109, Nietzsche further explains what this battle is about: the old, metaphysical ways of viewing the world and oneself need to be replaced by the perspective of will to power. Nature needs to be dehumanized and de-deified, and the human needs to be naturalized.

In *The Joyous Science* 110, Nietzsche explains why this battle is so difficult. Originally, the drive for error was the only precondition for life. Only very recently, a drive for truth has become one of the human drives as well. It has become party in the ongoing battle between drives that determines our perception and experience. Now, "the thinker is the being in which the drive for truth and these life-sustaining errors fight their first battle. [. . .] Compared to the importance of this battle, everything else is unimportant" (JS 110). Nietzsche concludes the aphorism by describing a dangerous new experiment: would it be possible to incorporate truth, rather than error? "To what extent does truth bear incorporation" (JS 110). Nietzsche speculates that if such a battle is won, the result could be "a higher organic system" (JS 113). In the notebook fragments of that period, Nietzsche toys with the idea that "the entire development of the spirit is perhaps a matter of the *body*: it is *the story—now becoming perceptible*—of a *higher body's shaping itself*. The organic rises to higher levels. Our thirst for knowledge of nature is a means, by which the body wants to perfect itself" (KSA 10, 24 [16]).

In *Beyond Good and Evil* 230, Nietzsche further addresses this fundamental battle that takes place in the thinker. He first discusses two forces that operate within the mind: on the one hand, the drive to incorporate, appropriate and assimilate new experiences—often by "editing" them: simplifying some aspects, overlooking other contradictory aspects, fitting them into existing structures. On the other hand, a sudden "decision to ignorance": the refusal to let in experiences and ideas that cannot be incorporated, that are too indigestible. Nietzsche adds that what the mind is capable of processing depends on its capacity for digestion: the mind resembles most of all a stomach.

Both of these drives are not concerned with truth. In the thinker, however, they are met by a third force: a drive to gain a deep and differentiated perspective on things, to unmask illusions, to translate man back into nature (this drive for truth needs to be distinguished from the will to truth that Nietzsche criticizes in *On the Genealogy of Morality* and elsewhere). Nietzsche describes this drive as cruel and its task as strange and foolish, but nevertheless it is his own chosen task—perhaps an expression of the unchangeable "granite of spiritual *fatum*" deep within him (BGE 231)? Thinkers such as Nietzsche willingly engage in a battle between the life-sustaining errors that they need to survive and the life-threatening truths that their intellectual integrity pursues. The willingness and the ability to engage in such a battle is for Nietzsche an important criterion for judging an individual: "How much truth does one *bear*, how much truth does one *dare*, that is more and more for me the actual measure of worth" (EH Foreword, 3).

In Nietzsche's notebook fragments of summer 1881, many fragments speak about such a process of incorporating truth. In August 1881, Nietzsche is overcome in an almost mystical way by the thought of the eternal recurrence. Very soon after this experience, he starts to speculate about incorporating this new perspective on life. A concept for a new book called *The Recurrence of the Same* can be found:

1. The incorporation of basic errors.
2. The incorporation of the passions.
3. The incorporation of knowledge and renunciatory knowledge [*verzichtendes Wissen*]. (Passion for knowledge)
4. The innocent one. The solitary one as an experiment. Life becoming lighter, more humble, weaker—transition.
5. The new *heavyweight: the eternal Recurrence of the Same.* Infinite importance of our knowledge, our mistakes, our habits, way of life, for all that comes after us. What do we do with the *rest* of our life—we, who have lived it for the largest part in essential ignorance? We *teach the teaching*—it's the most effective way to *incorporate* it ourselves (KSA 9, 11 [141]).

The first three chapters all deal with incorporation. Chapter one presumably aims to describe the existing state of affairs in the average human being: his perceptions and judgments of the world are only made possible by the incorporated basic errors that allow him to function in life. Chapter two would describe how those basic errors change the individual and give him his passions. Not only how one thinks, but also how one feels is the result of incorporated judgments about life. One's incorporated errors and passions allow one to function as a knowing and feeling creature. As Nietzsche adds in KSA 9, 11 [144]: "The opinions and errors change the individual and give him his drives—or: the incorporated errors."

Chapters three and four would presumably speak about the confrontation of incorporated illusions and passions with the drive for truth in the thinker (similar to Nietzsche's description in *The Joyous Science* 110). The incorporation of renunciatory knowledge [*verzichtendes Wissen*] refers to becoming aware of how untrue many incorporated judgments are and developing a healthy mistrust of those judgments. This already partially negates their instinctual power over the individual. But realizing the erroneous character of those judgments is not sufficient, as Nietzsche notes: "in order to act, you must believe in errors; and you will still act on these errors once you have seen through them as errors" (KSA 9, 11 [102]). The new "knowledge drives" are still powerless in comparison to the ancient erroneous instincts that have become deeply incorporated over time: "how powerless all physiological *knowledge* so far has been! While the old physiological *errors* have acquired spontaneous force" (KSA 9, 11 [173]).

The process of incorporation of truth has a negative quality: it is not so much a matter of substituting true judgments for incorporated errors. One can at most incorporate the insight into the erroneous nature of one's present incorporated judgments, such as ego, permanence, and substance, and aim to gradually dislodge them. One of the ways in which Nietzsche attempts to do this is to confront them with the reversed perspective of will to power:

> Extreme positions are not replaced by moderate ones, but by other extreme—but reversed—positions. And so belief in the absolute immorality of nature, in a lack of purpose of meaning, is the psychologically necessary *affect* when belief in God and an essentially moral order is no longer tenable. (KSA 12, 5 [71])

This process of undoing one's present incorporated errors might only be partially successful, Nietzsche suspects: "the final truth of the flow of things doesn't bear *incorporation*, our *organs* (to *live*) are designed for error. [. . .] To live is the precondition for knowledge. To err is the precondition for living, even to err fundamentally. Insight into our errors does not overrule them!" (KSA 9, 11 [162]). But Nietzsche doesn't think this is a reason for bitterness: "We must love our errors and cherish them, they are the womb out of which our knowledge grows. [. . .] To love and stimulate life for the sake of knowledge; to love and stimulate errors and delusions for the sake of life. [. . .] To want to know and to want delusion are like ebb and flow. If *one of them* rules absolutely, man will be ruined" (KSA 9, 11 [162]).

Within these limitations, the best one can do is to continually strive to understand everything as becoming, to deny our existence as individuals, and to look into the world out of many eyes.

> Our striving after seriousness consists in understanding everything as becoming, denying ourselves as individuals, looking into the world through as *many* eyes as possible, *living* in drives and activities *in order to* make ourselves eyes for that, giving oneself over to life *from time to time* so that one can later rest one's eyes on it: *entertaining* the drives as the foundation of all knowing, while being aware of where they oppose knowledge—in short, *to wait* and see to what extent *knowledge* and *truth* can be *incorporated.* (KSA 9, 11 [141])

Chapter five speaks about the result of this training process: the incorporation of Nietzsche's new teaching, the eternal recurrence. Incorporating this thought will transform us: "When you incorporate the thought of thoughts, it will transform you. The question in everything that you will do, "do I want to do this infinitely often" is the *greatest* heavyweight (KSA 9, 11 [143]). The thought of the eternal recurrence is incorporated when it "manifests itself spontaneously and doesn't have to wait for a stimulus anymore"

(KSA 9, 11 [164]), when it has become instinctual. But such a spontaneity is the result of a long and arduous training process.

Nietzsche's book project never saw the light of day. But he did publish *Thus Spoke Zarathustra*, which can be read as a description of Zarathustra's efforts to incorporate the thought of the eternal recurrence. According to some interpretations, Zarathustra's eventual success at this task indicates his final redemption (see chapter 8).[21]

THE CULTIVATION OF THE BODY: EDUCATING THE DRIVES

For Nietzsche, the way to study the mind is by the body. "Nothing good has come yet out of mental introspection. Only now, when one tries to learn about all mental phenomena (e.g., thought), guided by the body, does one begin to get anywhere" (KSA 11, 26 [374]). To start with introspection is unfruitful (KSA 11, 26 [432]).

Nietzsche put this also into practice himself: he often composed his books not sitting behind a desk or writing table, but during eight hour walks through nature. He claims that the figure of Zarathustra came to him during those long walks. In *Ecce Homo* he writes, "Do not believe any idea that was not born in the open air of free movement—in which the muscles do not also revel" (EH II, 1). Nietzsche wants to philosophize *am Leitfaden des Leibes*, with the body as a guide: "Important: to proceed from the body and use it as a guide [*Leitfaden*]. It is the infinitely richer phenomenon which is tangible and allows for clearer observation. The belief in the body is better established than the belief in the spirit" (KSA 11, 40 [15]).

If our bodily drives interpret the world for us, how can we bring about a shift in perspective? How can we shift from one "reading" of the world to another? Since our perception of an ordered world is fundamentally related to our bodily activity, Nietzsche's answer is, through cultivation of the body (seen as will to power): the development of different physiological habits, perform physiological practices, diet, climate: "In order to transform the soul, one has to transform the body" (KSA 10, 17 [6]). In *Twilight of the Idols,* Nietzsche stresses that any cultivation does not start with the "soul" but with the body:

> It is decisive for the lot of a people and of humanity that culture should begin in the *right* place—*not* in the "soul" (as was the fateful superstition of the priests and half-priests): the right place is the body, the gesture, the diet, physiology; the *rest* follows from that . . . Therefore the Greeks remain the *first cultural event* in history: they knew, they *did*, what was needed; and Christianity, which despised the body, has been the greatest misfortune of humanity so far. (TI 9, 47)[22]

For Nietzsche, "psychology is now again the path to the fundamental problems" (BGE 22), but the term *psychology* now refers to a proper physio-psychology that explains thoughts, feelings and convictions as a product of the various constellations and interplays of bodily drives. Such a physio-psychology is further described by Nietzsche as "morphology and the doctrine of the development of the will to power" (BGE 23).

In his book *Composing the Soul*, Graham Parkes shows how Nietzsche speaks about such a cultivation in terms of an education of the drives.[23] In *Daybreak*, Nietzsche describes cultivation of the bodily drives with the metaphor of the gardener:

> *What we are at liberty to do.*—One can dispose of one's drives like a gardener and, though few know it, cultivate the shoots of anger, pity, curiosity, vanity as productively and profitably as a beautiful fruit tree on a trellis; one can do it with the good or bad taste of a gardener. (D 560)

Such gardening work requires weeding and pruning and cultivation through nourishment. In *Daybreak* 109, for example, Nietzsche describes six methods to combat the vehemence of a drive. One can avoid its immediate cause, strictly regulate its fulfillment, abandon oneself intentionally to its wild fulfillment, attach a very painful thought to its fulfillment, exert oneself physically and thus redirect one's energies, or weaken one's total physical and psychological organization. Yet, Nietzsche goes on to relativize the gardener allegory, which suggests an "I" that is in charge of the cultivation process: the fact "*that* one *desires* to combat the vehemence of a drive at all, however, does not stand within our power," as "at bottom it is one drive *which is complaining about another*" (D 109).

This education of the drives is for Nietzsche strongly connected with the incorporation of new perspectives on reality, oneself and life as a whole. In the later notebook fragments, a program for such an education of the drives can indeed be found:

> *Overcoming the affects?* No, not if that means their weakening and annihilation. *But to take them into service*: which may involve tyrannizing them for a long time (not even as an individual, but as a community, a race, etc.). Eventually one gives them back their freedom with confidence: they love us like good servants and ultimately go where our best inclines. (KSA 12, 1 [122])

Only sustained cultivation over a long time will create the kind of discipline and mastery that will make it possible to achieve true spontaneity, where the drives will naturally function for the benefit of the entire organism.

> *Summa: mastery* over the passions, *not* their weakening or extirpation! The greater the will's power of mastery, the more freedom may be given to the passions. The "great human being" is great by virtue of the range of free play of his desires and of the still greater power that is able to take these magnificent monsters into service. (KSA 12, 9 [139])

THE BUDDHIST SELF-CULTIVATION OF BODY-MIND

A process of self-cultivation, seen as a practical project aiming at the enhancement of the personality (seen as the five *skandhas*), is essential to Buddhism. In early Indian Buddhism, such self-cultivation took place primarily through the mind (*citta*). Through cultivating the mind (*citta-bhāvanā*), the Buddhist practitioner could develop self-awareness or mindfulness.[24] In such a conception, the mind is used to cultivate the body: weed out certain traits, cultivate those worthy of cultivation, and bring new drives into being.[25] Morrison compares this with Nietzsche's gardener analogy. Also Mistry has pointed out many affinities between early Buddhist and Nietzschean views on self-cultivation. Both aim at a creative transformation of suffering.

In Japanese Buddhism the somatic aspects of mindfulness are stressed more. Not the mind but the body is the primary locus of Japanese Buddhist practice: not *citta-bhāvanā* but *shugyō* (personal cultivation): "a practical project aiming at the enhancement of the personality and the training of the spirit by means of the body."[26] In Japanese culture, it is commonly held that

> the human being can gain control of the spirit or intellect only through the consummation of physical form by way of mastery of the body. In the beginning, considerable effort is required to make all actions and passions of the self conform to a definite concrete pattern; but by shackling oneself with such a form, it is possible to shape the body, which otherwise remains one-sidedly instinctual in its nature, into a proper and appropriate agent.[27]

Although this formulation still hints at a dualism between mind and body, the very character of the dualistic mode in the relationship between the mind and the body will gradually change through the process of cultivation, and make room for a non-dualistic perspective on body and mind. Cultivation itself reverses the way we understand the world in ordinary experience. The integration of mind and body is only partial in the average human being. Full integration is the result of prolonged, assiduous cultivation. The goal of such cultivation is the development of the extraordinary human being: "Cultivation is to impose on one's own body-mind stricter constraints than are the norms of secular, ordinary experience, so as to reach a life beyond that which is led by the average person."[28]

The first phase in such a process of cultivation, a phase characterized by discipline, asceticism, and self-mastery, is to place the body into a special form or posture. Gradually, the posture becomes second nature—second nature in Nietzsche's sense as a protective skin that allows the first nature to develop unhindered (see chapter 7). A process of incorporation, in Nietzsche's terms, takes place, a movement from consciousness to instinct. This instinct is further refined through protracted discipline (as is apparent for example in martial arts practice).

The second phase of self-cultivation consists of relaxing the discipline ("giving the drives free reign"), and trusting a natural spontaneity to emerge. One allows the first nature to play out freely. In Nietzschean terms, the "I," a dominant drive which usually controls the other drives, has been dissolved into a plurality of drives, that has learned to function harmonically (or more accurately, agonistically: their continued mutual struggle allows for a dynamic equilibrium). Therefore, a dualistic approach to self-cultivation (where the mind seems to cultivate the body) is the beginning but not the end. As mentioned earlier, the notion of *shinjin ichinyō* serves to overcome body-mind dualism. Nagatomo describes how, in the course of Zen cultivation, the aspirant may understand *shinjin ichinyō* to mean

> "making the body and mind one" or "reaching the oneness of the body-mind," which is for the aspirant an ideal to be achieved. On the other hand, through deepening his Zen cultivation, the aspirant comes to understand the oneness of the body-mind [. . .] At such a time, there is no distinction between achieving an ideal and the ideal achieved, between practice and theory. [. . .] the understanding of *shinjin ichinyō* undergoes, we may surmise, an epistemological reorientation through the transformation of the somaticity.[29]

According to Yuasa, in the end only the mind-body unity can lead to true mastery, and even to true knowledge:

> True knowledge cannot be obtained simply by means of theoretical thinking, but only through "bodily recognition or realization" (*tainin* or *taitoku*), that is, through the utilization of one's total mind and body. Simply stated, this is to "learn with the body," not the brain. Cultivation is the practice that attempts, so to speak, to achieve true knowledge by means of one's total mind and body.[30]

Graham Parkes and Robert Morrison disagree on where to look for affinities between Buddhist and Nietzsche's thought of self-overcoming. According to Parkes, "it is precisely Nietzsche's insistence on the deep wisdom of the body, and on the fact that almost all of our 'drive-life' goes on beneath the level of consciousness, that brings him close to the Buddhists' insistence on the somatic aspects of mindfulness and their efforts to circumvent or undercut conceptual thinking."[31] In response to Parkes, Morrison contends that Nietzsche's emphasis on the body "has little or no connection with Buddhist doctrine or practice. Although in Buddhism there is no "soul," the locus of Buddhist practice is citta, or "mind." [. . .] To say that the body is such a locus is simply wrong."[32] In his reply to Morrison, Parkes specifies that the priority of *citta* is a doctrine of early Buddhism and that the later Mahāyāna Buddhism focuses more on the body. He adds that "what brings Mahāyāna Buddhism closer to Nietzsche is its this-worldly concern with "attaining enlightenment in this very body."[33]

DŌGEN'S SOMATIC PRACTICE OF ZAZEN

However, how to go about attaining such an enlightenment in this very body? Although he rejects the separation between body and mind, Dōgen provisionally distinguishes between intellectual-spiritual practice and somatic practice:

> There are two methods of learning the Buddha Way: learning with the mind and learning with the body. Spiritual practice means learning with all the capabilities of the mind [. . .] Somatic practice means learning with the body, and practicing especially with the body of flesh and blood. The Buddha-body emerges only out of the practice of the Buddha Way, and what emerges out of the practice of the Buddha Way is called the Buddha-body.[34]

Spiritual practice (practice with the mind) has to do with the cultivation of wisdom. Somatic practice can be external (practicing the Buddhist precepts, the regulations governing everyday life) or internal (zazen, seated meditation practice). In zazen one can, through "forgetting" limited conscious thought (Nietzsche's small reason) recognize oneself as the body, which is inseparable from the great world of nature (great reason). In this meditation practice, the everyday attitude toward body and mind is reversed:

> The everyday attitude attempts to master the body by means of the mind, on the premise that the subject of consciousness, the I, is able to control to some extent what goes on with the brain, the mouth, and other movements of the body. Dōgen's approach to the mind-body relationship reverses this everyday attitude, insofar as he advocates the mastery of the mind by means of the body.[35]

In zazen, a situation is created in which the drives cultivate themselves. As Yuasa puts it, "the departure point of cultivation assumes not the mind dominating the body, but rather, the body's dominating the mind. To sit in meditation is to carry out this attitude."[36] Zazen facilitates an attitude where the conscious mental process can take a step back, and the body can dominate the mind. The question could arise, what is it that puts the body in the right situation? And what recognizes what is the right situation? The Buddhist answer to this would be: *bodaishin*, the drive toward awakening. *Bodaishin* manifests itself as a conscious intention to practice zazen but is itself a result of a particular configuration of bodily drives. Therefore, *bodaishin* cannot be cultivated directly; it will develop as the body is further cultivated.

Nagatomo speculates that Dōgen's zazen practice somatically transforms one of the five *skandhas*, the *samskāras* (dispositional tendencies as a potential formative energy). Through sitting immovably and maintaining a mental attitude of positionlessness, the *samskāras* are slowly purified, and like and dislike come to an end.[37] Dōgen speaks about "letting drop off the body-mind" (*shinjin totsuraku*). According to Nagatomo, this phrase should not be interpreted as any kind of "Zen enlightenment" experience in the sense of an *unio mystica*, an emancipation from delusion or an epistemic state of "seeing things as they are," but as a switching of perspectives: body and mind are no longer dualistically experienced as two separate entities, but body-mind is experienced as a nondual unity. What is dropped is the dualistic everyday perspective on body and mind.[38]

Although from the everyday perspective, body and mind are experienced as two separate things, a higher perspective is possible where body-mind is experienced as a continually changing configuration of *dharmas*, that doesn't contain any "I." In Nietzschean terms, it is possible, through cultivation of the body, to replace the experience of an "I" (a life-sustaining error for the average individual) with a more pluralistic experience of a community of drives without an "I." Such a higher perspective is called "samadhic awareness" by Dōgen, as Nagatomo explains:

> The "oneness of the body-mind" cannot be understood from the perspective of our everyday existence. Epistemologically, this means that the function of external perception as it is directed towards the natural world, is incapable of experiencing, much less understanding, the oneness of the body-mind, and hence is useless in articulating the meaning of the oneness of the body-mind. [. . .] There must necessarily be an epistemological apparatus that operates in samadhic awareness quite distinct and different from the order that is operative in the everyday perceptual consciousness.[39]

Such an epistemic shift from a relative, provisional dualism that operates in our everyday existence to the nondualism that operates in samadhic awareness is not the result of some psychological breakthrough, but connected with a transformation of the body.

The perspectives of "everyday perceptual consciousness" and "samadhic awareness" can be compared to Zarathustra's perspectives of the child and the awakened one. In Nietzschean terms, a dualistic perspective "from below" is replaced by a nondualistic perspective "from above" (BGE 30), which is made possible by the body's enhanced capacity for incorporation and digestion. Seen from below it appears that the mind is holding these perspectives; seen from above it becomes clear that these perspectives belong to the body itself. A "higher body" is exactly higher in the sense that it is capable of holding and incorporating a wider variety of perspectives, including those "from above." Such a perspective "from above" is not "true" in the sense of adequately representing reality, but more inclusive in the sense of encompassing both truth and delusion.

DISCUSSION

Both Nietzsche and Dōgen ultimately aim at the incorporation of new and liberating perspectives through the body. Dōgen offers a specific somatic practice for this (zazen), whereas for Nietzsche, this somatic practice is more implicitly apparent from his long daily walks that could be seen as serving a similar purpose as zazen. For both, such a somatic practice is complemented by the subsidiary intellectual practice of philosophy *am Leitfaden des Leibes*: not a process of discovering "truths" by means of introspection and thinking, but a means to increase the body's capacity for incorporation.

For Dōgen as well as for Nietzsche, metaphors, images, and symbols no longer refer to an external world, but are purely used for their soteriological impact. As Kim remarks, for Dōgen, "words are no longer things that the intellect manipulates abstractly and impersonally, but rather, things that work intimately in the existential metabolism of one who uses them philosophically and religiously in a special manner and with a special attitude."[40] Also for Nietzsche, his metaphors are not meant to refer to "actual" reality, but function as tools to incorporate new and more liberating perspectives. Nietzsche's philosophy can be interpreted as one huge effort to improve the intellectual metabolism of his readers.

Dōgen can be useful to support such a reading of Nietzsche in several ways. He also rejects Cartesian dualism (see his quote about the Seneki heresy). He stresses the need for a practice of self-overcoming. And such a self-cultivation of the body allows the practitioner to inhabit more elevated perspectives. It is also important, however, to delineate some differences between Nietzsche's thought and that of Dōgen.

First of all, Nietzsche emphasizes that his project of incorporating truth is an experiment. Its chances for success or failure are unknown (perhaps, if one considers Nietzsche's biography, one should deem it a failure in his own case). Buddhist philosophy, on the other hand, is a soteriology that stresses the importance of faith in the reality of enlightenment. Of course, Dōgen's thought can help us in our interpretation of what Nietzsche's experiment consisted of. But from within Nietzsche's own philosophy, many questions arise (some of which were also asked by Nietzsche himself) about the viability and internal consistency of his project of incorporating truth. Nietzsche speaks about overcoming life-preserving errors. But is his own project of "translating man back into nature" not also a form of manipulation of reality? Why is Nietzsche's project of "incorporating truth" better than the common life-preserving errors? In *The Joyous Science* 344 Nietzsche seems to ask himself the same questions: to what extent are we still pious? Why this unconditional will to truth? Is it the will, not to let oneself be deceived? But why not let oneself be deceived? Interestingly enough, as we will see, Dōgen also problematizes the Buddhist ideal of "seeing things as they are," and speaks about enlightenment and delusion as two sides of the same coin (see chapter 8).

Second, although Nietzsche would seem to agree with Dōgen about the need for a practice of self-cultivation of the body in order to bring more elevated perspectives within reach, he is vague about what such a practice would look like. Although he stresses the importance of incorporating new perspectives, in his writings no clear instructions for any somatic practice can be found. Although Nietzsche himself often walked eight hours a day while writing his books, anything like zazen remained utterly foreign to him. We could charitably interpret Nietzsche's daily walks as a practice of self-cultivation of the body, creating a situation where the drives are able to cultivate themselves freely. Nevertheless, Dōgen's zazen constitutes a much more systematic somatic practice. It is interesting (but futile) to speculate whether such a somatic practice would have given Nietzsche a better opportunity to realize self-overcoming in his own life.

Finally, there is the question whether the perspective on the self-cultivation of the body would ultimately be the same for Nietzsche and Dōgen. Although both may consider body-mind dualism as a preliminary perspective that will be superseded as a result of the self-cultivation of body-mind, it seems that their "elevated" perspectives on self-cultivation differ widely. For Nietzsche, self-cultivation seems a matter of will to power, a notion that is replete with the metaphors of struggle, overpowering, and exploitation. The Japanese notion of *shinjin ichinyō* suggests a harmonious underlying unity, far removed from the overpowering and exploitation of will to power. According to Arifuku, for example, Nietzsche differs from Dōgen in that his conception of the body still retains certain features of individuality, and that he speaks about the body in a context of evolutionary biology.[41]

To a large extent, these differences are real. It is of no use to try to make a Buddhist out of Nietzsche. Let us, however, attempt to go a little further in attempting to interpret Nietzsche's thought through a Buddhist lens. In the next chapter, I will turn to Nietzsche's criticism of the notion of ego and individuality, and attempt a non-anthropocentric interpretation of the will to power. Perhaps, it might be possible to relegate Arifuku's remarks on Nietzsche to a self-oriented, or "lion stage" interpretation of Nietzsche's thought.

NOTES

1. John C. Maraldo, "The Practice of Body-Mind: Dōgen's Shinjingakudō and Comparative Philosophy." In *Dōgen Studies*, ed. William R. LaFleur, 112–30 (Honolulu: University of Hawai'i Press, 1985).

2. Kōgaku Arifuku, "The Problem of the Body in Nietzsche and Dōgen," in *Nietzsche and Asian Thought*, 214–25.

3. According to Conway, we need to read Nietzsche from the "standpoint of the physiologist": man needs a new set of instincts, and Nietzsche sees himself as the physiologist who can bring about such a transformation. Dan Conway, personal communication, 5/23/2008.

4. In the quotes in this chapter, *Leib* is used in the German original for "body," unless indicated otherwise.

5. Hutter, *Shaping the Future,* 26f.

6. As Parkes notes, this is literally the reverse of Plato, who wrote in the *Phaedo* 80a that the soul was the master of the body: the soul, as divine, "is by nature fitted to rule and lead," while the body, as mortal is "to obey and serve." Quoted in: Graham Parkes, *Composing the Soul: Reaches of Nietzsche's Psychology* (Chicago: University of Chicago Press, 1994), 254. See also the notebook fragment: "Your body contains more reason than your reason. And that which you call your wisdom—who knows what your body needs just this wisdom for" (KSA 10, 4 [240]).

7. See also the notebook fragments: "Behind your thoughts and feelings stands your body and your bodily self: the terra incognita. For which purpose do you have these thoughts and feelings? Your bodily self wants something with them" (KSA 10, 5 [31]).

8. Mistry, *Nietzsche and Buddhism*, 65.

9. *Sokushin jōbutsu* ("this very" + "body" + "attain" + "Buddha") literally means "this very body attaining Buddha." According to Kūkai, esoteric practice enabled one to be enlightened here and now. See David Edward Shaner, *The Bodymind*

Experience in Japanese Buddhism: A Phenomenological Study of Kūkai and Dōgen (Albany: State University of New York Press, 1985), 75f.

10. Kim, *Eihei Dōgen—Mystical Realist*, 101.

11. Kasulis, "Editor's Introduction," in: *The Body: Toward an Eastern Mind-Body Theory*, Yasuo Yuasa (Albany: State University of New York Press, 1987), 13. This calls to mind Nietzsche's discussion of the artist, the genius and the saint in *Schopenhauer as Educator*.

12. Kasulis, *Editor's Introduction*, 1.

13. Kasulis, *Editor's Introduction*, 1f.

14. Shigenori Nagatomo, *Attunement through the Body* (Albany: State University of New York Press, 1992), 123.

15. Dōgen, *Shōbōgenzō, Juki.* Quoted in: Kim, *Eihei Dōgen—Mystical Realist*, 101.

16. Dōgen, *Shōbōgenzō, Bendōwa*. Quoted in: Kim, *Eihei Dōgen—Mystical Realist*, 102.

17. Shaner, *The Bodymind Experience in Japanese Buddhism*. Shaner uses Husserl's phenomenological method to empirically verify the bodymind experience described by Kūkai and Dōgen. His study has received mixed reviews. Faure, for example, criticizes his "halfbaked philosophical comparativism," which turns Kūkai and Dōgen into precursors of Husserl.

18. Brian Leiter has argued that Nietzsche's naturalism is not substantive (the view that the only things that exist are natural or physical things) but methodological: "Although many philosophers simply equate 'naturalism' with substantive naturalism of one variety or another, this seems to me a mistake: what distinguishes the naturalist is the eschewal of a priori inquiry as the primary philosophical method, not a particular substantive commitment." Brian Leiter, "The Paradox of Fatalism and Self-Creation in Nietzsche," in *Nietzsche*, ed. J. Richardson and B. Leiter (Oxford: Oxford University Press, 2001), 303.

19. See *The Antichrist* 1 for Nietzsche's explicit reference to the Hyperboreans, and to have found the exit of the millennia of the labyrinth. In *The Antichrist* 2 it becomes clear that this exit is connected with viewing the world as will to power.

20. Cox, *Naturalism and Interpretation*, 241.

21. This is, for example, Heidegger's interpretation (Martin Heidegger, *Nietzsche I* (Pfullingen: Neske, 1961), 331f. According to Brusotti, Zarathustra's challenge is exactly the reverse: to call up the thought of the eternal recurrence from the depths of his unconscious to the surface of his consciousness (Marco Brusotti, *Die Leidenschaft der Erkenntnis: Philosophie und ästhetische Lebensgestaltung bei Nietzsche von* Morgenröthe *bis* Also sprach Zarathustra (Berlin/New York: de Gruyter, 1997), 595.

22. See Daniel W. Conway, *Nietzsche & the Political* (London/New York: Routledge, 1997), 114 for more on this passage.

23. Parkes, *Composing the Soul*, 1994. The discussion below is greatly indebted to chapters 8 and 9 of this work.

24. See Morrison, *Nietzsche and Buddhism,* 105.

25. Morrison, "Response to Graham Parkes' Review," *Philosophy East and West* 50/2 (2000), 276.

26. Yuasa, *The Body*, 85.
27. Arifuku, *The Problem of the Body in Nietzsche and Dōgen*, 218f.
28. Yuasa, *The Body*, 98.
29. Nagatomo, *Attunement Through the Body,* 126f.
30. Yuasa, *The Body*, 25.
31. Graham Parkes, *Nietzsche and Early Buddhism,* 265.
32. Morrison, *Response to Graham Parkes' Review*, 275.
33. Graham Parkes, "Reply to Robert Morrison," *Philosophy East and West* 50/2 (2000), 281.
34. Dōgen, *Shōbōgenzō, Shinjingakudō*. Quoted in: Arifuku, *The Problem of the Body in Nietzsche and Dōgen,* 218.
35. Arifuku, *The Problem of the Body in Nietzsche and Dōgen,* 219.
36. Yuasa, *The Body*, 119.
37. Nagatomo, *Attunement through the Body.*
38. Nagatomo, *Attunement through the Body,* 131.
39. Nagatomo, *Attunement through the Body,* 129.
40. Kim, *Eihei Dōgen—Mystical Realist*, 88.
41. Arifuku, *The Problem of the Body in Nietzsche and Dōgen*, 224.

Chapter 7

The Self-overcoming of the Ego

From an other-oriented perspective, the path of self-overcoming is seen as a path toward the realization of truth. Chapter 4 showed the challenges connected with self-overcoming from this perspective: doing battle with the ascetic ideal and the will to truth. Chapter 5 showed a self-oriented perspective on realizing truth: not working toward *discovering* truth, but toward *being* truth, being able to incorporate truth. Chapter 6 showed how such an incorporation of truth would be possible through the cultivation of the body, in which one becomes healthy enough to inhabit more elevated perspectives. However, there is a problem: in the process of incorporation, who is doing the incorporating? From a conventional perspective, this is the self. But from Nietzsche's perspective of will to power, this sense of self is nothing but one drive calling itself "I." And from the Buddhist perspective of *anātman*, the self is a fiction. Ultimately, as the notions of "I" and "will" are recognized to be illusory, self-overcoming must take place without a self.

SEEING THROUGH THE FALLACIES OF THE EGO

As formulated by Descartes, thinking is a function of the rational "I," without which it would be impossible. For Nietzsche, however, thinking is not an activity performed by a subject but an autonomous activity: "a thought comes when 'it' wants to, not when 'I' want it to" (BGE 17). We add a doer to the deed, but that is a projection performed afterwards. Actually it is the body that thinks, and consciousness is an impotent by-product instead of a causally effective agent. The importance that we tend to give to consciousness is misplaced: it operates in function of a "much higher and overviewing intellect," in whose service the conscious ego is but a tool (KSA 10, 24 [16]). Self-consciousness arrives very late on the scene as an almost superfluous afterthought. It is very imperfect compared to the inborn and incorporated unitary activity of the bodily functions. The most important activities are carried out subconsciously (KSA 9,11 [316]). Our conscious representations, intentions and goals are a sign language for a completely different process. Our conscious "I" is an instrument of this other process. For Nietzsche, conscious thought is nothing but the expression of a multiplicity of drives.

From a Cartesian perspective, self-overcoming looks like the mind cultivating the body and mastering the passions. But from a perspective of will to power, it's a matter of the body dominating the mind, and drives mastering drives. There is no voluntaristic master agent that can perform a process of self-enhancement. Consciousness is not an independent causal agent, but is a by-product of subconscious bodily drives. Conscious thought is nothing but the expression of the many drives that make up the individual as will to power. The practice of educating the "subterranean" drives cannot be directed by consciousness, since consciousness has no access to those realms (it is itself a by-product of those drives). Therefore, the gardener analogy becomes ever more problematic. Who will perform such a task? The subject is for Nietzsche not so much a unity but a multiplicity of bodily drives.

According to Nietzsche, our perspective on reality will change radically once we manage to liberate ourselves from the incorporated fallacy of the ego: we can then learn what it means to "experience cosmically":

> *Main Thought!* [. . .] the *individual* himself is a *fallacy*. Everything which happens in us is in itself *something else* which we do not know. [. . .] "the individual" is merely a sum of conscious feelings and judgments and misconceptions, a *belief*, a piece of the true life system or many pieces thought together and spun together, a "unity," that doesn't hold together. We are buds on a single tree—what do we know about what can become of us from the interests of the tree! But we have a consciousness as though we would and should be *everything*, a phantasy of "I" and *all* "not I." *Stop feeling oneself as this phantastic ego!* Learn gradually to *discard the supposed individual*! Discover the fallacies of the ego! Recognize *egoism* as *fallacy*! The opposite is not to be understood as altruism! This would be love of *other supposed* individuals! No! **Get beyond** "*myself*" and "*yourself*"! **Experience cosmically!** (KSA 9, 11 [7])

We find references to such cosmic experiencing throughout Nietzsche's work. Already in his early essay *Schopenhauer as Educator* we read

> There are moments and, as it were, sparks of the brightest fire of love in the light of which we no longer understand the word "I"; beyond our being there lies

> something which in these moments becomes a here-and-now, and therefore we desire from the bottom of our hearts to bridge this distance. (SE 5)

Zarathustra sometimes speaks from a quasi-mystical perspective in which the "I" has undergone dissolution. In "Before Sunrise," he describes an experience of the world from a horizon that transcends an anthropocentric view (see chapter 9). And such a perspective can also be found in Nietzsche's notebook fragments: "I am too full: thus I forget myself, and all things are in me, and beyond all things there is nothing more: where have *I gone*" (KSA 10, 5 [1] 238).

As we saw earlier, the overcoming of the ascetic ideal involved assuming a non-essentialist and non-teleological perspective. Now it is clear that a world-oriented perspective needs to be non-anthropocentric as well. Nietzsche stresses the need for practice in overcoming the anthropocentric perspective:

> We want to cure ourselves from the great basic insanity, *to measure everything after ourselves* [. . .] as if everything *revolves around us*. One walks on the street and thinks every eye is aimed at oneself. [. . .] What is needed is *practice* in seeing with *other* eyes: practice in seeing apart from human relations, and thus seeing *objectively* [sachlich]! To cure human megalomania! (KSA 9, 11 [10])

The result of such a process is a transformed way of perceiving ourselves:

> To describe the history of *the sense of I* [. . .] Perhaps it will end with our recognizing instead of the I the relationships and enmities among things, thus *multiplicities* and their laws: with our *seeking to free* ourselves from the *fallacy* of the I [. . .] Transform the sense of the I! Weaken the personal tendency! Accustom the eye to the actuality of things! (KSA 9, 11 [21])

And later on: "The task: to *see* things *as they are*! The means: to be able to see with a hundred eyes, from many persons" (KSA 9, 11 [65]).

THE THREE BODIES OF THE BUDDHA

Since Buddhism is a philosophy of no-self, where else to look for inspiration when it comes to seeing through the fallacies of the ego? In a sense, this task lies at the heart of the Buddhist path. So how does Buddhism describe the world from a non-anthropocentric and world-oriented perspective? In early Buddhism, the doctrine of *pratītya-samutpāda* attempts to express the interrelatedness and interconnectedness of all things. In Mahāyāna Buddhism, the theory of the three bodies of the Buddha attempts to describe the world as the cosmic Buddha body.

Mahāyāna Buddhism operates from a worldview that differs radically from our currently prevalent Newtonian preconceptions of time and space. It subscribes to the *trikāya* doctrine of the three bodies of the Buddha. According to this theory, the Buddha manifests himself in three bodies, modes, or dimensions. First, in his historical manifestation as Shākyamuni, the Buddha has a *nirmānakāya*, a created body which manifests in time and space. Second, as an archetypical manifestation, the Buddha can manifest himself as a sublime celestial form in splendid paradises, using a *sambhogakāya* or body of mutual enjoyment. Third, as the very principle of enlightenment, the Buddha manifests himself as a *dharmakāya*, the reality body or truth body, also interpreted as ultimate reality.[1]

According to the Mahāyāna Buddhist worldview, reality (the *dharmakāya*) should not be seen as a collection of lifeless objects, but as a vital agent of awareness and healing. Reality itself is continually co-active in bringing all beings to universal liberation. The sacred is immanent in space and time. Such a worldview has great soteriological consequences for spiritual practice. Rather than aiming at achieving higher states of personal consciousness, or therapeutic calm, the point of spiritual practice becomes to embody, or appreciate, or participate in, or achieve a liberating intimacy with reality itself.

According to Dōgen, the ultimate reality of the *dharmakāya* should not be interpreted ontologically as a transcendent cosmic Being that contains or projects the world, but should be seen as the fundamental activity of the world itself. For Dōgen, all of existence is itself buddhahood. Self-overcoming results in the realization of what he calls a "true human body" (*shinjitsu-nintai*): the body that has been transformed through self-cultivation.[2] For Dōgen, body and mind are not only interwoven with each other, they are also united with the world as a whole: "The whole earth is the true body of the Buddha, the whole earth is the gateway to liberation, the whole earth is the eye of Vairocana Buddha, and the whole earth is the *dharmakāya* of the Buddhist self."[3]

The individual psycho-physical constitution is extended to a cosmic dimension. Dōgen uses phrases as "the body-mind of Dharma," "the body-mind of the Buddhas and ancestors." Therefore, understanding is only possible when we participate in this totality. Then the true human body functions freely and authentically in harmony with the entire universe[4]: "The entire universe is precisely this very human body (*shinjitsu-nintai*); birth-and-death and coming and going are the true human body."[5]

For Dōgen, the way we construct our experience in thinking and language is not excluded from universal buddhahood—the latter is not a metaphysical notion of some supreme Being, but rather describes an ongoing activity that is intrinsic to the temporality of all phenomena.[6] Although it could be described as a form of "immanent transcendence," it also differs from Western notions of immanence (e.g., the notion of an immanent order in nature that can be understood and explained on its own terms, regardless of the existence of a transcendent, supernatural creator beyond it.)[7]

Can such a cosmic way of viewing the world also be found in Nietzsche? Perhaps, if we interpret his notion of will to power as a cosmic body. Graham Parkes has proposed exactly such an interpretation: will to power should be understood as a non-substantial force field of interpretive drives, in which mind, body and world are inextricably interpenetrated. Such an interpretation of will to power runs parallel to Mahāyāna Buddhist notions of reality as a cosmic body.

WILL TO POWER AS A COSMIC BODY

Graham Parkes points to a redivinization of nature that can be found in *Thus Spoke Zarathustra.*[8] Will to power is presented as a non-anthropocentric perspective that sees nature and the inanimate world ("the earth") as itself divine. Zarathustra exhorts his listeners to "stay faithful to the earth." Parkes argues that Nietzsche's notion of will to power can be interpreted as pointing to the divinity of the cosmos as part of a new Dionysian pantheism. Life is continual self-overcoming and will to power, however,

> while this would mean that the transcendent God of morality is refuted, a pantheistic cosmos full of immanent Gods is not. But to experience the world this way, as a play of will to power engaged in perpetual self-overcoming, one has to understand from experience the thought of eternal recurrence.[9]

Anyone who is able to incorporate the thought of eternal recurrence experiences the world as a force field of divine play.[10] Parkes argues that Nietzsche's understanding of the world as will to power "gives us a picture of the cosmos as a force field of interpretive drives. This understanding, which is consonant with a number of Daoist and (Mahāyāna) Buddhist ideas, is eminently conducive to reducing anthropocentrism."[11]

Interpreting will to power as a "cosmic body" would make sense of Nietzsche's notebook fragment where he refers to the possibility of experiencing ourselves cosmically as buds on a single tree (KSA 9, 11 [7]). It might also shed more light on a puzzling and challenging aspect of Nietzsche's thought that Parkes calls attention to: the multiplicity of drives may extend further than we would imagine. Nietzsche speculates (as part of the experimental philosophy that he has just announced in *The Joyous Science* 51) in *The*

Joyous Science 54 that our bodily drives may be transpersonal and connected with archaic sources: "I have *discovered* for myself that ancient humanity and animality, indeed the entire age and past of all sentient being continues in me to create [*fortdichtet*], to love, to hate, to infer." (JS 54). As Parkes comments,

> The experiment Nietzsche would have his readers undertake involves supposing that the drives that constitute our present experience have their roots in the archaic past: not only in our personal prehistory, but in the past of the human race—and on back beyond the animal past behind that.[12]

This quote points to the thoroughly non-anthropocentric nature of Nietzsche's views on self-overcoming. As Nietzsche writes in *The Joyous Science* 349, as a researcher into nature, one should come out of one's human corner. Self-overcoming is not a personal project for Nietzsche: ultimately it is a matter of life overcoming itself in and through the individual. The individual is merely the arena in which such an impersonal process plays itself out. For Nietzsche, the task of self-overcoming is not undertaken by a subject; it is part of the self-overcoming of life.[13] And since the individual, conceived as a constellation of drives, is ultimately part of his entire archaic heritage and part of entire nature, self-overcoming ultimately turns out to be a cosmic affair. Therefore, when Nietzsche introduces the notion of will to power in part II of *Thus Spoke Zarathustra*, he does so in the chapter called "On Self-Overcoming" (TSZ II, 12). However, this is no longer a personal self-overcoming, but a non-anthropocentric self-overcoming of life itself. Earlier, Zarathustra had already said that "man is something that shall be overcome" (TSZ Prologue, 3). Now, he reveals that life is "*that which must always overcome itself*" (TSZ II, 12).

This continual flux of self-overcoming is fundamentally a creative activity: "Becoming as inventing, willing, negating the self, as self-overcoming: no subject, but a doing, positive, creative" (KSA 12, 7 [54]). Individual self-overcoming now comes down to allowing this flux of self-overcoming to work through oneself, unhindered by any notion of teleology.[14] As Parkes points out, a full engagement with this creative activity is the source of all creative will:

> For Zarathustra, as long as human beings feel themselves subordinated to transcendent forces in the form of divinities they will lack confidence in their own will to create. But if they are able to face up to the impermanence of "becoming" and fully engage the cycles of death and rebirth and destruction and creation that characterize the world of a deity like Dionysus, such self-overcoming will allow the forces of the creative will to work and play—perhaps even dance—through them.[15]

The world-oriented perspective of will to power looks at nature without the categories of subject and object. And yet the very grammar of the language we use already presupposes subject and object. Interestingly enough, the Japanese language doesn't presuppose this. Often only the verb is explicitly used, which could be a great asset for imagining a world view that doesn't reify the world. As Ōkōchi points out, the Japanese term for nature, *shizen*, originally didn't mean anything objective or objectified that takes place in front of or outside human beings, but was rather an expression of the spontaneous way of being of all things. In its original usage it does not take on a substantive but only an adjectival or adverbial form, connected to our terms *naturally* or *by nature*.[16] Seen from such a perspective, people are not essentially distinguished from other beings, but are grasped as a part of the realm of beings.

PRACTICING SELF-OVERCOMING WITHOUT A SELF: LETTING GO OF THE GARDENER

However, a world-oriented description of the world as will to power is only a theoretical solution. How is self-overcoming without a self as a philosophical *áskēsis* even possible, and what would it look like? As we have seen, in his comparison between Nietzsche and Buddhism, Morrison uses the Buddhist practice of *citta-bhāvanā* to interpret Nietzsche's "gardener analogy" of cultivating the drives. The question in all this is, however, who decides to employ those selfless drives in the service of self-discipline? Who or what is behind the steering wheel? Nietzsche makes it very clear that it is not the individual itself. Therefore, according to Parkes,

> Morrison fails to see the inconsistency of his supposing that it is the "I" that is doing the self-overcoming, since he never asks the (very Buddhist) question Nietzsche so often poses: Who, or which drive, or what group of affects is the agent of willing, disciplining, or whatever, in this particular situation?[17]

In his earlier work, Nietzsche often uses various active metaphors to describe self-overcoming. In his later work, we find many passive and even fatalistic formulations suggesting a process of ripening, pregnancy, organic growth, and the absence of struggle, emphasizing the allowance of transcendence and openness. This is expressed metaphorically by Zarathustra as "the lion must go under." The lion needs to let go of the sense of "I will." It must unlearn its heroic will, let go of its will to knowledge and truth, since "A labyrinthine human being never seeks the truth, but—whatever he may try to tell us-always and only his Ariadne" (KSA 10, 4 [55]).

For Nietzsche, the attainment of self-mastery is only the first step on the way to self-overcoming. The first phase is a "preschooling in spirituality [*Geistigkeit*]," which consists of "gaining control over the restraining instincts" (TI 8, 6). One loses such spirit and self-control when one has become strong enough and no longer needs it (TI 10, 14). At that point, one can "give back to the drives their freedom" so that they will now "go where our best inclines" (KSA 12, 1 [122]). Therefore, whereas self-mastery is the first step, forgetting the self is the second and final step of self-overcoming. As Parkes puts it,

> The final stage of self-overcoming, then, consists of daring, after prolonged practice of self-mastery, to relax the discipline and trust to natural spontaneity. [. . .] The eventual relaxation takes place because the ego, which would otherwise control the process, has been overcome—dissolved into a plurality of drives—in the course of the protracted self-discipline. What is responsible for the disciplining are various (groups of) drives, and there comes a point where the discipline is no longer necessary because these various groups have learned to live in harmony with each other.[18]

As we saw in chapter 6, the drives must be brought under control by a dominant instinct so that one functions as a coherent whole. Nietzsche praises Goethe, for example, for having disciplined himself into a whole. From a self-oriented perspective, self-overcoming means to overcome the disgregation of the will, a kind of anarchy in which the instincts are no longer controlled.

Nietzsche increasingly comes to write about such a disgregation of the will in terms of decadence: "Nothing has preoccupied me more profoundly than the problem of decadence—I had reasons" (CW Foreword). The logic of decadence consists in an ultimate "no" to life: "decadence is the will to something else, the will to change the world, the will that opposes life—the will to salvation."[19] To be decadent means to be against life. Nietzsche had read Paul Bourget's essay on decadence[20] and followed his analysis: decadence manifests through a lack both of energy and of a central, organizing drive to control that energy. It denotes decline or decay from a previous state of vitality.[21] However, the problem with decadence is that it ultimately cannot be overcome through conscious, willful attempts to overcome it. As Benson notes,

> Decadence in effect operates with a kind of centripetal force that constantly sweeps one back into its center. No matter how much one attempts to overcome decadence, one can never really escape its overwhelming pull. Even the self-aware attempt to overcome decadence still ends up being one more manifestation—and perhaps even the most *virulent* manifestation—of decadence.[22]

The more one reacts to decadence, the more vicious the reaction. Therefore, the only possibility is not to react to it, to somehow take a step back from this downward spiral, to forget the self, and let unconscious processes do their work. Nietzsche tries to articulate how such a process can be thought:

> Every perfect action is exactly unconscious and no longer willed, consciousness is an expression of an imperfect and often morbid personal state. The personal perfection as dependent upon the will, as a being conscious [. . .] is a caricature, a kind of inner contradiction . . . For the degree of being conscious renders perfection impossible . . . (KSA 13, 14 [128])

All conscious attempts to become what one is actually only interfere with this process. From this point of view any self-oriented model of self-overcoming becomes very problematic. Once the "I" is recognized as illusory, every conscious attempt at self-overcoming is therefore recognized as necessarily in vain. Instead, what is needed is a willingness to surrender to chaotic reality, letting go of the boundaries of the "I."

When it comes to cultivation, there is no conscious subject that prunes a garden of drives according to some blueprint. Drives have their own telic structure. Self-overcoming takes place in the context of a hierarchical organizational process of the drives. Some individual drives form a hierarchy that allows some drives to redirect others so that the total can achieve a singular expression. One metaphor for such a process would be a football team, in which the players can adjust each other and players can take the role of captain in turn.

From such a perspective, to educate the drives would in fact amount to a self-education of the body. This is a reversal of the normal attitude of using the subject of consciousness to control the drives of the body. The whole operation is overseen by what Nietzsche calls "a kind of directing committee in which the various *dominant desires* make their voices and power effective" (KSA 13, 11 [145]).

The aim of such a cultivation of the body is not physical health per se, but to become capable of "looking into the world through as *many* eyes as possible," and be able to "make ourselves eyes for that" (KSA 9, 11 [141]). Such new ways of seeing will enable us to overcome the fixed modes of thinking, feeling, and doing that result from the illusion of an autonomous ego. One can then incorporate a radically new "awakened" perspective in which the ego acknowledges its status as a mere instrument of the "great reason" of the body.

DŌGEN ON FORGETTING THE SELF

For Dōgen, the challenge of describing self-overcoming without a self is present throughout his whole work. In his essay *Genjōkōan*, he attempts to describe the difference between a self-oriented perspective on self-overcoming and a world-oriented perspective that goes beyond the self: "Carrying the self forward to verify-in-practice (*shushō*) the myriad things is delusion; for the myriad things to come forth and verify-in-practice the self is enlightenment."[23]

For Dōgen, the experiential realization (embodied understanding) of such a world-oriented perspective is a matter of self-forgetfulness. In zazen, one can, through forgetting the small self, recognize oneself as the Self, which is inseparable from the great world of nature: "To study the Buddha Way is to study the self. To study the self is to forget the self. To forget the self is to be verified by the myriad things [of the world]."[24] Dōgen's view of such a self-overcoming without a self is described by Davis as

> an ongoing practice of enlightening, as an unending path of discovery, [. . .] a nondualistic and nonwilling perspectivism. It is a perspectivism insofar as reality only shows itself one aspect at a time. From a deluding standpoint, this aspect gets determined by the will of an ego-subject that goes out and posits a horizon that delimits—filters or "schematizes"—how a thing can reveal itself. From an enlightening perspective, the aspect is allowed to reveal itself through an event wherein the self has "forgotten itself" in an engaged yet nonwillful openness to the presencing of things.[25]

Nietzsche might describe this as follows: in forgetting oneself, one no longer attempts to grasp nature by projecting one's own anthropomorphic illusions onto it, but is able to embody the perspective that one's own body-mind organism is a part of nature, no more and no less, a nature understood as a purposeless, meaningless whole (will to power). Such a perspective allows for true affirmation. Zazen, as a somatic practice, aims to extinguish the incorporated "basic error" of an ego-centered perspective, in which one experiences oneself as an isolated subject separate from the objective world, so that the constellation of wills to power that constitute one's body-mind organism will act spontaneously and in accordance with "nature." This means that there will no longer be a static sense of self but only a continuous shedding of skin, a perpetual becoming, an endless play of wills to power in their mutual struggle. The transformation does not arise out of a willful self-assertion, but is an event in which one can at most willingly participate. The process of interpretation and incorporation never stops; a world-oriented practice of self-overcoming allows one to participate unobstructedly in this process of illuminating and creating reality in mutual dependence.

Dōgen's notion of openness to the presencing of things and his radically immanent embodied perspective on enlightenment reveal a rather different perspective on Zen and Zen practice than has been common in the West: not so much a universal spirituality that leads up to a transcendent mystical religious experience "beyond the mind," but an immanent affirmation and even sacralization of this very mind and this very body. But although Dōgen's notion of enlightenment as the embodiment of universal buddhahood points to a radical ontological immanence, he does also speak about the realization of enlightenment in terms of a radically transformed new relationship to the world, indicating the possibility of an epistemological transcendence. It is possible to transcend our ordinary ways of experiencing the world.

Is Dōgen's notion of ongoing practice of forgetting the self a useful perspective from which to view Nietzsche's philosophy of self-overcoming? Are there any similar notions to be found in Nietzsche's work?

HOW ONE BECOMES, WHAT ONE IS

Nietzsche's way of speaking about self-overcoming is perhaps most surprising and strange in *Ecce Homo*. Nietzsche speaks here about how his education of his drives has made him into what he is in strictly non-moral and physiological terms. Daniel Conway describes this as follows:

> Here he speaks not of his momentous and lasting achievements, but of "all these small things which are generally considered matters of complete indifference" (EH II, 10). When expressly dispensing the basic tenets of "his morality," he speaks not of the *Übermensch*, the Antichrist, active forgetting, or virile warriors, but of his insights into *diet* (EH II, 1). When accounting for "everything that deserves to be taken seriously in life," he turns not to the questions that exercise kings, judges, and priests, but to the more fundamental "questions of nourishment, abode, spiritual diet, treatment of the sick, cleanliness and weather" (EH IV, 8). Through his seemingly idle experiments with nutrition, location, climate, and recreation, he gradually became what he is.[26]

Self-overcoming seems to be all about creating the right circumstances for body and spirit. The advice that Nietzsche gives is in terms of nutrition (in the widest sense of the word): "how do *you* personally have to nourish yourself in order to attain your maximum of strength, of *virtù* in the Renaissance style, of moraline-free virtue" (EH II, 1). This is followed by a discussion of German and English cooking. But we shouldn't forget that in *Beyond Good and Evil* 230, Nietzsche has said that the mind resembles most of all a stomach. Nietzsche continues to take on the subjects of place, climate, and relaxation.[27]

Nietzsche stresses the absence of any struggle and describes self-overcoming as a physiological and subconscious process, something that grows within us underneath the surface of consciousness. Nietzsche describes "know thyself" as a recipe for ruin. In order to become what one is, one has to have no idea of who one is and keep a distance from all the great imperatives.

> Becoming what you are presupposes that you have not the slightest inkling *what* you are. From this point of view even life's *mistakes* have their own sense and value, the temporary byways and detours, the delays, the "modesties," the seriousness wasted on tasks which lie beyond *the* task. [. . .] where *nosce te ipsum* [know thyself] would be the recipe for decline, then forgetting yourself, *misunderstanding* yourself, belittling, constricting, mediocritizing yourself becomes good sense itself. [. . .] You need to keep the whole surface of consciousness—consciousness *is* a surface—untainted by any of the great imperatives. Beware even every great phrase, every great pose! With all of them the instinct risks "understanding itself" too soon—Meanwhile, in the depths, the organizing "idea" with a calling to be master grows and grows—it begins to command, it slowly leads you *back* out of byways and detours, it prepares *individual* qualities and skills which will one day prove indispensable as means to the whole—it trains one by one all the *ancillary* capacities before it breathes a word about the dominant task, about "goal," "purpose," "sense." (EH II, 9)

The metaphors of self-cultivation and self-overcoming, which suggest a conscious pursuit of emancipation and authenticity, leading up to a sovereign individual, give way to a metaphor of forgetting oneself, misunderstanding oneself, in order to not interfere with the "regulating idea" that grows below the surface of consciousness. For Nietzsche, it seems, any conscious effort at becoming what one is, is ultimately in vain.[28] He even views his own self-overcoming from such a non-anthropocentric perspective:

> I lack any memory of ever having exerted myself—there is no trace of a *struggle* evident in my life, I am the opposite of a heroic nature. "Wanting" something, "striving" for something, having in view a "purpose," a "wish"—I know nothing of this from experience. [. . .] I have not the slightest wish for anything to be other than it is; I myself do not want to be different. But this is how I have always lived. I have never wished for anything. (EH II, 9)

This is a baffling quote. It is historically incorrect, and even seems disingenuous. Nietzsche himself must know that these statements about himself are patently untrue. But let us try to connect this perspective on self-overcoming with another metaphor that Nietzsche uses, that of pregnancy. Nietzsche speaks about "that state of profound tension to which pregnancy condemns the spirit"(EH II, 3). In *Daybreak* 552, he had already written on "the holy condition of pregnancy":

> Is there a more holy condition than that of pregnancy? To do all we do in the unspoken belief that it has somehow to benefit that which is coming to be within

> us! [. . .] Everything is veiled, ominous, we know nothing of what is taking place, we wait and try to be *ready*. [. . .]—*it* is growing, *it* is coming to light: *we* have no right to determine either its value or the hour of its coming. All the influence we can exert lies in keeping it safe. "What is growing here is something greater than we are" is our most secret hope [. . .]—It is in *this state of consecration* that one should live! It is a state one can live in! [. . .] (D 552)

Nietzsche's remarks on pregnancy should be read with Diotima's views from the *Symposium* (Nietzsche's *Lieblingsdichtung*) in mind:

> All humans are pregnant, Socrates, both in body and in soul, and on reaching a certain age our nature yearns to engender offspring [. . .] Therefore when one who is pregnant approaches the beautiful [. . .] he becomes so exhilarated as to overflow with bringing forth and begetting [. . .] and one is pregnant and teeming ripe he is excited by the beautiful because its possessor can relieve him of his heaving pangs.[29]

Müller-Lauter points out that Nietzsche calls procreating the real achievement of the individual and hence his "highest interest"; he understands procreation as "the highest expression of power" from "the center of the whole individual" (KSA 12, 7 [9]). On the other hand, Müller-Lauter notes, procreation is the ultimate surrender of power: the entire body surrenders power in favor of the origination of a new body.[30] As Müller-Lauter points out, this fundamentally contradicts Nietzsche's fundamental understanding of the conflicting wills to power.

Diotima does not distinguish between the male begetting and the female giving birth aspect of procreation. She describes procreation as a process of opening up so that what one carries within oneself can manifest. The perspective on "becoming what one is" in *Ecce Homo* is about such an opening up and giving birth to what is inside.

BUDDHA NATURE

This idea that something is born within would perhaps fit well with the Mahāyāna Buddhist notion that when the Buddha became enlightened, he realized that all beings without exception have the same nature and potential for enlightenment. All sentient beings possess Buddha nature, the intrinsic potential to realize enlightenment. Buddha nature should not be interpreted as a kind of inherent self, but as empty of any defining characteristics. The notion can be traced to some early Buddhist schools of thought but was only fully developed within the *tathāgatagarbha* tradition in Mahāyāna

Buddhism. It became a widespread and important doctrine in East Asian Buddhism.

"Garbha" can mean both "embryo" or "womb" ("Tathāgata" means "Buddha"). Not only is everyone deep within a buddha, the entire world is one great womb where buddhas are being produced. According to one interpretation, through Buddhist practice one can realize one's Buddha nature (in the sense of actualizing it and demonstrating it). According to another one, the Buddha's enlightenment brought about the enlightenment of the whole world. At the time of his enlightenment, the Buddha is said to have declared that he and the great earth were simultaneously enlightened, and that mountains, rivers, grasses, and trees had all realized their intrinsic Buddha nature.

In the Zen tradition, this notion of Buddha nature be became very important. Bodhidharma famously claimed that Zen was about "direct pointing at the mind, seeing into one's nature and attaining buddhahood." Zen practice was about seeing into one's true nature[31]. For Dōgen, however, such a formulation is too suggestive of a kind of true self. For him, Zen practice is not about seeing into one's true nature (realizing one's inherent Buddha nature as an essence buried within oneself), but about the ongoing realization that all of existence is Buddha nature (awakening to the fundamental interrelatedness of all of existence). Dōgen disagrees with those who view the Zen *áskēsis* as aiming at a direct insight into the nature of reality, breaking through to one's true nature, or seeing one's true nature, indicated in Japanese as *kenshō*. Therefore, he rereads the standard Mahāyāna claim that "all sentient beings have the Buddha nature" to mean that "entire being/all beings is/are the Buddha nature."[32]

Nietzsche would most likely have agreed with Dōgen in his rejection of any claims of such kind of ultimate insight. But would he have any affinity with the notion of Buddha nature? In various places in his writings, Nietzsche addresses the topic of first and second nature as an interpretation of what a process of self-overcoming could entail. In the course of his work his interpretation of first and second nature changes from an other-oriented to a self-oriented to a world-oriented perspective.

FIRST AND SECOND NATURE

In the second *Untimely Meditation*, Nietzsche speaks about second nature in a negative way: attempting to overcome the errors of the past leads at best to the construction of new instincts, of a second nature, that causes our inherited, inborn first nature to scorch and shrivel up: "We plant a new habit, a new instinct, a second nature, in order for the first nature to shrivel up"

(TU II 3). He adds, however, that also this first nature once started out as a second nature, and that any triumphant second nature will become a new first nature.

We could call this an other-oriented perspective on first and second nature. The seeker after wisdom needs to build up a second nature, which overgrows his first nature and alienates him from it. All education is the development of such a second nature. In the other-oriented stage, the seeker is alienated from his first nature by his education. The morality of society keeps him from realizing who he is. Society puts before him all kinds of elevated goals to strive after. Nietzsche was driven by Schopenhauer's and Wagner's idealism. The beginning Zen practitioner may be driven by conventional Buddhist goals: a longing for enlightenment, a desire to end suffering. The camel that goes off into the desert refers to Nietzsche's own asceticism of the spirit in *Human, All Too Human*, and his ascetic attempt at emancipation from Wagner and Schopenhauer. The camel-lion transformation constitutes his own free-spirited liberation of conventional morality.

Although the second nature eventually needs to be overcome and the first nature needs to be recovered, building up a second nature is a necessary stage on the way to wisdom.

> *The first nature.*—The way in which we are educated nowadays, we first acquire a *second nature:* and we have it when the world calls us ripe, mature and useful. Some are snake-like enough to shed this skin one day, when underneath this cover their *first nature* has ripened. In most people it shrivels up however. (D 455)

Education provides us with a second nature as a protective snake skin that allows our first nature to develop unhindered and to ripen underneath. Most people, however, prove unable to shed this skin when their first nature has ripened. Therefore, their first nature will eventually shrivel up. Only very few people are snake-like enough to keep their first nature from shriveling up under the second skin of the second nature, and shed their skin one day.

Such a passive *ripening*—and eventual revelation—of one's first nature should be distinguished from the active *development* of one's second nature. In his notebook fragments Nietzsche writes, "My being *reveals* itself—whether it *develops*? From childhood on overloaded with outside nature and imported knowledge. I'm discovering myself"(KSA 8, 28 [16]). And in *The Wanderer and His Shadow*, he says, "One day, when in the eyes of the world one has completed one's education a long time ago, one *discovers* one*self*: this is where the task of the thinker starts; now it is time to enlist his help—not as an educator, but as a self-educated person who has experience"

(WS 267). Whereas in the other-oriented stage one needs a teacher and educator, in the self-oriented stage one simply needs a model. Perhaps Nietzsche portrays himself as such a model in *Ecce Homo* for some of his (future) readers.

But the relationship between first and second nature is more complex. In December 1882, Nietzsche uses in two letters the distinction between first and second nature to answer some critical remarks from his friend Erwin Rohde, presumably about *The Joyous Science* that appeared that year. Apparently, Rohde was not all that impressed by Nietzsche's newfound life-affirming demeanor. In a letter to Hans von Bulow, Nietzsche writes,

> What do I care when my friends say that my current free-spirited demeanor [*Freigeisterei*] is an eccentric, teeth-gritting *decision*, that is forced upon my own inclination? It may indeed be a "second nature:" but I will prove that only with this second nature I have come into the actual *possession* of my first nature. (KSB 6: 344)

According to this interpretation, Nietzsche thinks Rohde has failed to differentiate between Nietzsche's *historical* first nature and his *actual* first nature (which now is able to manifest itself through an acquired second nature). In Nietzsche's letter to Rohde himself, he expresses himself slightly differently:

> Yes, I do have a "second nature," but not in order to destroy the first but to *stand* it. I would have long ago perished from my "first nature"—I almost did perish from it. What you say about an "eccentric decision" is by the way completely *true*. I could name you place and time. But—who was it that *made the decision*?—For sure, my dearest friend, it was the *first* nature: **it** *wanted* "to live." (KSB 6: 345)

Nietzsche suggests here that it was his first nature that decided to adopt the second nature in order to protect the organism "Nietzsche" from itself. In *Ecce Homo*, Nietzsche writes about the re-emergence of his first nature: "That nethermost self, as if buried alive, as if made mute beneath the constant *need* to pay heed to other selves (—which is what reading is!) awoke slowly, shyly, hesitantly—but finally *it spoke again*" (EH III HAH, 4).

Nietzsche also writes about *The Wanderer and His Shadow* and *Daybreak* as a return to himself. So the second nature is not an alienation from the first nature, but serves as a protective skin, in order to not perish from it prematurely. In retrospect, Nietzsche realizes that his own asceticism of the spirit served an important function: to protect his own first nature. It even was his first nature that made him seek out this second nature as a protective skin. A second nature can function in service of a first nature.

The question remains how such a first nature should be read. Rather than some kind of inner essence, we could interpret it as nothing else than life itself. Returning to one's first nature would then mean that life breaks through in oneself. When the ego, one's acquired second nature, has been overcome, one gives birth to life itself in all its Dionysian vitality. One becomes the site where the self-overcoming of life plays itself out. This is what self-overcoming without a self would mean.

In Part II, I have conducted a dialogue between Nietzsche and various representatives from the Zen tradition on the topic of philosophical *áskēsis*, its deconstructive and constructive aspects, and its qualities of non-essentialism, non-teleology, and non-anthropocentrism. However, the question remains: what is the purpose of such an *áskēsis*? Is there a *summum bonum*, some kind of redemption or salvation, that can be reached or realized? In the Buddhist traditions, this *summum bonum* seems to be, without question, enlightenment. What would Nietzsche have said about Buddhist enlightenment? He did reject one conception of it, the notion of nirvana as it appears in the Pali Canon (obviously, as we have seen in chapter 1, through the lens of its nineteenth-century Western interpreters such as Oldenberg). And what would Dōgen say about Nietzsche's critique of redemption? Does Nietzsche's *áskēsis* perhaps culminate in some kind of Zen enlightenment, or non-enlightenment? In part III I will critically examine such questions.

NOTES

1. Damien Keown, "trikāya." *Encyclopedia.com: A Dictionary of Buddhism.* www.encyclopedia.com/doc/1O108-trikya.html (accessed September 6, 2010).

2. Nagatomo, *Attunement Through the Body,* 165.

3. Dōgen, *Shōbōgenzō, Yuibutsu Yobutsu.* Quoted in: Arifuku, *The Problem of the Body in Nietzsche and Dōgen*, 223.

4. Kim, *Eihei Dōgen—Mystical Realist*, 104.

5. Dōgen, *Shōbōgenzō, Shinjingakudō.* Quoted in: Kim, *Eihei Dōgen—Mystical Realist*, 104.

6. Kim notes that, although Dōgen could be described as a "mystical realist" (Kim, *Eihei Dōgen—Mystical Realist*), his mysticism is a far cry from Western and Eastern forms of apophatic mysticism where God, Dao, Brahman are said to be ineffable, only to be known by systematically negating language and thought. For Dōgen, the embodiment of universal buddhahood takes place precisely through language and thought (Kim, *Dōgen on Meditation and Thinking*, 90).

7. Charles Taylor, *A Secular Age* (Cambridge: The Belknap Press, 2007), 15.

8. Graham Parkes, "Nature and the human "redivinized": Mahāyāna Buddhist themes in *Thus Spoke Zarathustra*," in *Nietzsche and the Divine*, 181–99.

9. Parkes, *Nature and the human "redivinized,"* 189.

10. Parkes, *Nature and the human "redivinized,"* 194.

11. Parkes, *Nature and the human "redivinized,"* 184.

12. Parkes, *Composing the Soul,* 305–7. See also Parkes, *Nietzsche and early Buddhism*, 262.

13. See Daniel W. Conway, "Life and Self-Overcoming," in *A Companion to Nietzsche*, ed. Keith Ansell Pearson, 532–47 (Oxford: Blackwell Publishing, 2006).

14. Müller-Lauter has called attention to a lingering ambiguity in Nietzsche's thought on teleology (Wolfgang Müller-Lauter, *Nietzsche: His Philosophy of Contradictions and the Contradictions of his Philosophy* (Urbana/Chicago: University of Illinois Press, 1999), 180). In describing Nietzsche's views on the body as a command structure, Müller-Lauter points to *Thus Spoke Zarathustra*, where the body is described as "a plurality with one meaning, a war and a peace, a herd and a shepherd" and "a great reason" (TSZ I, 4). Plurality and unity, purposelessness and purpose seem to go hand in hand here. And in a long note in 1884, Nietzsche assumes "that a purposefulness rules events on the smallest level," and speculates that this could be due to "*tremendously much higher and more comprehensive intellects* than the one we are conscious of" (KSA 10, 24 [16]). By 1885, Müller-Lauter adds, Nietzsche has overcome this "teleological temptation."

15. Parkes, *Nature and the human "redivinized,"* 187.

16. Ryogi Ōkōchi, "Nietzsche's Conception of Nature from an East-Asian Point of View," in *Nietzsche and Asian Thought*, 204.

17. Graham Parkes, *Nietzsche and Early Buddhism*, 264.

18. Graham Parkes, *Nietzsche and Early Buddhism*, 264.

19. Benson, *Pious Nietzsche*, 9.

20. Paul Bourget, "Théorie de la décadence," in *Essais de psychologie contemporaine, vol. I.* (Paris: Plon, 1926), 3–33.

21. For more on Nietzsche's use of the term decadence, see Benson, *Pious Nietzsche,* 8 and 55–61.

22. Benson, *Pious Nietzsche*, 59.

23. Dōgen, *Shōbōgenzō, Genjōkōan*. Quoted in: Bret W. Davis, "The Presencing of Truth: Dōgen's Genjōkōan," in *Buddhist Philosophy: Essential Readings*, 256.

24. Dōgen, *Shōbōgenzō, Genjōkōan.* Quoted in: Davis, *The Presencing of Truth,* 257.

25. Davis, *The Presencing of Truth,* 254.

26. Conway, *Nietzsche & the Political,* 115f.

27. Duncan Large suggests that *Ecce Homo* can be read as an instruction manual for "how to become what you are." See Duncan Large, "Introduction," in Friedrich Nietzsche, *Ecce Homo. How To Become What You Are* (Oxford: Oxford University Press, 2007), xv. Such an instruction would have to be compatible with Nietzsche's conception of human individuality as the particular configuration of a person's drives. Becoming what one is would refer to an individual process of educating the

drives, in which what is optimal for one person is not necessarily optimal for another. Nietzsche's own life is not a recipe to be followed but serves as a model or example (*Vorbild*). I argue, however, that *Ecce Homo* is not meant as a self-help book but as an explanation of how Nietzsche has become a person that is capable of perceiving what is true and capable of performing a revaluation of values (see chapter 12).

28. Nietzsche's affirmation of his own "byways and detours" could therefore be seen as not only an artistic form of self-creation, involving a retrospective reinterpretation which inevitably involves bending the historical truth a little bit (Large, *Introduction*, xviii) but also as part of a more general theory on illness and health, which explains why Nietzsche's health is a form of "the great health," which makes him uniquely suited for performing a revaluation of values.

29. Plato, *Symposium* 206c–e. Quoted in: Parkes, *Composing the Soul*, 240. For more on Nietzsche's use of the metaphor of pregnancy, see Parkes, *Composing the Soul*, 238–47.

30. Müller-Lauter, *Nietzsche*, 182.

31. According to Yoshizu Yoshihide, "The Relation between Chinese Buddhist History and Soteriology," in *Paths to Liberation*, 328, the phrase "seeing the nature" originally did not refer to the individual seeing his own nature, but to the practice of Buddhas and bodhisattvas as they saw the Buddha nature of all sentient beings.

32. Dōgen, *Shōbōgenzō, Busshō*. Quoted in: Davis, *The Presencing of Truth*, 252f.

Part III

Enlightenment

Chapter 8

The Self-overcoming of Redemption and Enlightenment

Can self-overcoming be thought of as a soteriology? Does self-overcoming culminate in redemption? One of the problematic aspects of both a Nietzschean and a Zen soteriology is that they are not to be interpreted as a teleological imperative. Their *áskēsis* cannot be grasped as a means to arrive at some end projected in the future. The very attempt to overcome the ascetic ideal would be a symptom of that ascetic ideal itself. This is why some researchers have interpreted Nietzsche's thought as an anti-soteriology: a call to continuous struggle, a call to intensify that struggle to the maximum. According to this interpretation, Nietzsche maintains that no redemption or liberation will be in store anytime now or in the future.[1] Yet there is a great sense of urgency that runs through all of Nietzsche's writings. He considers it imperative that his readers become what they are. But if Nietzsche's view on self-overcoming is non-teleological, is there any need for practice? Rather than become what we are, we could simply be what we are and live happily.

Redemption, like many concepts, has a negative as well as a positive meaning for Nietzsche. On the one hand, a longing for redemption runs through his work. On the other hand, he tries to genealogically deconstruct and unmask that longing out of intellectual integrity. Nietzsche continuously thinks against himself. If Nietzsche has a soteriology, then it is skeptical in two ways: skepticism plays an important role as a way to redemption, and as a soteriology, it continuously puts itself skeptically into question. Is redemption possible? Can we be redeemed, or redeem ourselves? Perhaps Nietzsche's redemption consists of there being no redemption. Perhaps living through nihilism constitutes redemption. Perhaps redemption is an abyss. Nietzsche seduces the reader to want to be redeemed and simultaneously problematizes this redemption.

Nietzsche's relationship to redemption can be compared to his relationship to morality. Although Nietzsche's "immorality" is often interpreted as the absence of any kind of morality, it actually implies a more severe morality than other types of morality. The liberation of morality is not a goal in itself, but a preparation for an alternative morality. In a similar way, the death of God, and the liberation of the Christian soteriology is not a goal in itself. Also the atheist has to be overcome. When the death of God is announced by the madman in *The Joyous Science* 125, his audience consists of atheists, not the Christian faithful. Just like Nietzsche the immoralist, who wants to overcome morality for the sake of morality, can be characterized as a postmoralist,[2] the antichrist Nietzsche, who wants to overcome religion for the sake of religion, can perhaps be characterized as a "postreligious" thinker.[3]

A parallel question runs through the Zen tradition. Standard Buddhist soteriology holds that Buddhist practice culminates in enlightenment.[4] But throughout the Zen tradition, the notion of attaining enlightenment or "becoming a Buddha" is problematized. We find much anti-enlightenment rhetoric. So does practice culminate in enlightenment? Yes, says early Buddhism: the Noble Eightfold Path offers a path from bondage to liberation, a way out of samsara into nirvana. No, says Nāgārjuna: samsara is not different from nirvana. Liberation is not an escape from bondage but a renewed perspective on it. Yes, say some Mahāyāna schools, the very insight that samsara is nirvana, that new and liberating perspective, constitutes enlightenment. Realizing emptiness becomes the goal of Mahāyāna Buddhist soteriology. No, say some Zen masters, also emptiness is empty.

There are three temptations that should be avoided in an interpretation of redemption: (1) essentialism, which is conceiving of redemption as some kind of static "state"; (2) teleology, which is conceiving of redemption in terms of some ultimate goal; (3) anthropocentrism, which is the tendency to speak in anthropomorphic and individualistic terms about redemption.[5]

Essentialism and teleology belong to an other-oriented perspective. From this perspective (in which the ascetic ideal still has not been seen through yet), redemption can only be conceived of as some kind of state that serves as the goal of a path toward wisdom, an ideal to aspire to. But from a self-oriented perspective, one has overcome the ascetic ideal and is able, through a practice of active nihilism, to deconstruct any essentialist and teleological notions and any ideals. From such a perspective, redemption can only be described in strictly non-essentialist and non-teleological terms. But the self-oriented seeker (Zarathustra's lion figure) is still anthropocentric in his clinging to his own sovereignty, expressed as "I will." Therefore, he can only conceive of redemption in a limited way, in terms of an individual transformation. If redemption can only be properly described in non-essentialist, non-teleological and non-anthropocentric terms, how to imagine it?

THE TRANSFORMATION OF REDEMPTION AND ENLIGHTENMENT

The German term *Erlösung* that Nietzsche uses can be translated as either "redemption" or as "salvation." Salvation (from the Latin *salus*, "health," "safety," "well being") can be defined as "a religious concept that refers either to the process through which a person is brought from a condition of distress to a condition of ultimate well being or to the state of ultimate well being that is the result of that process."[6] Ideas of salvation may or may not be linked to the figure of a savior or redeemer or correlated with a concept of God. In Christianity, salvation is variously conceived. One prominent conception emphasizes justification—the process through which the individual, alienated from God by sin, is reconciled to God and reckoned just or righteous through faith in Christ.

Though closely allied to salvation, redemption is more specific, for it denotes the means by which salvation is achieved, namely, by the payment of a ransom. There are many passages in the New Testament which represent Christ's sufferings under the idea of a ransom or price, and the result thereby secured is a purchase or redemption.[7] In the payment made for our redemption, the debt against us is not viewed as simply cancelled, but is fully paid. Christ's blood or life, which he surrendered for them, is the "ransom" by which the deliverance of his people from the servitude of sin and from its penal consequences is secured.

Redemption is related to the Greek secular concept of *apolutrosis*, buying the freedom of a slave.[8] It refers to a purchase back of something that has been lost by the payment of a ransom. It has been used as a metaphor to describe the action of God: Christ the Redeemer delivered people from the consequences of their sins, bearing the cost himself.[9] The modern secular meaning of redeeming coupons goes back to this theological origin.

The meaning of the term *Erlösung* needs to be seen from within its German context. I will use the overview of Claus-Dieter Osthövener.[10] In German culture, according to Osthövener, the term used to have a strictly Christian meaning. Especially Luther's theology is all about redemption and man's neediness for redemption. Schleiermacher extended the use of the term to also include non-Western religions. Schopenhauer and Wagner extended its use even further. For Schopenhauer, redemption referred to the liberation from suffering through asceticism (ethical redemption) and art (aesthetic redemption). Wagner took over the concept of aesthetic redemption. Schopenhauer used redemption as well to indicate the Buddhist state of enlightenment, nirvana.

Osthövener claims that Nietzsche definitively transformed the notion of redemption that had already been enlarged in the nineteenth century by Schopenhauer and Wagner.[11] He also points out, however, the problematic nature of the notion in Nietzsche's work. On one hand, Nietzsche uses the notion, like Luther and others, both in a privative sense (liberation *from* something, with the emphasis on freeing oneself from a situation that is valued negatively) and in a positive sense (transformation *into* something, with the emphasis on the positive new state that is being achieved). Often both meanings are closely related. This tension between "redemption from" and "redemption to" is connected to affirmation and negation in Nietzsche's whole work.[12] On the other hand, Nietzsche's criticism on the notion of redemption in Christianity and Wagner is connected to attempts to construct his own notion of redemption, in the sense of emancipation and self-overcoming, also and especially from (the need for) Christian and Wagnerian "redemption." According to Willers and Theierl, redemption is even a key notion in Nietzsche's entire work.[13]

There is only a limited match between the concept of redemption/salvation and the Buddhist notion of bodhi/nirvana/enlightenment. The economic and legal meaning of redemption, for example, is absent in enlightenment. Yet enlightenment has been conceived as a type of Buddhist salvation, understood as liberation from the *duhkha* of existence. But just as Nietzsche has undertaken a genealogy of redemption, there is a need for a Buddhist genealogy of enlightenment. In the Nietzschean sense of the word, a genealogy is the search not so much for the validity or truthfulness as it is for the origins of certain notions, customs, or practices. A genealogical investigation reveals that concepts with seemingly fixed meanings are in actuality the result of a contingent series of consecutive reinterpretations, none of which can be privileged as the "original" or "true" interpretation. Enlightenment can be seen as one of these fixed notions whose solidity is in dire need of a genealogical deconstruction. As Zen scholar Albert Welter remarks, "Zen propagandists and apologists in the twentieth century sold the world on the story of Zen as a transcendental spiritualism untainted by political and institutional involvements."[14] Zen enlightenment has been presented as a transcendent, pure experience. However, the notion of enlightenment within the Zen tradition is the product of a complicated historical development.

THE HERMENEUTICS OF REDEMPTION AND ENLIGHTENMENT

In this chapter, I will explore a parallel between Nietzsche's ambivalent relationship to redemption and Zen's relationship to enlightenment.[15] I will explore this parallel in terms of the other-oriented, self-oriented, and world-oriented perspectives.

The type of redemption that Nietzsche criticizes takes place within an other-oriented perspective. It is hostile to life and connected with the ascetic ideal in seeking refuge in a higher "true" world. According to the Zen tradition, such a type of redemption can be found in Buddhist soteriologies that separate samsara and nirvana and that view enlightenment as a state of absorption that can be reached through meditation.

The emancipation from this kind of redemption leads to a self-oriented perspective that provides a "redemption from redeemers" [*Erlösung von Erlösern*]. From Nietzsche's perspective, life is seen as will to power, as a continual agonal self-overcoming. From a Zen perspective, the separation between samsara and nirvana is empty. For both, the practice of self-overcoming consists therefore in active nihilism and strong skepticism.

There is also a world-oriented type of redemption that constitutes an "emancipation from the emancipation" (Nietzsche's letter to Lou Salome that was mentioned earlier), redemption in the sense of amor fati: an affirmative perspective on life where all of life appears "redeemed" (in the sense of justified). The logic of redemption (something is wrong and lacking and needs to be fixed) is replaced by the logic of amor fati (nothing is lacking and nothing needs to be fixed or overcome).[16] Or, as Zarathustra puts it, the lion goes under and gives up its "I will." What is left is ecstatic philosophy from "the tragic-Dionysian state as the highest state of affirmation of life" (KSA 13, 17 [3]).

World-oriented enlightenment in Zen refers to the realization of the emptiness of emptiness. In contemporary Japanese Buddhism, nirvana is interpreted as a "dynamic dialectic of reaffirmation through double negation."[17] The first negation is the ascetic overcoming of the craving and ignorance that bind us. This could be likened to the nihilistic view of nirvana as an escape from samsara. However, this negation has to be followed up by an equally necessary second negation: a negation of any attachment to a transcendent repose in the realm of nirvana. As Davis puts it: "The event of nirvana thus paradoxically completes itself only in a movement through its own negation."[18] Any dualistic perspectives on nirvana, as a state separate from and superior to samsara, have to be overcome, and a nondualistic perspective on nirvana needs to be realized.

The dynamic dialectic of reaffirmation through double negation can be likened to Nietzsche's emancipation from the emancipation. The first negation (nirvana as a liberation from samsara) can be likened to Nietzsche's self-redemption. However, this self-redemption needs to be overcome as well. This is the second negation: the self-oriented perspective has to be left behind in order to make room for a dynamic reaffirmation of existence just as it is (amor fati). The dialectic of double negation could be seen as first a self-redemption that constitutes a "redemption from redemption" [*Erlösung von Erlösung*], followed by a redemption from this very self-redemption itself.

NIETZSCHE'S AND LINJI'S CRITIQUE OF OTHER-ORIENTED REDEMPTION

Nietzsche's critique of redemption can be interpreted as his critique of specific notions of redemption given so far by Christianity, Schopenhauer, Wagner, and (early) Buddhism. Christianity has intensified the experience of individuality and has defined human lack in a subjective, individual way: it introduced the concept of "sin" to explain our experience of lack. Christian morality is an attempt to deal with our experience of lack. By purifying not only our actions but also our intentions, our sense of guilt can be reduced. Redemption of our guilt as a liberation of lack is now defined as "deliverance from sin." Such a deliverance can only be attained through grace, not through merit.

Nietzsche distinguishes two forms of redemption that he considers inadequate and even damaging answers to the reality of existential suffering. The first is redemption as a narcotic anesthetic for the weak who cannot handle suffering. Both religion and art offer such anesthetic, for example, by promising an *unio mystica*, the Wagnerian intoxication, or Schopenhauer's aesthetic form of redemption. Secondly, redemption also refers to an escape from suffering for the stronger persons, those with a will strong enough to dedicate themselves to ascetic practices. This kind of redemption originates from a weak pessimism, that judges life as negative. Escaping suffering can take place by hygienically restraining it, as in Buddhism, or by letting the will die off and die out, as in Schopenhauer's ascetic way to ethical redemption.

Nietzsche's critique is multi-layered. First of all, starting with *Human, All Too Human* and continuing into the later work, Nietzsche gives a psychological critique of the notion of redemption. He attempts to give a non-mythological and purely psychological explanation of the need for redemption—it is based on fantasy and fiction (HAH I 135, 476). He also explains the feeling of redemption as a false interpretation of well being (KSA 11, 44 [6]).

Redemption is connected with the idea of "sin," which for Nietzsche is just as much an imaginary concept as redemption (KSA 9, 5 [33], 9, 7 [251]). The term *redemption* refers to a psychological state that Nietzsche rejects as an illusion (JS 335), an imaginary "impact and transformation" (KSA 9, 4 [89], AC 15), as "lies and counterfeiting" (AC 38), and as a psychological reality based on the imagination (KSA 13, 11 [383], AC 33).

Later on, Nietzsche's psychological critique of redemption is joined by a genealogical critique. He critically examines how such a concept could arise in the first place. Redemption is viewed as an expression of resentment. Through its connection with sin, redemption serves to stimulate submission to the priests (AC 26). It also serves to condemn life (HAH I, 16, KSA 13, 11 [265], KSA 13, 14 [89]). Redemption functions as a reward for suffering: by suffering here on earth one can experience redemption in the afterlife. As Nietzsche analyzes in *On the Genealogy of Morality*, the Christian priest develops a new way to deal with suffering by reinterpreting it as sin and redirecting resentment within. The notions of sin and redemption point the blame for suffering back at the sufferer. Suffering is reinterpreted as a necessary pathway to redemption. By giving this meaning to suffering, it is made bearable. For the priests, resentment came to be built into the very fabric of redemption. They developed a theology of guilt, sin, and redemption, which allowed them to be the mediators of a complex mechanism of reward and punishment. Redemption became an instrument of violence and revenge.

In his late work, Nietzsche's psychological and genealogical critique is joined by a physiological critique: the need for redemption is a sign of decadence (CW Afterword 1). Nietzsche now also criticizes redemption on "medical grounds." Redemption is claimed to be healing, but in reality, it makes the patient even more ill. The Christian "training of repentance and redemption" [*Buss- und Erlösungtraining*] leads to epileptic symptoms (GM III, 21) and to "redemptive hysterics" [*Erlösungs-Hysterie*] (EH IV, 8). As a "systematization of the instinct for destruction" (KSA 13, 14 [164]), redemption is a symptom of a morality of decadence (KSA 13, 14 [210]). For Nietzsche, Christian redemption doesn't liberate and heal people; it reinforces their bondage.

For the late Nietzsche, redemption is connected with nihilism. According to Nietzsche, both Christianity and Buddhism define redemption as the absence of pain and suffering. The state of redemption is a state of total "collective hypnotizing and stillness" (GM III, 17), a state of deep sleep, whether interpreted as becoming one with Brahman or as an *unio mystica* (GM III, 17). Redemption becomes synonymous with "nothing" (AC 7).

Also in the Zen tradition, such an other-oriented notion of enlightenment is criticized as too essentialist and teleological. Zen agrees with Nāgārjuna's equation of nirvana with samsara. Enlightenment is empty. We have seen in chapter 5 that Linji criticizes his disciples for seeking enlightenment as a goal outside themselves. That enlightenment (i.e., becoming a Buddha) should not be conceived as an essentialist and teleological notion is clearly expressed in the following well-known Zen koan:

> Mazu Daoyi [. . .] did zazen all day long. Knowing that Mazu was a Dharma vessel, Nanyue went to him and asked, "Great monastic, what do you intend by doing zazen?" Mazu said, "I am intending to be a buddha." Nanyue picked up a brick and started polishing it. Mazu said, "What are you doing?" Nanyue said, "I am trying to make a mirror." Mazu said, "How can you make a mirror by polishing a brick?" Nanyue said, "How can you become a buddha by doing zazen?"[19]

SELF-ORIENTED REDEMPTION: GRADUAL AND SUDDEN ENLIGHTENMENT

At the same time, the emancipation from such a faulty notion of redemption constitutes another type of redemption. The free spirit does not need redeemers to be liberated; it can emancipate itself from the need for redemption. When he speaks about redemption as part of Christian morality, Nietzsche envisages self-liberation (*Selbsterlösung*) as an emancipation from the need for redemption (HAH 134). Realizing that "everything is necessity" can liberate the free spirit from its (imaginary) sense of sinfulness and guilt and its need for redemption of this sinfulness (HAH 107).[20] A redeemer becomes superfluous, just like in the time of the Buddha, the teacher of the religion of *Selbsterlösung* (D 96). By unlearning the moral prejudices, the free spirit can liberate itself from the greatest illness of humanity: Christian morality (KSA 9, 4 [315]).[21]

In order to criticize other-oriented perspectives on enlightenment, in the Zen tradition a distinction has often been made between gradual enlightenment (*jianwu*) and sudden awakening (*dunwu*). This contrast draws on the work of second- and third-century Daoist writers who contrasted "sudden" teachings, which were direct and immediate, with "gradual" teachings that were indirect, metaphorical, or analogical, relying on various expedient means (*upāya*) to guide people to wisdom. According to Chinese Buddhist schools, the most profound teachings of the Buddha were delivered to advanced audiences capable of sudden awakening, whereas teachings that relied on expedient means were for the sake of people requiring gradual cultivation before they would be capable of bearing the fruit of enlightenment.[22] Gradual teachings that talk about realizing emptiness as an essentialist goal use an other-oriented perspective; sudden awakening means to see through essentialism and teleology. According to Hershock,

> "*dunwu*" might be rendered as "readiness to awaken" or "readiness to awaken." The ambiguity of this phrase works well in rendering the Chinese into English. It accurately leaves unclear whether you yourself are ready to awaken, whether you are ready to awaken someone else, or whether we are all poised in a situation that is itself ready for awakening.[23]

The readiness to awaken does not refer to a particular state of consciousness free from impure impulses and defiling activity, but to an ongoing practice of responsive virtuosity, together with all things in the world performing the work of enlightenment, that is, illuminating and bringing to full expression the enlightening character and non-duality of all things.

ZARATHUSTRA'S ENLIGHTENMENT: DIONYSIAN REDEMPTION

Can something like "sudden awakening" also be found in Nietzsche? Throughout his work, Nietzsche tries to come to an alternative, "Dionysian" form of redemption, that would be life-affirming rather than hostile to life. In his early work (1868–1876), Nietzsche tries to conceive of redemption as the unification of the Dionysian primal chaos of life with the beautifying Apollonian images of art. Dionysian redemption refers to a shift from an individual mode of experiencing to a world-oriented mode of experiencing, to a transcendence of the principium individuationis. In *The Birth of Tragedy*, Nietzsche distinguishes two forms of Dionysus: the suffering Dionysus Zagreus, individuated, fragmented, and Dionysus Iacchus, the reborn transfigured Dionysus.

> Dionysus appears in a variety of forms, in the mask of a fighting [tragic] hero, and entangled, as it were, in the net of the individual will [. . .] In truth, however, the hero is the suffering Dionysus of the mysteries, the god experiencing in himself the agonies of individuation [. . .] But the hope of the epopts looked toward the rebirth of Dionysus, which we must now dimly conceive as the end of individuation. (BT 10)

But in his later, skeptical phase (1876–1882), he rejects his early attempts as an "artist metaphysics." This skeptical phase leads up to his famous description of the death of God in 1882. However, the death of God does not mean the end of redemption.

In *Thus Spoke Zarathustra*, his self-declared "fifth gospel," Nietzsche tries to come to another positive definition of redemption. By some, *Thus Spoke Zarathustra* has been interpreted as an initiatory writing, in which not only the nature of redemption is described, but in which redemption is also embodied and evoked in the reader.[24] Karl Löwith considers redemption the central theme of *Thus Spoke Zarathustra*: "the whole of Zarathustra, from his first performance to the final ass festival, is the continuous history of an ever postponed redemption."[25]

In his later works, Nietzsche sometimes seems to suggest that Zarathustra could be seen as a redeemer. In *Twilight of the Idols*, Zarathustra appears at the end of the history of Western metaphysics, at the moment when the idea of a "true world" behind all appearances has been fully seen through (TI 4, 6). In *On the Genealogy of Morality*, Nietzsche looks forward to the redeeming person (*der erlösende Mensch*), a redeemer (who has not yet appeared on earth), who will come to liberate man, the sick animal, from nihilism (GM II, 24 and 25). In *Ecce Homo*, Nietzsche describes Zarathustra as a new kind of human being in which all opposites are combined into a new unity: a Dionysian type that says and does "No" to an unheard-of degree and nevertheless is the antithesis of a no-saying spirit (EH III Z, 6).

In "On Redemption" (TSZ II, 20), Zarathustra speaks about three different forms of redemption.[26] The first form of redemption refers to Zarathustra's privative notion of a true liberation of all that was past from a state of imprisonment, coupled with a positive notion of redemption into affirmation. This redemption is a creative reinterpretation of the past in order to justify it. "To redeem that which has passed away and to re-create all "It was" into a "Thus I willed it"—that alone should I call redemption" (TSZ II, 20). This type of redemption is reminiscent of Nietzsche's early attempt to conceive redemption as a creative reinterpretation.

Such a creative reinterpretation becomes impossible, however, once the will discovers that it is powerless to change the past. Resentment sets in. The will now becomes infected with the spirit of revenge. The world is seen as a negative affair that we need to be redeemed from. Redemption now refers to a liberation from this life and a refuge in annihilation, which culminates in nihilism and the attempt to not will anymore: "'Unless the will should at last redeem itself and willing should become not-willing—': but you know, my brothers, this fable-song of madness"(TSZ II, 20). The second form of redemption refers to such a criticized privative redemption, the yearning, fed by resentment, for liberation from a life that is experienced as a burden.

The third form of redemption refers to Zarathustra's description of a process of Dionysian redemption. Redemption has here on the one hand a privative meaning, a liberation from false redemption and redeemers, morality, the irreversibility of time, revulsion, and revenge. On the other hand, redemption refers to the realization of the affirmative relationship to life of amor fati. Zarathustra starts to speak about such Dionysian redemption as follows:

> Has the will yet become its own redeemer and joy-bringer? Has it unlearned the spirit of revenge and all gnashing of teeth? And who has taught it reconciliation with time, and something higher than any reconciliation? Something higher than any reconciliation the will that is will to power must will—yet how shall this happen? Who has yet taught it to will backwards and want back as well? (TSZ II, 20)

Zarathustra equals the creative will with the will to power. But what is this "something higher than any reconciliation" that the will must will? This question doesn't receive any answer here. Zarathustra suddenly falls silent and looks terrified. According to Lampert, this is because it refers to the thought of eternal recurrence, which is too terrifying yet for Zarathustra to contemplate:

> Although reconciliation and "something higher" are both necessary if revenge is to be overcome, it is that ""something higher" that the will to power must learn to will if there is to be redemption. The highest will does not will mere reconciliation, however that may be in the face of the long history of revenge. [. . .] the will to power that wills the past, and hence wills what is higher than all reconciliation, wills eternal return. [. . .] The will to power as redeemer overcomes and replaces the will to power as revenge when it wills the eternal return of beings as they are. Redemption comes not through the abandonment of the will to power, but through an enactment of the most spiritual will to power. As an agent of redemption, the will to power learns the most affirmative willing of itself and all that is and has been."[27]

The relationship between redemption and the eternal recurrence is complicated. According to Heidegger, redemption is only possible when the will wants the eternal recurrence.[28] But according to Brusotti it is the other way around: the will can only will the eternal recurrence once it is liberated from the "ill will toward time." Only a liberated will who has learned to "will backwards" is able to affirm the eternal recurrence.[29]

Dionysian redemption refers to being healed from the spirit of revenge and resentment. Revenge, an attitude that refuses to justify the past,[30] needs to be replaced by amor fati: an attitude that considers all of life justified and worthy of ecstatic affirmation. But in order to realize such an attitude of amor fati, the will itself (which is for Nietzsche always will to power) must be liberated from revenge. It must be able to passionately embrace the horrifying thought of eternal recurrence: everything will recur ad infinitum, exactly as it is right now. Such a redemption is seen by some commentators as the extreme self-overcoming of the will to power[31]: the final goal of Nietzsche's philosophy.[32] Most commentators interpret Zarathustra's redemption as his transformation into a child.[33]

Expressed in religious terms, Nietzsche's Dionysian redemption refers to the capacity to experience and embrace the reborn Dionysus as the coming God.[34] Nietzsche speaks in explicitly religious terms about Dionysian redemption as a justification of life, which he opposes to Christian redemption as a liberation from sins. He describes Dionysus as "a type that takes into itself and *redeems* the contradictions and questionable elements of existence," as opposed to the type of "the Crucified," the redeemer that Paul created (KSA 13, 14 [89]). Both the suffering of Christ and that of Dionysus redeem, but in a different sense. The suffering of Christ serves to liberate man from sin; the suffering of Dionysus is an ecstatic expression of the fullness and richness of life, not an objection to life but its celebration. In this way, life is redeemed in the sense of justified.[35]

Dionysian redemption goes beyond the self-oriented perspective, and therefore implies a kind of de-individuation. But whereas in *The Birth of Tragedy* de-individuation referred to the restoration of the world to a metaphysical underlying oneness (the Dionysian ground of being), de-individuation now has a different meaning: going-under, letting go of the self in order to embrace the chaos of the drives.[36]

This late notion of redemption is both collective and individual. On the one hand, Nietzsche speaks about a world-redemption, in which the world is justified (KSA 12, 10 [203]; TI 6, 8) and its contradictions and questionable elements are taken in (KSA 13, 14 [89]). On the other hand, this redemption refers individually to a self-redemption. Nietzsche describes himself as self-redeemed (KSA 13, 25 [7]). Redemption refers here to an affirmation of life where all eternity is "sanctioned, redeemed, justified, and affirmed" (KSA 12, 7 [38]). This leads to the faith in the redemption and justification of the whole. At the end of *Twilight of the Idols*, Nietzsche stresses the affirmative aspect of this redemption:

> Such a *liberated* spirit stands with a joyful and trusting fatalism in the midst of everything, in the faith that only the individual is reprehensible, that in the whole, everything redeems and affirms itself—*he does not negate anymore* [. . .] But such a faith is the highest of all possible faiths: I have baptized it with the name of Dionysus. (TI 9, 49)

THE STRUGGLE BETWEEN CRITIQUE AND CONSTRUCTION

As Osthövener describes it, after *Thus Spoke Zarathustra*, the notion of redemption gets into a crisis, an ambivalence between critique and construction.[37] On the one hand, Nietzsche intensifies his critique on both the

Christian and the romantic notion of redemption, not only psychological but also historical, physiological, and moral. Nietzsche criticizes the notion of other-oriented redemption from a self-oriented perspective. From this perspective, there is no redemption. Yet, Nietzsche attempts to articulate a constructive notion of redemption by speaking about affirming reality and letting reality appear as existentially justified and therefore intrinsically worthy of affirmation. The realization of such a constructive notion of redemption (a world-oriented redemption), however, requires not becoming too firmly entrenched in the self-oriented perspective.

Such a struggle between criticizing other-oriented enlightenment from a self-oriented perspective and the attempt to construct a world-oriented notion of enlightenment also runs through Zen. The Zen tradition is rooted in two Indian Buddhist philosophical traditions: the *tathāgatagarbha* tradition and the Madhyamaka thought of Nāgārjuna. Its discourse on enlightenment contains elements of both kataphasis (making use of positive, affirmative statements) and apophasis (making use of negative and deconstructive statements). A kataphatic discourse stresses *upāya*: many roads lead to the goal. An apophatic discourse stresses that there is no goal and that any notion of a goal leads to further illusion and bondage.[38]

The kataphatic strains in Zen thought are connected with the notion of Buddha nature from the *tathāgatagarbha* tradition. "Buddha nature," however, is but one of the many Buddhist terms and concepts, such as *nirvana* and *śūnyatā*, that are to be properly used in a soteriological way, not a metaphysical way. In order to avoid their reification, they need to be deconstructed again and again. Therefore, apart from the kataphatic strain in Zen thought, a continuous apophatic strain can be discerned, which goes back to Madhyamaka thought and its emphasis on *śūnyatā*.[39]

Youru Wang describes the inner struggles within the evolution of Zen discourse on enlightenment as an ongoing dialectic between kataphasis and apophasis, between the substantialization of Buddha nature and its deconstruction.[40] In Chinese Buddhism, the Indian Buddhist discourse on enlightenment was transposed into the Chinese philosophical discourse of *ti* (substance, essence) and *yong* (function). The early Chinese Zen tradition conceived of realizing one's Buddha nature in terms of contemplating and seeing the essence (*ti*) of the mind.

The first internal Zen struggle regarding the orthodox view of enlightenment is portrayed in *The Platform Sutra* in the famous story of the verses of Shenxiu (606?–706), head monk of the fifth Zen patriarch, and Huineng (638–713), the later sixth Zen patriarch.[41] Shenxiu had presented his understanding of enlightenment in the following verse:

The body is the tree of enlightenment,
The mind is like a bright mirror's stand;
Time after time polish it diligently
So that no dust can collect.[42]

Huineng had followed this up with his own verse:

Enlightenment is not a tree,
The bright mirror has no stand;
Buddha nature is always clean and pure—
What place could there be for dust?[43]

According to Wang, Shenxiu portrayed enlightenment as *linian* (being free from thoughts). Wang calls this a "quasi-reifying interpretation" that leaves room for a logocentric hierarchy that privileges pure over impure, the true mind over the ordinary mind, *ti* over *yong*.[44] Enlightenment is consequently conceived as entering into a pure and quiet state, possibly leading to a dangerous Zen escapism. Huineng famously corrected Shenxiu's interpretation. Huineng speaks of *wunian* (no-thought or no-thinking), referring not so much to an empty mind as to an apophatic emptiness of deluded thought. As Huineng puts it, "no-thought means not to be carried away by thought in the process of thought."[45] *Wunian* refers to an attitude of flowing together with thoughts and things.

Wang investigates a second moment of internal struggle in the evolution of the Zen discourse on enlightenment among two descendants of Huineng: his self-professed disciple Shenhui (684–758), a well-known Zen popularizer and speaker, and Mazu (709–788), the founder of the Hongzhou School. According to Wang, Shenhui gave an interpretation of Huineng's notion of *wunian* that is problematic. He privileged intuitive knowledge over ordinary, discriminative cognition. He taught "establishing awareness and cognition" (*li zhijian*) and in this way favored *ti* over *yong*. Wang argues that the Hongzhou school rejected Shenhui's logocentric hierarchy of *ti* and *yong*. With its motto "let the mind be free" (*renxin*), it emphasized flowing together with ever-changing reality and being free (*renyun zizai*). Enlightenment is not about realizing a fixed and unchanging essence within; it refers to being harmonious with change and flux.[46]

Mazu stressed that Buddha nature manifests in function (*yong*). The essence of the mind is seen through its external functioning. The ultimate realm of enlightenment manifests itself everywhere in human life. Mazu ultimately denied any kind of awakening, even the awakening of the ordinary mind to itself, since the ordinary mind is already Buddha nature. No cultivation is therefore necessary; Mazu advocated to simply let the mind be free and to follow along with the movements of all things or circumstances (*renyun*). This change in focus from contemplating the internal essence of the true mind to its external functioning has been seen as the essential divide between the early and the classical Zen tradition in China.

DIONYSUS VERSUS THE CRUCIFIED: AN ALTERNATIVE NIETZSCHEAN SOTERIOLOGY?

In the Nietzsche literature, it has been debated whether the Dionysian "teaching of redemption"[47] of the late Nietzsche can be interpreted as an anti-Christian soteriology. Willers, for example, attempts to reconstruct both Nietzsche's critique of redemption as his Dionysian redemption as an anti-Christian soteriology in order to facilitate a dialogue with Christian theology.[48] In recent years, Fraser and Benson have engaged in a discussion on this question.

According to Fraser, Nietzsche was obsessed with the matter of redemption because of his upbringing in a Lutheran environment and tried to develop an anti-Christian soteriology free from resentment and external transcendence.[49] Fraser thinks Nietzsche fails because he does not take suffering seriously enough.[50] However, according to Fraser, Nietzsche uses redemption in the sense of liberation from suffering.[51] But for Nietzsche, it could be argued *pace* Fraser, redemption refers to a justification of existence including pain and suffering.

Benson argues in opposition to Fraser that Nietzsche hopes to escape from the logic of soteriology and to be saved from the perceived need for redemption, in the sense of overcoming suffering.[52] It is the reactive logic of decadence that creates the need for salvation—that something needs to be made right. Decadence is the will to something else, the will to change the world, the will that opposes life. But from an affirmative standpoint, the world has already been "redeemed," just as it is. Benson describes the overcoming of decadence not as some final redemptive state, but as a getting back into step with life.

He points to the influence of German Pietism on Nietzsche, which emphasizes emotional piety much more than salvation through grace. According to Benson, Nietzsche's positive notion of redemption—embracing amor fati—carries the opposite meaning as usual. There is not something wrong that needs to be fixed. Not thinking there is something wrong is already a liberation from redemption, a liberation of the notion that the world should and could be saved. The "logic of amor fati" is opposed to the "logic of redemption."[53] If a soteriology can be detected in Nietzsche's work at all, it can only be a "soteriology *from* soteriology, a soteriology that insists on abandoning soteriology,"[54] Benson concludes.[55]

DELUSION VERSUS ENLIGHTENMENT: A ZEN SOTERIOLOGY?

If it is problematic to speak of a Nietzschean soteriology, can we speak of a Zen soteriology? Can we, for example, view enlightenment as the overcoming of delusion? It seems clear that delusion belongs to a self-oriented perspective on the world, whereas the enlightened perspective would be world-oriented. As we have seen in chapter 7, Dōgen makes a distinction between delusion and enlightenment: "Carrying the self forward to verify-in-practice (*shushō*) the myriad things is delusion; for the myriad things to come forth and verify-in-practice the self is enlightenment."[56] Therefore, the transformation from a self-oriented to a world-oriented perspective is interpreted by Davis as a shift from a deluded/deluding to an enlightened/enlightening engagement with the world:

> Delusion occurs when the ego posits itself as the single fixed center—rather than understanding itself as one among infinitely many mutually expressive focal points—of the whole. In delusion, the myriad things are seen, not according to the self-expressive aspects through which they show themselves, but rather only as they are forced into the perspectival horizon of the self-fixated and self-assertive ego. The deluded and deluding ego willfully projects its categories of perception onto the world.[57]

However, all kinds of teleological and essentialist undertones present themselves. Should delusion be overcome for the sake of enlightenment? Dōgen therefore also problematizes such a standard view on delusion and enlightenment: "Buddhas are those who greatly enlighten delusion; ordinary sentient beings are those who are greatly deluded amid enlightenment."[58]

Dōgen describes various possible perspectives on the relationship between delusion and enlightenment. Enlightenment is not opposed to delusion, but refers to the continuous and endless process of overcoming delusion. Delusion and enlightenment differ from each other only perspectivally:

> When the various things (*dharmas*) are [seen according to] the Buddha Dharma, there are delusion and enlightenment; there is [transformative] practice; there is birth/life; there is death; there are ordinary sentient beings; and there are Buddhas.
>
> When the myriad things are each [seen as] without self [i.e. without independent substantiality] there is neither delusion nor enlightenment; there are neither Buddhas nor ordinary sentient beings; and there is neither birth/life nor death.

> Since the Buddha Way originally leaps beyond both plentitude and poverty, there are arising and perishing; there are delusion and enlightenment; and there are ordinary sentient beings and Buddhas.
>
> And yet, although this is how we can say that it is, it is just that flowers fall amid our attachment and regret, and weeds flourish amid our rejecting and loathing.[59]

The first statement can be said to reflect the other-oriented perspective on self-overcoming, or conventional truth. There is a clear differentiation between delusion and enlightenment. Delusion must be overcome, and enlightenment is the ideal that the practitioner aspires to. The second statement perspective reflects the realization of emptiness: there is neither delusion nor enlightenment; both are empty. This is the self-oriented perspective. The third statement reflects the world-oriented perspective: the emptiness of emptiness. Conventional and ultimate truth are both mutually dependent. In the fourth statement, very characteristic for Zen, we are returned to this life, to this earth. Mountains are just mountains again.[60]

In this chapter, I have laid out some structural similarities between Nietzsche and Zen in their (anti-)soteriological notions of redemption and enlightenment. Both struggle between kataphasis and apophasis. For Nietzsche, one kataphatic image in particular is very important, in his struggle to describe the highest perspective on his *áskēsis*: the child. It is this image that I will turn to in the next chapter.

NOTES

1. See for example, Benson, *Pious Nietzsche* and Paul J. M. van Tongeren, *Reinterpreting Modern Culture: An Introduction to Friedrich Nietzsche's Philosophy* (Lafayette: Purdue University Press, 2000).
2. See Schacht, *Nietzsche's Postmoralism.*
3. Roberts, *Contesting Spirit*, 204.
4. See Van der Braak, *Enlightenment Revisited*, for an overview of how *enlightenment* came to be the Western term of choice as a translation for the Buddhist soteriological goal.
5. As we have seen, also the Buddhist soteriological tradition has had to contend with the temptations of essentialism, teleology, and anthropocentrism. In a way, the Zen tradition can be seen as a continuous corrective response to such a temptation. However, as we will see, also within the Zen tradition itself, these temptations are by no means absent.
6. "Salvation, Soteriology." *Believe.* mb-soft.com/believe/text/salvatio.htm (accessed September 20, 2010).
7. "Redemption." *Believe.* mb-soft.com/believe/txw/redempti.htm (accessed September 20, 2010).

8. See E. Schott, "Erlösung," in *Historisches Wörterbuch der Philosophie* II, ed. J. Ritter a.o., (Basel/Stuttgart: Schwabe & Co Verlag, 1972), 717f.

9. A much-cited formulation can be found in Charles Hodge, *Systematic Theology II* (London: Thomas Nelson and Sons, 1871), 520: "Christ saves us neither by the mere exercise of power, nor by his doctrine, nor by his example, nor by the moral influence which he exerted, nor by any subjective influence on his people, whether natural or mystical, but as a satisfaction to divine justice, as an expiation for sin, and as a ransom from the curse and authority of the law, thus reconciling us to God by making it consistent with his perfection to exercise mercy toward sinners."

10. Claus-Dieter Osthövener, *Erlösung: Transformationen einer Idee im 19. Jahrhundert* (Tübingen: Mohr Siebeck, 2004).

11. Osthövener, *Erlösung*, 244.

12. Willers, *Nietzsches antichristliche Christologie*, 166f.

13. Willers, *Nietzsches antichristliche Christologie*, 166; Herbert Theierl, *Nietzsche: Mystik als Selbstversuch* (Würzburg: Königshausen und Neumann, 2000), 9.

14. Albert Welter, *Monks, Rulers, and Literati*, 4.

15. See also André F. M. van der Braak, "Nietzsche on Redemption. A Mahāyāna Buddhist Perspective," in *Nietzsche—Philosoph der Kultur(en)?*, ed. Andreas Urs Sommer (Berlin/New York: de Gruyter, 2008), 519–27.

16. Benson, *Pious Nietzsche*, 51.

17. Davis, *Zen After Zarathustra*, 99.

18. Davis, *Zen After Zarathustra*, 99.

19. This story occurs in many places. This citation is from John Daido Loori, "Nanyue Polishes a Tile," in *The Art of Just Sitting: essential writings on the zen practice of shikantaza*, ed. John Daido Loori (Boston: Wisdom Publications, 2002), 127.

20. See Brusotti, *Leidenschaft der Erkenntnis*, 11.

21. Brusotti, *Leidenschaft der Erkenntnis*, 109.

22. Hershock, *Chan Buddhism*, 101f.

23. Hershock, *Chan Buddhism*, 103.

24. Carl G. Jung, *Nietzsche's Zarathustra Vol I and II. Notes of the Seminar Given in 1934–1939* (Princeton: Princeton University Press, 1988); Van der Braak, *Hoe men wordt, wat men is*.

25. Karl Löwith, *Nietzsches Philosophie der Ewigen Wiederkunft des Gleichen* (Stuttgart: Kohlhammer, 1956), 334.

26. See Robert Gooding-Williams, *Zarathustra's Dionysian Modernism* (Palo Alto: Stanford University Press, 2001), 205–14.

27. Laurence Lampert, *Nietzsche's Teaching: An Interpretation of* Thus Spoke Zarathustra (New Haven: Yale University Press, 1986), 147.

28. Martin Heidegger, *Was heisst Denken?* (Tübingen: Niemeyer, 1984), 43.

29. Brusotti, *Leidenschaft der Erkenntnis*, 574f. Redemption as incorporation of eternal recurrence is discussed by Heidegger, *Nietzsche I*, 331f; Brusotti, *Leidenschaft der Erkenntnis*, 587–618; Gooding-Williams, *Zarathustra's Dionysian Modernism*, 269–308; Kee, *Nietzsche Against the Crucified*, 133–36; Lampert, *Nietzsche's Teaching*, 147.

30. Brusotti, *Leidenschaft der Erkenntnis*, 569.

31. E.g., Brusotti, *Leidenschaft der Erkenntnis,* 574. However, the phrase "self-overcoming of the will to power" does not occur in Nietzsche's work itself. See chapter 10.

32. Brusotti, *Leidenschaft der Erkenntnis,* 571.

33. Löwith, *Nietzsches Philosophie der Ewigen Wiederkunft des Gleichen*, 76ff; Harold Alderman, *Nietzsche's Gift* (Athens: Ohio University Press, 1977); Lampert, *Nietzsche's Teaching*, 210–23. According to Gooding-Williams, *Zarathustra's Dionysian Modernism*, 291–302, Zarathustra only reaches the child stage at the end of TSZ IV. Lampert, *Nietzsche's Teaching*, 210–23 claims that Zarathustra's redemption in TSZ III, 13 is expressed in the last three chapters of TSZ III as a transformation into an attitude of amor fati through a creative reinterpretation. Martin Heidegger ("Wer ist Nietzsches Zarathustra?" in *Vorträge und Aufsätze*, 99–124 (Frankfurt am Main: Klostermann, 2000), 117ff) concludes that Zarathustra's redemption ultimately fails, since it implies an antipathy against time and impermanence, and therefore is still subject to the spirit of revenge. Müller-Lauter, *Heidegger und Nietzsche, Nietzsche-Interpretationen III* (Berlin/New York: de Gruyter, 2000), 135–58 disagrees and holds that Heidegger interprets Nietzsche's redemption incorrectly as too metaphysical.

34. Already in his early work Nietzsche refers to Dionysus with his Greek name ὁ λύσιος, the liberator. According to Rethy, Dionysus refers here to a "release not from but into life" (Robert Rethy, "The Tragic Affirmation of *The Birth of Tragedy*." *Nietzsche-Studien* 17 (1988), 40). See also Kee, *Nietzsche Against the Crucified* and Gerd Schank, *Dionysos gegen den Gekreuzigten: eine philologische und philosophische Studie zu Nietzsches "Ecce homo"* (Bern: Peter Lang, 1993) on "Dionysus against the Crucified" in Nietzsche.

35. Nietzsche's aphorism about Dionysus against the "Crucified" is followed two pages later by: "*Buddha against the "Crucified."* Within the movement of nihilism one should always make a distinction between *Christian* and *Buddhist* varieties: the *Buddhist* variety expresses a *beautiful evening*, a completed sweetness and mildness,—it is grateful towards what lies behind it, everything included, it lacks bitterness disappointment, rancor" (KSA 13,14[91]). Although Nietzsche is much more positive here on Buddhism than on Christianity, he still considers it a form of nihilism.

36. This Dionysian redemption includes the various kinds of redemption from *The Birth of Tragedy*, also the Apollonian, although this term is mostly absent from the later work (Ivan Soll, "Schopenhauer, Nietzsche, and the Redemption of Life through Art," in *Willing and Nothingness: Schopenhauer as Nietzsche's Educator*, ed. Christopher Janaway, (Oxford: Clarendon Press, 1998), 112; for more on Dionysus and redemption, see Fraser, *Redeeming Nietzsche*, 54–58.

37. Osthövener, *Erlösung*, 239–43.

38. There are also approaches that hold that, as the practitioner goes the Way, his perspective changes. Finally, there are those who claim that all perspectives, both kataphatic and apophatic, ultimately fall short and can be potential sources of bondage.

39. According to Robert Magliola, the Zen tradition contains a logocentric, absolutist strain, connected with the Northern School of Chan rooted in the kataphatic Yogācāra philosophy, and a differential strain, connected with the Southern School of Chan rooted in the apophatic Madhyamaka tradition. See Robert Magliola, *Derrida on the Mend* (West Lafayette: Purdue University Press, 1984). According to Youro Wang, however, the Southern School of Chan, especially Huineng and the Hongzhou school, deconstructs not only the Northern School of Chan, but also logocentric tendencies within the Southern Chan school itself. See Wang, *Linguistic Strategies in Daoist Zhuangzi and Chan Buddhism.*

40. Wang, *Linguistic Strategies in Daoist Zhuangzi and Chan Buddhism.* For a summary of Wang's argument, see van der Braak, *Toward a Philosophy of Chan Enlightenment.*

41. See Philip B. Yampolsky, *The Platform Sutra of the Sixth Patriarch* (New York: Columbia University Press, 1967).

42. Addiss, Lombardo, and Roitman, *Zen Sourcebook*, 23.

43. Addiss, Lombardo, and Roitman, *Zen Sourcebook*, 25.

44. Wang, *Linguistic Strategies in Daoist Zhuangzi and Chan Buddhism*, 67.

45. Yampolsky, *The Platform Sutra*, 138.

46. The Hongzhou school was controversial even in Chan circles. Chan historian Guifeng Zongmi (780–841), a follower of Shenhui, criticized the Hongzhou view for focusing too much on *yong* and ignoring *ti.* In this way, the Hongzhou school collapsed essence into function, which represented a dangerous antinomianism. But according to Wang, such criticism is not justified. The Hongzhou school also engaged in self-deconstruction. He refers to Mazu's famous self-effacement of his teaching "this mind is Buddha" by replacing it with "neither mind nor Buddha."

47. See Herbert Theierl, *Nietzsche: der Verkünder einer Erlösungslehre* (Unpublished Dissertation. Heidelberg: Ruprecht Universität, 1949) and *Nietzsche: Mystik als Selbstversuch.*

48. Willers, *Nietzsches antichristliche Christologie.*

49. Fraser, *Redeeming Nietzsche*, 24–44; 75–79.

50. Fraser, *Redeeming Nietzsche*, 122.

51. Fraser, *Redeeming Nietzsche*, 61.

52. Benson, *Pious Nietzsche*, 9.

53. Benson, *Pious Nietzsche*, 51.

54. Benson, *Pious Nietzsche*, 200.

55. Tyler Roberts holds that Nietzsche is wrong to condemn Christianity in itself with the claim that *the* Christian response to suffering is always hostile to life (*Contesting Spirit*, 174). Roberts claims that, in some forms of theology of the Cross, Christians demonstrate an affirmative practice of suffering that comes close to Nietzsche's affirmation. According to Roberts, "a theology of the Cross directs human beings to a life, like Christ's, that, out of love, opens itself to the world and all its suffering and refuses to flee from it" (*Contesting Spirit*, 176). A theology of the Cross can affirm a God who suffers with humanity, who is immersed out of love, in the worldly reality of the human. Such a life-affirming suffering God is closer to the

repeated suffering and dying of Nietzsche's Dionysus, Roberts maintains (*Contesting Spirit*, 183). See André F. M. van der Braak, "Nietzsche, Christianity and Zen on Redemption," in *Studies in Interreligious Dialogue* 18/1 (2008): 5–18.

56. Dōgen, *Shōbōgenzō, Genjōkōan*. Quoted in: Davis, *The Presencing of Truth*, 256.

57. Davis, *The Presencing of Truth*, 252f.

58. Dōgen, *Shōbōgenzō, Genjōkōan*. Quoted in: Davis, *The Presencing of Truth*, 256.

59. Dōgen, *Shōbōgenzō, Genjōkōan*. Quoted in: Davis, *The Presencing of Truth*, 256.

60. Chapter 3 recounted the story of Zen Master Qingyuan about mountains and rivers.

Chapter 9

The Child

> Seeing the world as a divine game and beyond good and evil: in this both the Vedanta and Heraclitus are my predecessors.[1]

Let us revisit what Zarathustra is saying exactly about the child in his speech on the three transformations of the spirit:

> Innocence the child is and forgetting, a beginning anew, a play, a self-propelling wheel, a first movement, a sacred Yea-saying. Yes, for the play of creating, my brothers, a sacred Yea-saying is needed: the spirit now wills *its own* will, the one who had lost the world attains *its own* world. (TSZ, I, 1)

Various commentators have noted the vague and insubstantial character of this description, especially compared to Zarathustra's more extensive description of the camel and the lion. Gooding-Williams and Benson conclude that this is because Zarathustra himself has not yet had the experience of becoming a child when he delivers his speech. Speaking of *Thus Spoke Zarathustra* in a letter to Franz Overbeck, Nietzsche himself says, "It contains an image of myself in the sharpest focus, as I am, *once* I have thrown aside my whole burden" (KSB 6: 326). The description of the child is therefore perhaps best interpreted as conjectural.[2]

Four aspects of the child image jump out: forgetting oneself, innocence, play, and a sacred Yes. Forgetting oneself has been extensively discussed in chapter 7. The sacred Yes is connected to Nietzsche's notion of amor fati, which I will discuss in the next chapter on Nietzsche and Nishitani. In this chapter I will focus on innocence and play.

FROM "I AM" TO "IT PLAYS"

The image of the innocent child conjures up all kinds of romantic associations. Together with Nietzsche's own ongoing obsession with romanticism, it seems to make sense that, as Gooding-Williams notes, Nietzsche commentators have often interpreted the figure of the child in essentially romantic terms.[3] For example, for Heller, Nietzsche's child is the symbol for paradise regained, a naiveté, innocence, and unity with nature that signify a dissolution of self-consciousness.[4] J. P. Stern also interprets the child in terms of a Wordsworthian innocence.[5] Löwith interprets the child as an immediate oneness with being.[6] According to Stambough, the child is "wholly immersed in its being."[7] These commentators support their interpretation with the textual claim that Nietzsche identifies the child with the motto "I am," thanks to the following notebook fragment: "Higher than 'thou shalt' ranks 'I will' (the heroes); higher than 'I will' ranks 'I am' (the gods of the Greeks)" (KSA 11, 25 [351]).

As Gooding-Williams notes, however, the expression "I am" occurs nowhere in the discussion of the child in *On The Three Transformations*. He therefore defends a different interpretation of the third transformation as

> a shift in self-understanding that involves a disappearance of the idea of a substantial subject (a so-called "doer behind the deed") to whom various acts of willing can be ascribed. The child, far from saying "I am" or "I will," does not say "I" at all. Rather, he "wills his own will," thereby appearing to acknowledge no substantial subject but only the act of willing itself.[8]

As opposed to both the camel's and the lion's perspective, where actions are performed by an ego that underlies but does not depend for its being on its actions, thoughts, and desires, the child perspective rejects the view that willing is the activity of a substantial subject. The doer-deed dichotomy and the fiction of a substantial subject have been overcome.

Günter Wohlfart's interpretation of this overcoming of the subject (the death of the ego) leads him to the interpretation of the child not as "I am" but as "it plays." According to Wohlfart, one could see in the "thou shalt" of the camel the articulation of the premodern, in the "I will" of the lion the articulation of the modern, and in the "it plays" of the child the articulation of the postmodern mind. He compares the "it plays" to Nietzsche's replacement of the "I think" with the "it thinks"—whereby the "it" is not hypostasized like the "I" before, but should be understood as a synonym for "thought." Thought processes play themselves out; the thinking, imagining subject is part of this play.

The metaphor of play can also be found in Dōgen's work. Dōgen speaks about enlightenment as "the samadhi of self-fulfilling activity" (*jijuyū-zammai*), translated as "playful samadhi." Although the term "samadhi" usually refers to a state of mental concentration, for Dōgen it refers to a mode of activity, a way of functioning where dualities and opposites are not so much transcended as they are realized. According to Kim,

> in Dōgen's view, the samadhi of self-fulfilling activity in its absolute purity was such that our daily activities are undefiled by and unattached to the dualistic categories, events, and things that our perceptions and intellect create, all the while living with and using those dualities.[9]

Dōgen's samadhi of self-fulfilling activity should not be understood as a kind of absorption in an undifferentiated realm, a kind of *unio mystica*. Dōgen condemns the classical Zen instruction texts for suggesting this: "Their formulations are examples of merely "returning to the origin, back to the source" (*gengen-hempon*) and are attempts at vainly "stopping thoughts in abysmal quietude" (*sokuryo-gyōjaku*)."[10] For Dōgen, the samādhi of self-fulfilling activity refers to the self-enjoyment of the *dharmakāya*. It is a state of mind that at once negates and subsumes self and other; a total freedom of self-realization without any dualism or antitheses. This does not mean that oppositions or dualities are obliterated or transcended, but that they are realized. Such a freedom realizes itself in duality, not apart from it.[11] "For playing joyfully in such a samādhi," Dōgen writes, "the upright sitting position in meditation is the right gate."[12] Dōgen's playful samadhi can be seen as another expression of "it plays": not an individual, but a cosmic play.

THE PLAY OF HERACLITUS' COSMIC CHILD: BEYOND ANTHROPOCENTRISM

Also for Nietzsche, the transformation from a self-oriented to a world-oriented perspective should not be seen as merely an individual transformation. I therefore argue for a trans-individual, "cosmic" interpretation of the child. A hint to such a cosmic interpretation can be found in a notebook fragment from 1885: "'Play,' the useless as the ideal of him who is overfull of strength, as 'childlike.' The 'childlikeness' of God, *pais paizon*" (KSA 12, 2 [130]). The expression *pais paizon* is a reference to a cryptic fragment of Heraclitus, fragment B-52: "The *aeon* [the game of life] is like a child, playing a board game; the child; the kingdom."[13]

From his early years in Basel all the way through *Ecce Homo*, Nietzsche senses a kinship with Heraclitus, in whose proximity he feels "altogether better and warmer than anywhere else" (EH III BT, 3). And fragment B-52 connects the early Nietzsche with the late Nietzsche, including his child transformation. The connection between the lion-child transformation and the early Nietzsche's interpretation of the B-52 fragment has been noticed in the Nietzsche literature from the beginning.[14]

Nietzsche refers to the B-52 fragment seven times in his essay *Philosophy in the Tragic Age of the Greeks* and six times in his lectures on the Pre-Platonic philosophers.[15] Nietzsche introduces Heraclitus' child image: "For what he invented here is a rarity even in the sphere of mystic incredibilities and unexpected cosmic metaphors. The world is the game Zeus plays . . ." (PTAG 6). He refers to it as "the beautiful innocent play of the Aeon." (PTAG 7).[16] Nietzsche describes the world according to Heraclitus:

> A becoming and ceasing to be, a construction and destruction, without any moral attribution, in forever equal innocence, can only be found in this world in the play of the artist and the child. And thus, like the child and the artist play, plays the eternally living fire, it builds and destroys, innocently—and this is the play that the Aeon plays with itself. (PTAG 7)

The playful cosmic child could be interpreted as a non-anthropocentric perspective on life, in which the world is experienced as a cosmic body, not separate from the self, but always already including the self:

> This playful cosmic child continually builds and knocks down but from time to time begins his game anew: a moment of contentment followed by new needs. His continuous building and knocking down is a craving, as creativity is a need for the artist; his play is a need. [. . .] Rejection of any teleological view of the world reaches its zenith here: the child throws away its toy, but as soon as it plays again, it proceeds with purpose and order: necessity and play, war and justice. (PPP 72f)[17]

In Nietzsche's early writings on Heraclitus, we find the seeds of his later formulation of will to power as a symbol for the cosmic play of the world. The world as play is looked at as a "monster of energy" with "the most complex forms arising out of the simplest structures [. . .] and then returning again to the simple, from the play of contradictions back to the delight of harmony" (KSA 11, 38 [12]).

THE INNOCENCE OF BECOMING: BEYOND TELEOLOGY

Also the innocence of the child should not be interpreted in a romantic way. It does not refer to having no knowledge of the past, or living in the here and now, or being naïve. It points to a non-essentialist perspective that doesn't assume any God or godlike essence that is the origin and ground of all else.[18] The liberation of such notions of godlike essence constitutes a redemption of the world as a whole:

> *There is nothing besides the whole*—That nobody is held responsible any longer, that the mode of being may not be traced back to a *causa prima*, that the world does not form a unity either as a sensorium or as "spirit"—*that alone is the great liberation*: with this alone is the *innocence* of becoming restored. The concept of "God" was until now the greatest *objection* to existence. We deny God, we deny responsibility in God: only *thereby* do we redeem the world. (TI 6, 8)

For Nietzsche, such a redemption implies leaving behind all teleological notions. In a notebook fragment from 1885, he defines his own philosophical project as trying to prove the innocence of becoming: "Since forever I have tried to prove to myself the perfect *innocence* of becoming! [. . .] I acquired a taste for denying all purposes [*Zwecke*] and sensed the unknowability of all causal relations" (KSA 11, 36 [10]). Nietzsche stresses the need to leave any and all notions of causality behind: "Most important point of view: to gain the innocence of becoming by expelling purposes. Necessity, causality—no more" (KSA 10, 7 [21]).

In order to transform into a child, the lion must give up all teleological and anthropocentric notions, in order to gather the courage to "go under." He must realize the liberating perspective of the innocence of becoming: "The absolute necessity to completely get rid of purposes: otherwise we won't dare to try to offer ourselves up and let go! Only the innocence of becoming gives us the greatest courage and the greatest freedom" (KSA 10, 8 [19]).

In "Before Sunrise", Zarathustra speaks about the innocence of becoming as a state of mind in which all things are experienced not as representations of a subject but rather, as it is called in Zen, in their own "suchness" (*tathātā*):

> But this is my blessing: to stand over each and every thing as its own Heaven, as its round roof, its azure bell and eternal security: and blessed is he who blesses thus! For all things are baptized at the fount of eternity and beyond good and evil; but good and evil are themselves mere intervening shadows and dampening sorrows and drifting clouds. Verily, a blessing it is and no blasphemy when I teach: "Over all things stands the Heaven Accident, the Heaven Innocence, the Heaven Contingency, the Heaven Exuberance."
>
> "Lord Contingency"—that is the oldest nobility in the world, which I restored to all things when I redeemed them from their bondage under Purpose. (TSZ III, 4)

The notion of the innocence of becoming goes back to Heraclitus. Nietzsche notes that Heraclitus "altogether denied being. For this one world which he retained—supported by eternal unwritten laws, flowing upward and downward in a brazen rhythmic beat—nowhere shows a tarrying, an indestructibility, a bulwark in the stream" (PTAG 5).

For Heraclitus, all existent forms are eternally becoming, and all becoming is equally justifiable. Strive is the natural law, generally productive of the world's coming into being, and thus just and good. The particular effects of such a life are either the direct creation of more definitive forms or destruction, which may serve, indirectly, as a condition of the possibility of new formulations. But this struggle is not always a hostile struggle. In a healthy structure, the self-mastered form will promote the sublimation of the agonal instinct. All forms struggle forever to seek new and more appropriate ways to "wage the war" of their own coming to be.

Heraclitus contested Anaximander, according to Nietzsche, by disclosing innocence rather than injustice in the nature of all becomings. Whereas Anaximander conceived of the *apeiron* [the indefinite] as separate from the world of time, space, and causal distinctions and felt that injustice characterized the transformation of things into their opposites, Heraclitus reaffirmed the Greek agon and viewed becoming as a continuing struggle.[19]

Whereas Anaximander judged all becoming to be injustice (and Parmenides responded to this judgment by denying the possibility of becoming at all), Heraclitus viewed all becoming as affirmed and justified. In Nietzsche's view, Heraclitus' thought had remedied Anaximander's two-world system; his subsequent retreat into the metaphysical domain; the weary concept of life as injustice. Therefore, realizing the innocence of becoming can serve the overcoming of morality. "*The Innocence of Becoming: a Guide to the Redemption from Morality*" is the title of one of Nietzsche's book projects (KSA 10, 8 [26]).

For Nietzsche, the flux of becoming is related to the interconnectedness of all things. As Zarathustra asks the dwarf, "And are not all things knotted together so tightly that this moment draws after it all things that are to come" (TSZ III, 2). And at the end of part IV, Zarathustra sings, "Did you ever say Yes to a single pleasure? Oh, my friends, then you said Yes to all pain. All things are interlinked, intertwined, enamored"(TSZ IV, 19).

The Heraclitean world of becoming has been compared by Thomas McEvilley to the Buddhist world of impermanence: "Heraclitus's thought bears close resemblance not only to the flux philosophy of early Buddhism but to the "middle position"—between yes and no—expounded later in the Buddhist tradition in the *Prajñāpāramitā* sutras and the Madhyamaka school."[20]

Buddhist impermanence is often expressed through the doctrine of *pratītya-samutpāda* (dependent origination), which states that all phenomena do not exist independently, but are dependent for their existence on complex networks of causes and conditions. Within the Abhidharma philosophical systems, *pratītya-samutpāda* is further elaborated as a causal model in terms of configurations and constellations of *dharmas*. In early Buddhism, enlightenment is seen as realizing the truth of *pratītya-samutpāda* and the world of interdependence that it reveals.

According to the Mahāyāna Buddhist view, however, *pratītya-samutpāda* points to the very lack of inherent causality. Also, the formulation in terms of *dharmas* carries the risk that these *dharmas* are interpreted as some kind of ultimate essence. Therefore, the Mahāyāna sutras interpret *pratītya-samutpāda* in terms of emptiness. From the perspective of emptiness, all dualities are only provisional, conceptual discriminations that may be functionally practical in specific situations, but are barriers to openness and awakening if conceived of as ultimately real. Therefore, the sacred does not exist separate from, or outside, the ordinary worldly realm. Nirvana, the serene salvation from all struggle, exists in the midst of samsara, the world of perpetual conflict and struggle, the world as a play of will to power engaged in endless self-overcoming, like a lotus blossoming out of muddy water. Seen from this perspective, the Mahāyāna view is an attempt to restore the innocence of becoming: nirvana is not some ideal that needs to be reached, but is already the case. Life is already justified as it is and does not need to be justified by anything else. However, the problem arises: then what is the point of any philosophical *áskēsis?*

THE ONENESS OF PRACTICE AND ENLIGHTENMENT

Especially in the esoteric Vajrayāna Buddhist tradition and its tantric practices, the insight into the oneness of nirvana and samsara led to the development of practices of transcendent faith and ritual enactment of buddhahood, dependent not on lifetimes of arduous practice, but rather on immediate, unmediated, and intuitional realization of the fundamental ground of awakening.[21] Such a replacement of a paradigm of spiritual cultivation by a paradigm of the leap into realizing inherent enlightenment was expressed in more devotional Buddhist traditions by a "leap of faith," and, as we have seen in chapter 8, in the Zen tradition by the notion of sudden enlightenment.

In the context of medieval Japanese Buddhism, such a leap paradigm was represented by the immensely influential Tendai Buddhist discourse of "original enlightenment" (*hongaku*), the assertion that all beings are Buddhas inherently.[22] Since Dōgen grew up in the Tendai school, this *hongaku* discourse also functioned as the intellectual matrix out of which his thought emerged (even though he was also critical of it).[23]

According to Dōgen, enlightenment is not the *result* or the *goal* of practice: it is the perspective from which practice should be carried out—not in order to realize enlightenment, but as an expression of enlightenment. This is reflected in Dōgen's notion of the oneness of practice and enlightenment:

> To think that practice and enlightenment are not one is a non-Buddhist view. In the Buddha-dharma they are one. Inasmuch as practice now is based on enlightenment, the practice of a beginner is itself the whole of original enlightenment. Therefore, in giving the instruction for practice, a Zen teacher advises his/her disciples not to seek enlightenment apart from practice, for practice points directly to original enlightenment. Because it is the very enlightenment of practice, there is no end to enlightenment; because it is the very practice of enlightenment, there is no beginning to practice.[24]

Zazen does not *lead* to enlightenment; zazen itself *is* enlightenment.[25] As Kasulis explains, "To say that one practices zazen in order to become an enlightened person is like saying one practices medicine to become a doctor. To practice medicine is to *be* a doctor. To practice zazen is to *be* enlightened."[26]

Dōgen uses the term practice-realization (*shushō*) in order to indicate how the two notions are mutually interwoven. The character for *shō*, which Dōgen usually uses for enlightenment, normally means to verify, prove, attest to, confirm, or authenticate something.[27] Therefore, *shō* means to verify ("showing to be true" and literally "making true") and hence realizing (in both senses of the term) that who one really is, is part and parcel of the universal Buddha nature. From such a perspective, practice is not about improving or redeeming oneself; rather, self-overcoming is the natural expression of life itself. Zazen is the natural expression of the ongoing enlightening activity of the true human body. For Dōgen, practice-enlightenment is seen not as achieving some kind of psychological state, but as a liberating activity, a liberating intimacy with all things. Enlightenment is not a matter of transcending the predicament of ordinary life, but of becoming more fully immersed in it from an affirmative perspective.

Zazen is not so much a psychological training aiming at particular states or experiences, but the ritual expression, embodiment, and enactment of buddhahood. In his *Fukanzazengi* (Universally Recommended Instructions for Zazen), Dōgen stresses that the zazen that he speaks of is not meditation practice and admonishes the practitioner to not try to become a Buddha.[28] Zazen is not about attaining a mental state of liberation, but about an ongoing transformation that is as much physiological as it is psychological, in which one "realizes" one's own buddhahood, in the sense of fully participating in it. It is not a state but an activity.

Zazen is a communal ritual and ceremonial performance that expresses ultimate reality (the *dharmakāya*). Dōgen stresses that all practitioners should practice zazen together: "standing out has no benefit; being different from others is not our conduct."[29] In such a way, he radically demythologizes standard Zen views on meditation and demythologizes it as a liberating expression and activity of Buddha nature. Zazen should not be practiced in order to gain therapeutic or religious benefits. Rather, for Dōgen, zazen is the prototype of ultimate meaninglessness. According to the twentieth-century Sōtō teacher Kōdō Sawaki (1880–1965), the practice of zazen requires leaving behind a means-end rationality: "Zazen is an activity that comes to nothing. There is nothing more admirable than this activity that comes to nothing. To do something with a goal is really worthless. [. . .] Because it takes you out of the world of loss and gain, it should be practiced."[30]

Zen practice takes place from the realization that everything is already perfect as it is. In the words of Norman Fischer, a contemporary American Zen teacher who teaches in the tradition of Dōgen,

> Birds sing, fish swim, and people who are devoted to zazen do zazen with devotion all the time although there is no need for it. Our life is already fine the way it is. Everything that happens is already a manifestation of our original enlightenment even though we don't know it. We don't need to enter another condition or improve or disprove anything. The gentle rain of the Dharma is falling all the time evenly and freely on everything, and each thing receives that rain and uses it in its own way, each in a different way. The whole world is unfolding in a beautiful and perfect interplay of forces.[31]

BACK TO THE MARKETPLACE

For Nietzsche, this might be a perfect description of the innocence of becoming and the experience of amor fati. However, there is another aspect connected to realizing the innocence of becoming for Nietzsche: it involves a great responsibility. In chapter 3, I mentioned Nietzsche's notebook fragment with the title "*The Way to Wisdom*—Hints for an Overcoming of Morality" (KSA 11, 26 [47]). In this fragment, Nietzsche distinguishes three stages as part of the process of overcoming morality. The description of the third stage reads as follows:

> *The third stage.* Great decision whether one is capable of a positive attitude, of affirmation. No longer any God, any man *above* me! The instinct of the creator who knows *what* he is creating. The great responsibility and the innocence. In order to enjoy a single thing, one has to affirm [*gutheißen*] *everything*. Give oneself the right to act. (KSA 11, 26 [47])

When there is no God above oneself, no one to abdicate responsibility to, the innocence of becoming is restored. But this is not a passive state of self-forgetfulness. Nietzsche speaks about a great responsibility, and about giving oneself the right to act. This might be the reason for Nietzsche's ambivalence toward Heraclitus. As all pre-Platonic thinkers, Heraclitus is greatly one-sided (PTAG 2). Nietzsche considers Heraclitus with his "hate against the Dionysian element" (KSA 7, 19 [61]) too much of an "Apollonian product" with an Apollonian ideal: "everything semblance and play" (KSA 7, 23 [8]). Other than Heraclitus, who lived in self-sufficient solitude and detested his fellow human beings, Zarathustra wants to share his wisdom. Heraclitus is "a star without an atmosphere" with "no powerful feeling of compassionate stirrings, no desire to help, heal and save. As a human being among human beings Heraclitus was impossible" (PTAG 8).[32]

As Nietzsche notes, in the Dionysian rapture, individuals are joined together and experience themselves as one (DW 1). Therefore, in order to do justice to the Dionysian aspect of the child, Nietzsche's Heracliteanism must be understood together with his Dionysianism as two expressions of the same fundamental conception.[33] Nietzsche's remarks on Heraclitus in *Ecce Homo* are telling:

> Before me one doesn't find this transformation of the Dionysian into a philosophical pathos: *tragic wisdom* is lacking—I have looked in vain for signs of it even among the *great* philosophical Greeks, those who lived in the two centuries *before* Socrates. I had a lingering doubt about *Heraclitus*, in whose vicinity I feel altogether warmer, better disposed than anywhere else. The affirmation of transience *and destruction*, the decisive feature of any Dionysian philosophy, saying "yes" to opposition and war, *becoming*, with a radical rejection of even the concept of "being"—in this I must in any event acknowledge ideas that are more closely related to mine than any that have hitherto been thought. (EH III BT, 3)

Even in a yes-saying book like *Ecce Homo*, Nietzsche keeps Heraclitus at a distance in the midst of all his praise for him. He merely "retained some doubt in the case of Heraclitus." Nietzsche likes Heraclitus' philosophical pathos and chooses to ignore his aversion to the communitarian aspect of the Dionysian. But the notion of community is an integral aspect of Nietzsche's child figure. Many Nietzsche interpreters argue that, although the early Nietzsche of *The Birth of Tragedy* looked toward the religious festivals of the Greek communities as a source of inspiration for contemporary European culture, he left such a religious communitarianism behind in his later works. Julian Young argues, however, that Nietzsche never abandoned his youthful aspirations for enlightened community. Therefore, the mature Nietzsche should not be read as an individualist or an existentialist, but as a religious communitarian.[34]

Also, the Zen master is not the iconoclastic individualist that he is often made out to be in popular literature. From the perspective of Mahāyāna Buddhism, enlightenment is always universal liberation, not individual. This is most clearly expressed in the notion of the *bodhisattva*, a being who has vowed not to personally settle into the salvation of final buddhahood until he can assist all others (the *bodhi* in the term means "enlightenment" or "awakening," while *sattva* means "being" or "warrior"[35]). He therefore continues to work in the world in order to help all human beings to realize enlightenment. The bodhisattva has a mysterious and auspicious aspiration to care for and awaken all beings (Sanskrit: *bodhicitta*; Jap. *bodaishin*; literally "enlightening mind"). This translates into the four inconceivable bodhisattva vows that embody a thorough, universal level of commitment:

> Living beings are infinite, I vow to free them
> Delusions are inexhaustible, I vow to cut through them
> Dharma gates are boundless, I vow to enter them
> The Buddha Way is unsurpassable, I vow to realize it.[36]

The bodhisattva's two main qualities are consummate wisdom and boundless compassion. Whereas wisdom is associated with an ascent out of the world of ignorance, compassion involves a descent back into the world for the salvation of all beings. The attainment of wisdom naturally leads to an abundant generosity and a re-engagement with the world. By liberating all sentient beings, bodhisattvas do the work of buddhas in the world.[37] The bodhisattva continuously saves all sentient beings, not out of pity but out of a natural resonance with all beings, sustained by the insight of universal interconnectedness. As a famous Zen koan puts it, the bodhisattva saves all sentient beings like a person who gropes at night for a pillow by reaching behind him.[38]

The bodhisattva has overcome the self-other distinction and naturally resonates with other sentient beings. Their suffering is his own suffering. The teaching of universal Buddha nature and interconnectedness describes how we do not exist in isolation. Rather, all beings are intimately interrelated in their effects on each other. When this deep connection between all sentient beings is realized, the dichotomy between self and other is exposed as a provisional fiction, a conventional truth. Ultimately, all beings are each distinct expressions of one whole, not separate competing entities.[39] The notion of a cosmic Buddha body is a provisional counter fiction that can help to overcome the fiction of separateness. From such a world-oriented perspective, the bodhisattva lives and practices with awareness of the illusory nature of the self-other separation that is continuously produced by his conditioned mentality.

The bodhisattva as a model for self-overcoming has been variously interpreted in the Mahāyāna Buddhist tradition. Some Mahāyāna schools that follow a *mārga* approach distinguish several stages of bodhisattvahood as stages of approaching Buddhahood. As we have seen, in Zen the *mārga* approach is rejected as a form of "gradual enlightenment." Also, Dōgen denies any distinction between Buddhahood and bodhisattvahood:

> All bodhisattvas are all Buddhas. Buddhas and bodhisattvas are not different types of being. Old and young, superior and inferior do not obtain. Even though this bodhisattva and that bodhisattva are not two beings, nor are they distinguished by the self and other, or by the past, present and future, to become a Buddha is the supreme model for the practice of the bodhisattva way. At the time of the initial desire for enlightenment, one becomes a Buddha, and at the final stage of Buddhahood one [still] becomes a Buddha.[40]

In Dōgen's interpretation, the ascending and descending aspects of the bodhisattva path become one and the same. One of the virtues of the bodhisattva is his unlimited giving: "When riches are what they truly are, they invariably become giving. The self gives the self for the sake of giving the self; the other gives the other for the sake of giving the other."[41]

This reminds one of Zarathustra's gift-giving virtue. Graham Parkes points out several other parallels between the bodhisattva and the figure of Zarathustra.[42] In the first section of the Prologue, Zarathustra descends from the mountain top where he has accumulated wisdom, saying "I am overburdened with my wisdom, like the bee that has gathered too much honey, I need hands outstretched to receive it" (TSZ Prologue, 1). Zarathustra's abundant generosity becomes clear when he says,

> I love him whose soul squanders itself, who wants no thanks and does not give back again: for he always bestows and would not preserve himself. [. . .] I love him whose soul is overfull, so that he forgets himself, and all things are in him: thus all things become his going-under. (TSZ Prologue, 4)

Also in part II of *Thus Spoke Zarathustra*, it is love that prompts Zarathustra to go down and pour out his self into the world: "My impatient love overflows in torrents, downwards, toward rising and setting. [. . .] Indeed a lake is within me, solitary and self-contained; but the river of my love draws it off—down to the sea" (TSZ II, 1).

Therefore, the child metaphor can be interpreted up to a point in terms of Heraclitus and his notions of the cosmic child and the innocence of becoming. From such a world-oriented perspective, Nietzsche's philosophical *áskēsis* consists in the continuing effort to remain faithful and restore the innocence of becoming (i.e., keeping it free from essentialism, teleology, and anthropocentrism). Such a practice can also be found in the Zen tradition: enlightenment is perpetually in danger of being turned into an essence (the state of enlightenment), a telos (the final result of all practice), and an anthropocentric personal accomplishment ("my enlightenment"). This is why Dōgen redescribes the Zen *áskēsis* in order to safeguard the innocence of becoming: practice is no longer separate from enlightenment. This could be helpful in suggesting what a Nietzschean perspective on *áskēsis* could look like. However, interpreting Nietzsche's child metaphor in terms of Heraclitus is insufficient because it leaves out the Dionysian aspect. An important aspect of the child is its "return to the marketplace."

At this point in our dialogue between Nietzsche and Dōgen on Nietzsche's child metaphor, let us turn to the most influential interpreter of Nietzsche's child figure in terms of Zen so far, Keiji Nishitani, member of the Kyoto School.

NOTES

1. KSA 11, 26 [193].
2. Whether Zarathustra or Nietzsche himself ultimately reached the child state or not is a question that will not be addressed here
3. Gooding-Williams, *Zarathustra's Dionysian Modernism*, 41.
4. Erich Heller, *The Disinherited Mind* (New York: Harcourt Brace Jovanovich, 1975).
5. J. P. Stern, *A Study of Nietzsche* (Cambridge: Cambridge University Press, 1979).
6. Löwith, *Nietzsches Philosophie der Ewigen Wiederkunft des Gleichen.*
7. Joan Stambough, "Thoughts on the Innocence of Becoming," *Nietzsche-Studien* 14 (1985), 174.
8. Gooding-Williams, *Zarathustra's Dionysian Modernism*, 41.
9. Kim, *Eihei Dōgen—Mystical Realist*, 64.
10. Dōgen, *Shōbōgenzō, Zazenshin.* Quoted in: Kim, *Eihei Dōgen—Mystical Realist*, 61.
11. Kim, *Eihei Dōgen—Mystical Realist*, 55.
12. Dōgen, *Shōbōgenzō, Bendōwa.* Quoted in: Kim, *Eihei Dōgen—Mystical Realist*, 55.
13. See Günter Wohlfart, "Also sprach Herakleitos." *Heraklits Fragment B52 und Nietzsches Heraklit-Rezeption* (Freiburg/München: Alber, 1991), 33–78 for an extensive commentary on Heraclitus' fragment B-52 and Nietzsche's reception of Heraclitus.
14. Wohlfart, "Nachwort. Wille zur Macht und ewige Wiederkunft: die zwei Gesichter des Aion," in *Friedrich Nietzsche: Die nachgelassenen Fragmente, eine*

Auswahl (Stuttgart: Reclam, 1996), 308–59 gives a helpful overview. He also points out that strangely enough there is no reference to the B-52 fragment in the KSA-commentary (see KSA 14, 286). The following discussion owes much to Wohlfart, *Nachwort.*

15. These lectures have not often been used in Anglo-Saxon Nietzsche research because they were not available in English and were deemed unimportant by Kaufmann. In 2001, however, an English translation was published: *The Pre-Platonic Philosophers.* Translated by Greg Whitlock (Urbana/Chicago: University of Illinois Press, 2001). References to this work will be indicated as PPP. Dale Wilkerson, *Nietzsche and the Greeks* (London/New York: Continuum, 2005) heavily draws on PPP.

16. Note Nietzsche's addition of innocence, which is not in the original Heraclitus fragment.

17. See also *The Birth of Tragedy*, 24: "Thus the dark Heraclitus compares the world-building force to a playing child that places stones here and there and builds sand hills only to overthrow them again."

18. Gooding-Williams, *Zarathustra's Dionysian Modernism*, 43.

19. As Wilkerson, *Nietzsche and the Greeks,* 138 suggests, the contest that Nietzsche draws between Heraclitus and Anaximander can be seen as an analogy for the intellectual struggle that Nietzsche saw himself carrying out against Schopenhauer's pessimism.

20. McEvilley, *The Shape of Ancient Thought,* 38.

21. Taigen Dan Leighton, *Visions of Awakening Space and Time: Dōgen and the Lotus Sutra* (Oxford: Oxford University Press, 2007), 7.

22. For an extended discussion of *hongaku* thought in medieval Japanese Buddhism, see Jacqueline I. Stone, *Original Enlightenment and the Transformation of Medieval Japanese Buddhism* (Honolulu: University of Hawai'i Press, 1999).

23. See Kim, *Eihei Dōgen—Mystical Realist,* xx for an overview of Dōgen's relationship to *hongaku* thought.

24. Dōgen, *Shōbōgenzō, Bendōwa.* Quoted in: Kim, *Eihei Dōgen—Mystical Realist*, 63f.

25. According to Masao Abe, we can interpret this oneness of practice and enlightenment in a dualistic way or a nondualistic way. The dualistic way would say that there are two perspectives, which in Buddhism would be called the standpoint of acquired enlightenment (*shikaku*) and that of original enlightenment (*hongaku*). The nondualistic interpretation would say that practice and enlightenment are not two but one and constitute a dynamic whole in which the horizontal dimension (practice) and the vertical (enlightenment) are inseparably united. As Abe puts it: "Both [enlightenment] [. . .] and practice [. . .] are indispensable; but the former is indispensable as the *ground* or *basis*, whereas the latter is indispensable as the *condition* or *occasion*." (Masao Abe, *A Study of Dōgen: His Philosophy and Religion* (Albany: State University of New York Press, 1992), 26).

26. Kasulis, *Zen Action / Zen Person*, 78.

27. Davis, *The Presencing of Truth*, 252. As Kim clarifies, "The three Sino-Buddhist characters, *go*, *kaku*, and *shō*, are read as *satori* in the native Japanese way;

the word *satori*, translated as "enlightenment," has become a household word in the West, thanks to D. T. Suzuki. [. . .] *Shō* (which means "to prove," "to bear witness to," "to verify") signifies the direct, personal verification of salvific reality/truth through the body-mind (*shinjin*), one's whole being. [. . .] in speaking of enlightenment (*shō*), Dōgen always presupposes the process of verification in which enlightenment entails practice, and vice versa" (Kim, *Dōgen on Meditation and Thinking*, 21f).

28. Dōgen, *Fukanzazengi*, in: Taigen Dan Leighton and Shohaku Okamura, trans., *Dōgen's extensive record: a translation of the Eihei Kōroku*, Boston: Wisdom Publications, 2008, 534, 533.

29. Taigen Dan Leighton, "Zazen as an Enactment Ritual," in *Zen Ritual: Studies of Zen Buddhist Theory in Practice,* ed. Steven Heine and Dale S. Wright, (Oxford: Oxford University Press, 2008), 170.

30. Arthur Braverman, *Living and Dying in Zazen: Five Zen Masters of Modern Japan* (New York: Weatherhill, 2003), 58f. Dale Wright comments, however, that some sense of purpose remains in spite of such disclaimers: "If you lack the purpose of Zen, you will also lack everything else about Zen, including *zazen*. This is so because the purpose of casting off all purposes in an exalted state of no mind still stands there behind the scenes as the purpose that structures the entire practice, enabling it to make sense and be worth doing from beginning to end" (Dale S. Wright, "Introduction: Rethinking Ritual Practice in Zen Buddhism," in *Zen Ritual: Studies of Zen Buddhist Theory in Practice*, ed. Steven Heine and Dale S. Wright (Oxford: Oxford University Press, 2008), 15.

31. Zoketsu Norman Fischer, "A Coin Lost in the River Is Found in the River," in *The Art of Just Sitting: essential writings on the zen practice of shikantaza*, ed. John Daido Loori (Boston: Wisdom Publications, 2002), 149f.

32. See Michael Skowron, *Nietzsches Weltliche Religiosität und ihre Paradoxien*, 33 for a fuller discussion of this.

33. Ted Sadler, *Nietzsche: Truth and Redemption: Critique of the Postmodern Nietzsche* (London/Atlantic Highlands, NJ: Athlone Press, 1995), 134.

34. Young, *Nietzsche's Philosophy of Religion.*

35. See Parkes, *Nature and the Human "Redivinized,"* 183.

36. The bodhisattva vows occur in many sutras. This quote is from Taigen Dan Leighton, *Faces of Compassion: Classic Bodhisattva Archetypes and Their Modern Expression* (Boston: Wisdom Publications, 2003), 33.

37. Leighton, *Faces of Compassion*, 41.

38. Blue Cliff Record, Case 89. See *Two Zen Classics: The Gateless Gate and the Blue Cliff Records.* Transl. Katsuki Sekida (Boston: Shambhala, 2005), 375ff.

39. Leighton, *Faces of Compassion*, 37.

40. Dōgen, *Shōbōgenzō*, *Shohō-jissō*. Quoted in: Kim, *Eihei Dōgen—Mystical Realist*, 204f.

41. Dōgen, *Shōbōgenzō, Bodaisatta-shishōhō.* Quoted in: Kim, *Eihei Dōgen—Mystical Realist*, 208.

42. Parkes, *Nature and the Human "Redivinized,"* 183.

Chapter 10

Nishitani on Nietzsche: the Self-overcoming of the Will to Power

> Ironically, it was not in his nihilistic view of Buddhism but in such ideas as *amor fati* and the Dionysian as the overcoming of nihilism that Nietzsche came closest to Buddhism, and especially to Mahāyāna.[1]

Whereas the fundamental question of the onto-theological mainstream of the West has been "what is being?," the counter question of the Kyoto School has been "what is nothingness?"[2] Rather than an ontology, the philosophy of the Kyoto School can be described as a meontology, a philosophy of non-being or nothingness.[3] However, the nothingness of the Kyoto School is not a relative nothingness, an absence of being, but an absolute nothingness (*zettai-mu*) that encompasses both being and not-being. The term *zettai* literally means a "severing of opposition," which implies the sense of "without an opposing other." Absolute nothingness must embrace, rather than stand over against, relative nothingness.[4] It is connected to the Zen notion of emptiness with its various connotations. Kasulis mentions two kinds of emptiness that recur throughout Zen literature:

1. Linguistic distinctions (and the concepts formulated through them) cannot be the medium of an adequate description of reality.
2. Experience (or, alternatively, reality) arises out of a source that cannot be described as either Being or Nonbeing, form or no form.[5]

The first type of emptiness, Nāgārjuna's *śūnyatā*, is primarily a critique of philosophical distinctions. It refers to the fact that all things come to being in *pratītya-samutpāda* (dependent origination) and are therefore empty of any independent self-nature. The second type of emptiness, the Daoist pre-ontology of *wu*, emphasizes an indeterminate, distinctionless reality, the origin of all things. This unnamable non-dualistic source of all being and relative non-being is also referred to as the *dao* (the Way). Both of those two strands of thought were combined in the Zen notion of nothingness.

Śūnyatā is technically translated as *kū* (*kong* in Chinese), and the Chinese *wu* is changed only in pronunciation into the Japanese *mu*.[6] The thinkers of the Kyoto School tend to favor the term *mu*, which is found predominantly in Zen. In his mature writings, however, Nishitani explicitly employs the Mahāyāna Buddhist term *śūnyatā* to refer to absolute nothingness.

NISHITANI'S "STANDPOINT OF ZEN"

Just like his teacher Nishida, Nishitani attempts to bring about a synthesis between Japanese Zen Buddhist philosophy and Western philosophy, but from the opposite end.[7] Nishida attempts to integrate nothingness in Western frameworks, to interpret the Zen experience in phenomenological and ontological terms. Nishitani, on the other hand, attempts to integrate being in Eastern frameworks. In his work he addresses the problem of nihilism and how Western thinkers and Buddhism can find ways to its overcoming.

Nishitani distinguishes three different perspectives: the standpoint of egoity, the standpoint of nihility (relative nothingness), and the standpoint of *śūnyatā* (absolute nothingness).[8] The standpoint of absolute nothingness refers to a perspective that reflects the spontaneous, unconditioned way of natural existence, the simultaneous unity and difference of all entities. Absolute nothingness is the standpoint from which all that is and is not emerges as it is grasped by the non-egocentric self. The egoistic self must be broken through in order to actualize the fundamental standpoint of "non-ego" or "no-self." Absolute nothingness signifies the fundamental unity that encloses all differentiation. Nishitani claims that

> on the field of sunyata, *the center is everywhere*. Each thing in its own selfness shows the mode of being of the center of all things. Each and every thing becomes the center of all things and, in that sense, becomes an absolute center. This is the absolute uniqueness of things, their reality. [. . .] Only on the field of sunyata can the totality of things, each of which is absolutely unique and an absolute center of all things, at the same time be gathered into one.[9]

To realize non-ego is to locate oneself not as a fixed identity but as a process in the greater process of existence, a drop in the sea apart from which the drop could not be. Non-ego is thus neither an ontological nor an epistemological position; it only has meaning in the context of the movement toward self-realization, which is possible only from the standpoint of absolute nothingness. The self thus realized is the self seen through *śūnyatā*, which allows nihilism free play and follows it to the end.

THE SELF-OVERCOMING OF NIHILISM

In his work *The Self-overcoming of Nihilism*, based mostly on a collection of lectures given in 1949 but only translated into English in 1990, Nishitani interprets Nietzsche's three transformations of the spirit as three stages of existence as nihilism. The stage of the camel involves "both immersing oneself in the teachings of traditional religion and metaphysics as well as a turn to nihilism which breaks through them."[10] The lion stage is the turn from the preliminary stage of masked nihilism to true nihilism, "which makes this world into a problematic 'X' by negating the beyond."[11] The lion engages in a practice of active nihilism, and in this process, according to Nishitani, "the self that has grown strong under the bonds of all that has been learned eventually 'breaks the revering heart' and sheds everything that had been acquired through reverent learning as an outer husk, casting it aside to make way for the true self."[12] According to Nishitani, Nietzsche conceives of such a true self as "a granite of spiritual fate" (BGE 231), a fate deep within our foundations, unreachable by teaching or learning. He compares this to the Zen transmission of teachings without dependence on scriptures by pointing directly to the human heart.[13] In the third child stage, nihilism overcomes itself. According to Nishitani, in this overcoming the body is restored as the standpoint of the creating and willing "I."[14] This I is "a manifestation of the 'will to power' which constitutes the essence of life. The so-called "I," what we normally take as the self, is merely a frame of interpretation added to this life process after the fact."[15]

After the death of God and the replacement of metaphysical truth with perspectivism, there is no absolute standard for truth anymore; there are only perspectives. However, such perspectives are not true but, strictly speaking, illusory. Human beings can live only through illusion: life functions in us through a will to deception. When truth is seen as the value standard of life, a will to truth arises. The constant creation of new perspectives (the fabrication of new lies) opens up further, broader horizons. This broadening of perspectives is a new illumination of the world and thus strengthens and enhances humanity. Only persons of strong will can stand existence in a world without purpose, unity, or truth.[16] Therefore, one has to relentlessly track down and negate all idealistic and other-worldly worldviews and moralities (*Hinterweltlerei*) in oneself and others. One needs to look into the abyss of nihility—descend into how deeply lies and fabrications make up life. This fictitious world without meaning or purpose is the only reality that exists.

When one sees the world from this perspective (which is, according to Nishitani, the world as will to power), the world process takes on the necessity of *fatum*: it could not be otherwise than it is.[17] Only if there would be another world behind this one, the world could be otherwise than it actually is. One has to submit oneself to this fate and deeply accept and embrace the necessity of the world process: this is the attitude of amor fati. Amor fati means understanding the world as play of the multiple perspectives of will to power.

Nishitani calls Nietzsche's fatalism an extreme fatalism, without room for providence, progress, or evolution. In ordinary fatalism, we are helpless victims of the way the course of all things is run by something or some process outside of us. Such a view destroys chance and creativity. But Nietzsche's fatalism is identical with chance and the creative. Chance and necessity are identical.[18]

Nishitani stresses that the self is an active part of this fatalism: every action of a person has an infinitely great influence on everything that is to come. He connects this to the Buddhist notion of karma. Every action of the self is influenced by all things and in turn influences all things.[19] The self and the world are one: they both are will to power.[20] The world and its necessity are affirmed out of a creative will to power. For Nishitani, the perspective of amor fati means attaining a height and a bird's eye view in observation. Every kind of imperfection and the suffering due to it belong together in the highest desirability.

Nishitani describes how one breaks through to amor fati. Once one descends into one's ultimate depths of nihilism, into the abyss of the great suspicion, one encounters what in Zen is called the Great Doubt and what Nietzsche calls the great suspicion, which is taught to us by the great pain that is the liberator of the spirit:

> Only the great pain is the ultimate liberator of the spirit, as the teacher of the *great suspicion* [. . .] Only the great pain [. . .] forces us philosophers to descend into our ultimate depths and to disabuse ourselves of all trusting, of everything good-natured, concealing, mild, mediocre, in which we have perhaps placed our humanity up until now [. . .] [and] out of the abyss of the *great suspicion* one returns newly born. (NCW Epilogue 1, 2)

The painful insight into necessity and contingency functions as the sharp, liberating pick axe that cuts through our second nature. One's innermost nature (our first nature) bursts forth like a natural spring from which the covering debris has been removed, like a giving birth. Absolute affirmation affirms even the deceptions that had blocked it; it has a love of what is inevitable.

As Nishitani puts it, "The very act of submitting to fate is a return to one's own innermost nature. It is to become oneself, shaking off what is not oneself and what prevents one from becoming oneself."[21] What is not oneself is appropriated into the self. The world becomes the perspective of the great love and the will that embraces all possible comprehensive horizons. Fate becomes one with one's own creative will. This means a radical transformation of the self's mode of being.

Amor fati is connected with the incorporation of the thought of eternal recurrence. Nishitani interprets eternal recurrence as the intuitive experience of insight into eternity from within this world of becoming, an ek-stasis, an experience of the eternal present.[22] Suffering is transformed into joy as lead is alchemically transformed into gold. There is divine life in a new and Dionysian sense in a world without God. One must have wings to get out of the abyss: the wings of eros.

Embracing the thought of eternal recurrence means stepping out of the frame of self. Conquering the spirit of gravity involves conquering the voice of skepticism that insists that escaping the boundaries of the self is not possible. The frame of the self, in which all things thrown high fall back on oneself, is broken through. The entire world process now becomes the activity of the self's will: "the world worlds," Nishitani adds with a Heideggerian flourish.[23] Those who can't step out of the frame of the self are invalids. One has to turn one's abyss inside out into the light.

Nishitani interprets the thought of eternal recurrence (because all things are tied together, this moment must recur) both as Nietzsche's extreme fatalism and as a counterweight to ordinary fatalism: the elimination of the concept of necessity, the will, "truth."[24] Eliminating will does not mean to return to the standpoint of a bystander, but to say "once more," fully immersed. Eliminating necessity means that ordinary necessity, as something that binds, disappears. Necessity as fate is play, the play of the child. Eliminating truth means that knowledge is negated only to be reaffirmed as a part of illusion. The negation is also negated, just like the doer is reabsorbed into the deed. This is, according to Nishitani, the self-overcoming of the will to power: both resistances and the striving against them have been overcome. Nietzsche's extreme fatalism means absolute freedom; the innocence of becoming is restored.

Thinking through the thought of eternal recurrence is the most extreme form of nihilism, a European Buddhism. This is why Nietzsche philosophizes with the hammer. Only those who can bear the thought of eternal recurrence courageously and without deception in order to consummate their nihilism will be able to attain the will to the revaluation of values and absolute affirmation.[25] Nihilism is both a crisis and a turning point. Breaking through to a Dionysian stance toward existence (amor fati) could be called the redemption of Nietzsche's new "religion." Nishitani stresses that this new religion is, just like Zen, a religion of laughter.[26] One is free to immerse oneself in the play of the samsaric world: samsara is nirvana (nirvana is also samsara: the last man will return endlessly). This is the standpoint of absolute nothingness. However, Nishitani concludes that Nietzsche's overcoming of nihilism ultimately falls short of such a perspective of absolute nothingness: "What is clear, however, is that there is in Mahāyāna a standpoint that cannot yet be reached even by a nihilism that overcomes nihilism, even though the latter may reach in that direction."[27]

RELIGION AND NOTHINGNESS

In his later work *Religion and Nothingness* (published in English in 1982; original Japanese publication in 1955), Nishitani is more explicitly practicing comparative philosophy. He uses the philosophy of Zen—as well as Heidegger, Eckhart, and Nietzsche—to shed light on the philosophical problematic of nothingness. In this work, Nishitani is much more critical of Nietzsche's work. Even though Nietzsche's notion of the innocence of becoming comes close to a "pure activity beyond the measure of a teleological gauge," it still remains bound to a "standpoint of will"[28] in two ways: will to power remains external to the self and is therefore not truly a standpoint of non-self, and Nietzsche's attempt to willfully overcome nihilism falls short of the standpoint of absolute nothingness.

Nishitani's first objection is that Nietzsche's notion of will to power is still too metaphysical; it still retains aspects of a new essence, a new metaphysical notion of being.[29] Undoubtedly, Nishitani was influenced in this by Heidegger's rejection of will to power as a hidden metaphysics. The self is still determined by the will to power and therefore not completely free. Therefore, the standpoint of the will to power falls short of what Nishitani calls "the self that is not a self," the self that stands out into a relation of dependent origination with others.

His second objection is that the notion of will to power is still too anthropocentric and self-centered. There is too much "will" left in "will to power." It does not break through all transmutations of self-centered willing. The standpoint of *śūnyatā* is oriented directly opposed to any kind of will. As Nishitani explains,

> in the conversion from [. . .] the standpoint of the self-centered will to the standpoint of the non-ego samadhi, [. . .] doing becomes a true doing, ecstatic of itself. This doing implies a responsibility to every neighbor and every other; [. . .] It is a doing on the standpoint of non-ego, of the "non-duality of self and other."[30]

Such a standpoint of *śūnyatā* is not achieved by willfully overcoming nihilism, but by what Nishitani calls "trans-descendence," stepping back through the relative nothingness of the field of nihility to the absolute nothingness of the field of *śūnyatā*. For Nishitani, Nietzsche remains stuck in a standpoint of "relative absolute nothingness."[31]

DAVIS: THE SELF-OVERCOMING OF THE WILL TO POWER?

Nishitani's reading of Nietzsche through Zen has been followed up on by contemporary philosophers more or less associated with the Kyoto School.[32] For example, in his article *Zen after Zarathustra*, Bret Davis takes up Nishitani's criticisms of Nietzsche. Davis focuses on the relation between nihilism and will. He seeks a confrontation between Nietzsche's radical affirmation and Buddhism's radical negation of the will. As we have seen, the Buddhist nirvana is not to be seen as a simple extinction of the will, as was assumed in the nineteeth-century reception of Buddhism. But could it be interpreted as an existential death that gives new life, a conversion to a way of being in the world radically other than will to power? Could it be seen as Nietzsche's lion–child transformation? Is there room in Nietzsche's thought for a transformation of action such that it is no longer determined by will? Can nirvana be understood as a great negation that makes possible a reaffirmation of another way of being in the world? As Davis puts it, "Is there a 'lion's roar' of the Buddha that says No to (the) life (of will) so that it can one day awaken children of tender Yeses to (the) life (of non-willing)?"[33]

Davis then goes on to discuss the role of the will in Nietzsche and Zen in nihilism and its overcoming. For Nietzsche, overcoming nihilism demands a revaluation of all values out of a revitalized strength of will. But as Heidegger puts it, overcoming nihilism by positing new values is like putting out a fire with kerosene. This is why, according to both Heidegger and Nishitani, Nietzsche ultimately remains entangled in nihilism.

There are indeed places in Nietzsche's work where the will to power seems to turn into a new essence and a new teleology, a new "thou shalt." Davis gives examples where Nietzsche calls the will to power "the ultimate ground and character of all change" (KSA 13, 14 [133]), "the innermost essence of being" (KSA 13, 14 [80]), and "the ultimate fact to which we come down" (KSA 11, 40 [61]). This seems to be a far cry from Buddhist notions of emptiness.

Moreover, a Buddhist critique of the will to power could claim that it is a form of *tanhā* (ego-centered craving). The will to power even becomes connected to the teleological imperative of cultivating the body, resulting in the coordination of drives under a single predominant drive. As Davis notes, "While for Nietzsche there is no ego *as a given*, there is *the task of constructing an ego*, of organizing the plurality of disparate impulses by submitting them to the rule of a commanding will to power."[34] As Nietzsche writes about the ego, "The ego subdues and kills, it operates like an organic cell: it is a robber and is violent. It wants to regenerate itself—pregnancy. It wants to give birth to its god and see all mankind at its feet" (KSA 10, 1 [20]). And yet, "At the risk of displeasing innocent ears I propose: egoism belongs to the nature of the noble soul—I mean that unshakable faith that to a being such as 'we are' other beings must be subordinate by nature and have to sacrifice themselves" (BGE 265). This seems again far removed from the Buddhist notion of extinguishing the ego.

Davis concludes that, from a Buddhist perspective, "The will to power as an egoistic force that expands the domain of the ego by subjugating others to its rule, is the root that needs to be cut in order to make possible a fundamental conversion of life to a radically other way of being-in-the-world,"[35] a way that is characterized by compassion.

However, Davis doesn't stop at this conclusion. He notes that a Buddhist characterization of Nietzsche as a "willful nihilist" would be just as one-sided as Nietzsche's characterization of Buddhism as a passive nihilism. As a possible solution, he suggests to relegate the will to power to the lion stage of Nietzsche's thought. In the lion–child transformation, the will to power itself would be overcome, which would mean moving beyond both the simple ascetic Schopenhauerian denial of the will to power and its simple lion stage affirmation:

> In its most radical possibility this movement of self-overcoming would not just lead to a dialectical *Aufhebung* of the will to power, but would be more akin to a Derridean deconstruction of the very regime of the language of will, that is to say, an overturning within and then breaking free of the binary opposition between assertion and denial of will. One could read Nietzsche's assertion of the doctrine of will to power as an *inversion* of the binary opposition that posits will-lessness as the ideal.[36]

On the one hand, will to power can be interpreted as Nietzsche's inversion of the nihilistic redemptive notion of will-lessness that dominates Christianity (and Buddhism, in Nietzsche's view): rather than to be extinguished, the will needs to be maximized. But Davis thinks that it would be inconsistent for Nietzsche to stop at a mere countermovement, a mere "anti." He suggests that perhaps, just like Heidegger said, Nietzsche's *Umdrehung* of Platonism turned into a *Herausdrehung*, "so too he would move beyond *both* the simple denial *and* the simple affirmation of the will to power."[37] This would be a fine example of "the dynamic dialectic of reaffirmation through double negation." First, the will to power serves as a counter notion in order to negate the ideal of will-lessness; then the notion of will to power itself has to be overcome as well. The camel, with its asceticism of the spirit and its ideal of will-lessness, denies the reality of the will to power. The lion, with its emancipation from the ascetic ideal, affirms the will to power—the doctrine of the will to power serves as an instrument to twist free of the camel's ascetic ideal. A second step of twisting free would involve going beyond both. Davis goes on to suggest that "perhaps, then, just as Nietzsche's thought would in the end twist free of the oppositions between the 'true' and the 'apparent' worlds, so too would he move beyond both the simple denial and the simple affirmation of the will to power."[38] The question is

> Does Nietzsche leave open the possibility of a movement from the subjective to the objective genitive in the phrase "the self-overcoming *of* the will to power?" *Must life ceaselessly overcome itself because it is in essence the will to power; or, might the will to power itself in the end be overcome because life is in essence self-overcoming?*[39]

Davis undertakes three attempts to answer this question. First, one could argue that egocentrism and exploitation depict only degenerate forms of the will to power. There is also an elevated egoism, a selfishness that is "whole and holy," which is the "gift-giving virtue" that forces "all things to and into yourself that they may flow back out of your well as the gifts of your love" (TSZ I, 22). Perhaps such an elevated egoism is a result of the lion–child transformation.

In Nietzsche's work, there certainly are passages to be found that suggest that the willfulness of the lion has to make place for the will-lessness of the child. Davis discusses section 13 in part II of *Thus Spoke Zarathustra* (the section following section 12, "On Self-Overcoming", where Zarathustra introduces the will to power). Zarathustra says about "the ascetic of the spirit,"

> *He must still unlearn even his heroic will*; he shall be elevated [*ein Gehobener*] for me, not merely sublime [*ein Erhabener*]: the ether himself should elevate him, the will-less one [*den Willenlosen*]! [. . .] To stand with relaxed muscles and *unharnessed* will: that is most difficult for all of you sublime ones. [. . .] For this is this soul's secret: only when the hero has abandoned her, she is approached, in a dream,—by the overhero. (TSZ II, 13; translation Bret Davis)

Such an unlearning of the heroic will would presumably constitute the transformation into the child. The soul is abandoned by the hero and approached in a dream by the overhero. Nietzsche alludes here to the myth of Ariadne, who was left behind by Theseus and approached in a dream by Dionysus.

However, Davis signals a fundamental ambivalence in Zarathustra's teaching. Would the elevated egoism of the overhero tolerate a plurality of perspectives out of a released willingness to let their irreducible and unappropriable otherness be, or out of a strength of commanding will that is able to subjugate them all? Is the will to power overcome in the lion-child transformation, or is the lion–child transformation made possible by a strong will to power, who performs the overcoming? To be an overhero seems to require the mutually exclusionary qualities of strength and openness.[40] Perspectivism demands an infinite openness to other interpretations: the world may include infinite interpretations. Yet, interpretation is itself a means of becoming master of something. Davis notes that there is a paradoxical ambivalence in the expression "self-overcoming *of* the will to power": it is the will to power that needs to have the strength to execute such an overcoming, yet is it the will to power itself that dissolves in an infinite openness.

In a second approach, Davis tries to go deeper into this ambivalence by probing into the nature of Nietzsche's *áskēsis* as a training of the will to power. Nietzsche proposes "to make *asceticism* once again *natural*: in place of the purpose of denial, the purpose of *strengthening*: a gymnastics of the will" (KSA 12, 9 [93]). This gymnastics of the will eventually results in the incorporation of the thought of eternal recurrence and the transformation into amor fati. However, the same ambivalence re-occurs here: is the will able to incorporate the thought of eternal recurrence because it has overcome itself and has been transformed or because it has become strong enough to say of the entire past, "Thus I willed it?" Does the incorporation of the eternal recurrence signify the transformation or the consummation of the will? This tension leads to

> two ways of understanding Nietzsche's "unrestricted Yes" to the eternal recurrence of the same. Does this unrestricted Yes, this amor fati, indicate that the wise man has learned to bless every moment and everything *for its own sake*? Or does it mean that the strong man succeeds in interpreting all existence, including that of the nauseating last man, as necessary for the "high point of the series," the moment of his own affirmation?[41]

Davis attempts a third way out of this dilemma by suggesting that Nietzsche himself recognized the unresolved tension in his thought and came up with the projection of the future Übermensch. However, also in the figure of the Übermensch the same ambivalence recurs. Müller-Lauter has shown how the Übermensch is caught in two incompatible images: that of the wise man, who is able to allow many perspectives to be, and that of the strong man, who is able to impose his will on many perspectives. Müller-Lauter argues that only an "incomprehensible qualitative leap" can explain the movement from strong man to wise man.[42]

Davis suggests that such a qualitative leap may be found in the Zen notion of "sudden awakening" (*dunwu*): "The Zen masters do indeed seem to suggest that strength and wisdom can be reconciled, and that a dynamic nondualism between autonomous mastery and compassionate servitude can be thought outside the horizon of a contest of wills."[43] Sudden awakening is not a leap into a state of awakening, but a shift to a new perspective, the perspective that one already is, and always has been, awakened. It can be compared to the world-oriented perspective in which the innocence of becoming is restored, the perspective in which, as Benson puts it, nothing needs to be fixed.

In the Zen tradition, many notions express the nonduality of self and world: Dōgen's forgetting the self, the notion of Buddha nature, the notion of the mutual interpenetration of all phenomena. Would Nietzsche have accepted such a notion of liberation, Davis asks, or would he have considered this yet another "fable song of madness?"[44]

DISCUSSION

Nishitani has been groundbreaking in his Nietzsche interpretation based on Zen.[45] His Nietzsche interpretation is remarkably astute, especially considering the state of Nietzsche research at the time his lectures were held (1949 and 1955, before Walter Kaufmann's influential English Nietzsche translations). His interpretation of Nietzsche's camel–lion–child has inspired many Nietzsche researchers. Nevertheless, some comments can be made about his Nietzsche interpretation. It also needs to be kept in mind that his interpretation of Nietzsche is only a stepping stone to his primary interest: to develop a philosophy of Zen that takes into account Western philosophical concepts. As Davis notes, Nishitani was in the habit of going as far along with a Western thinker as he could. When he could go no further, he simply marked the differences and moved on.[46]

Thomas Kasulis has drawn an interesting contrast between two sets of Kyoto School thinkers. Masao Abe and D. T. Suzuki, who attempted to introduce Zen to a Western audience, tended to emphasize the immediate, mystical experience of *śūnyatā*. Nishida and Nishitani, on the other hand, tended to avoid references to *śūnyatā* as a foundation for their philosophies. For them, *śūnyatā* is something to be explained philosophically, not something that explains (away) the problems of philosophy. Without the clarity of that experience, philosophy runs into unavoidable obstacles.[47] Since they primarily wrote for Japanese, the reality of the *śūnyatā* experience was not in question. The issue for them more often was how that experience could enrich Western philosophy with new and useful categories.

Therefore, Nishitani's approach generally is to take on Western philosophical problems and try to present better, Zen Buddhist answers to those problems. As part of this approach, he tends to accentuate the apophatic aspects of Zen that are both most different from Western traditions and most distinctively Japanese: insight into *śūnyatā*, non-duality, absolute nothingness. He writes less about *mārga* and self-cultivation. Therefore, in his comparison with Nietzsche, he does not say much about the importance of a *practice* of continual self-overcoming. And yet, it is such a conception of Zen as a practice of continual self-overcoming (as can be found in Dōgen's thought) that might make for the most fruitful dialogue between Nietzsche and Zen. Zen is also and primarily about practices of self-cultivation and self-overcoming conducive to spiritual development.[48]

The main difference between Nishitani's Nietzsche interpretation and my own lies in the status of the will to power. Nishitani ultimately concludes that Nietzsche remains stuck in the notion of will to power, failing to realize the Zen "standpoint of *śūnyatā*." The centrality of the will to power that Nishitani ascribes to Nietzsche's thought is in line with the Nietzsche research of the period in which his engagement with Nietzsche's thought took place. However, the past sixty years have seen great progress and refinement in Nietzsche philology and interpretation. The will to power is no longer interpreted as his "main thought." Colli and Montinari have proven that *The Will to Power* is not Nietzsche's *Hauptwerk*, that Nietzsche abandoned such a work, and that his sister revived and reconstructed the work.

Also, and again perhaps related to the time he originally held the talks, Nishitani tends toward an individualist, existentialist Nietzsche interpretation. Nishitani's Nietzsche is a radical individualist, engaged in a heroic battle with nihilism. Nishitani interprets amor fati as an individual redemption, whereas Nietzsche also speaks in places about the Dionysian redemption of reality as a whole, not of an individual, which comes close to the Zen affirmation of the original "suchness" of reality. Although Nishitani recognizes such trans-individualist impulses in Nietzsche's philosophy, he does not think Nietzsche went far enough. Recent Nietzsche interpreters, however, stress his critique of the "I" and the pre-postmodernist aspects of his thought, which makes his thought more in agreement with the Buddhist philosophy of non-self (see chapter 2).

Finally, Nishitani's focus on "the standpoint of *śūnyatā*" tends to underemphasize the importance of the body and the earth. According to translator Jan van Bragt, in Nishitani's later work, an evolution beyond the thought of *Religion and Nothingness* can be detected: not only an emphasis on emptiness, but also on "transcendence in the earth." He argues that, in his later work, "Nishitani now pays special attention to aspects of reality to which he had not allotted full weight in his earlier system: the dark, nondiaphanous sides of human existence in its connection with the body and the earth."[49] Unfortunately, Nishitani did not return to Nietzsche in his later work; it would have been interesting to see which parallels between Nietzsche and Zen he would have elucidated with regard to the importance of embodiment.

We are left with the question of the self-overcoming of the will to power. It is important to keep in mind that the notion of the self-overcoming of the will to power is a construction of some Nietzsche researchers.[50] The expression does not occur in Nietzsche's own work. To argue that Nietzsche's child should be read as the result of a self-overcoming of the will to power is therefore certainly a defensible interpretation but not an interpretation that Nietzsche himself seems to have intended.

Perhaps any comparative effort between Nietzsche and Zen that continues to give the will to power this central place in Nietzsche's thought and interprets the purpose of Nietzsche's *áskēsis* as the self-overcoming of the will to power is bound to conclude that there remains an unbridgeable gap between Nietzsche and Zen. But what is the ontological status of the will to power? Let us turn to a different approach and apply the Mahāyāna Buddhist hermeneutic of *upāya* to Nietzsche's notion of will to power, that is, interpret it as a form of skillful means. This is what the next chapter will investigate.

NOTES

1. Nishitani, *The Self-Overcoming of Nihilism,* 180.
2. General information on the Kyoto School in this chapter has been taken from Davis, *The Kyoto School.*
3. Davis, *The Kyoto School,* 3.1
4. Davis, *The Kyoto School,* 3.3.
5. Kasulis, *Zen Action / Zen Person,* 14.
6. Kasulis, *Zen Action / Zen Person,* 39.
7. Jan van Bragt, "Translator's Introduction," in *Religion and Nothingness,* xxxii.
8. This overview is based on the summary of Nishitani's thought in Brian Schroeder, "Dancing Through Nothing: Nietzsche, the Kyoto School, and Transcendence," *Journal of Nietzsche Studies* 37 (2009): 44–65.
9. Nishitani, *Religion and Nothingness,* 146.
10. Nishitani, *The Self-Overcoming of Nihilism,* 82.
11. Nishitani, *The Self-Overcoming of Nihilism,* 83.
12. Nishitani, *The Self-Overcoming of Nihilism,* 91.
13. Nishitani, *The Self-Overcoming of Nihilism,* 92.
14. Nishitani, *The Self-Overcoming of Nihilism,* 95.
15. Nishitani, *The Self-Overcoming of Nihilism,* 96f.
16. Nishitani, *The Self-Overcoming of Nihilism,* 47.

17. Nishitani, *The Self-Overcoming of Nihilism,* 48.

18. Nishitani, *The Self-Overcoming of Nihilism,* 49.

19. This is similar to the notion of mutual interdependence and interpenetration of Huayan Buddhism.

20. Nishitani, *The Self-Overcoming of Nihilism,* 50.

21. Nishitani, *The Self-Overcoming of Nihilism,* 51.

22. Nishitani, *The Self-Overcoming of Nihilism,* 54.

23. Nishitani, *The Self-Overcoming of Nihilism,* 59.

24. Nishitani, *The Self-Overcoming of Nihilism,* 61.

25. Nishitani, *The Self-Overcoming of Nihilism,* 64.

26. Nishitani, *The Self-Overcoming of Nihilism,* 66.

27. Nishitani, *The Self-Overcoming of Nihilism,* 180.

28. Nishitani, *Religion and Nothingness,* 258; Nishitani, *Religion and Nothingness,* 265.

29. Nishitani, *Religion and Nothingness,* 216.

30. Nishitani, *Religion and Nothingness,* 255.

31. Nishitani, *Religion and Nothingness,* 66. See also Schroeder, *Dancing Through Nothing*, 51.

32. See, for example, David Jones, "Empty Soul, Empty World: Nietzsche and Nishitani," in *Japanese and Continental Philosophy: Conversations with the Kyoto School*, ed. Bret W. Davis, Brian Schroeder, and Jason M. Wirth (Bloomington & Indianapolis: Indiana University Press, 2011), 102–19.

33. Davis, *Zen After Zarathustra,* 96.

34. Davis, *Zen After Zarathustra,* 112.

35. Davis, *Zen After Zarathustra,* 113.

36. Davis, *Zen After Zarathustra,* 115.

37. Davis, *Zen After Zarathustra,* 115.

38. Davis, *Zen After Zarathustra,* 115.

39. Davis, *Zen After Zarathustra,* 116.

40. For an attempt to combine these two qualities of strength and openness, see van der Braak, *Hoe men wordt, wat men is.*

41. Davis, *Zen After Zarathustra,* 124f.

42. Wolfgang Müller-Lauter, *Nietzsche.*

43. Davis, *Zen After Zarathustra,* 125.

44. In a recent publication, Davis concludes that intimations of a self-overcoming of the will to power in Nietzsche's thought "remain at least underdeveloped, and perhaps irredeemably ambivalent." Bret W. Davis, "Nishitani after Nietzsche: From the Death of God to the Great Death of the Will," in *Japanese and Continental Philosophy: Conversations with the Kyoto School*, ed. Bret W. Davis, Brian Schroeder, and Jason M. Wirth (Bloomington & Indianapolis: Indiana University Press, 2011), 96.

45. See the publications by Graham Parkes: "Nietzsche and Nishitani on the Self through Time," *The Eastern Buddhist* 17/2 (1984): 55–74; "Nietzsche and Nishitani on the Self-Overcoming of Nihilism," *International Studies in Philosophy* 25/2 (1993): 51–60; "Nietzsche and Nishitani on Nihilism and Tradition," in *Culture and*

Self: Philosophical and Religious Perspectives, East and West, ed. Douglas Allen (Boulder: Westview Press, 1997), 131–44.

46. Davis, *Zen after Zarathustra*, 90.

47. Thomas P. Kasulis, "Masao Abe as D. T. Suzuki's Philosophical Successor," in *Masao Abe: A Zen Life of Dialogue*, ed. Donald W. Mitchell, 251–59 (Boston/Rutland, VT/Tokyo: Charles E. Tuttle, 1998), 257.

48. As Bret Davis notes, for Nishitani himself, (Zen) practice and philosophy went very much together: "He saw philosophy's rational pursuit of wisdom and Zen's embodied 'investigation into the self' as mutually supportive endeavors in a life of 'sitting [in meditation], then thinking; thinking, then sitting.'" (Bret Davis, "Nishitani Keiji's "The Standpoint of Zen: Directly Pointing to the Mind," in *Buddhist Philosophy: Essential Readings*, ed. William Edelglass and Jay L. Garfield (Oxford: Oxford University Press, 2009), 93.

49. Jan van Bragt, "Foreword," in *On Buddhism,* Keiji Nishitani (Albany: State University of New York Press, 2006), viii. However, Bret Davis has pointed out that these were lectures held at the Pure Land Otani University and may therefore have been addressed specifically to a Pure Land Buddhist audience (Bret Davis, personal communication, 4/10/2010).

50. See chapter 8, note 31.

Part IV

The Self-overcoming of Philosophy

Chapter 11

Exoteric and Esoteric

What is the philosopher, who wants to encourage his readers to incorporate more truthful perspectives on life, to do? How can he educate them to the point where they are able to realize a world-oriented perspective? He cannot simply feed them more truthful ideas; his readers will not be able to incorporate them. Various types of individuals differ in their capacity to digest certain insights and perspectives. Certain books can serve as nutrition for the higher type of person but be poisonous for a lower type of person (BGE 30).

Philosophical thought is itself also an expression of the multiplicity of drives, of will to power. For Nietzsche, the philosophical systems of earlier philosophers need to be seen for what they are, namely a symptom of the overall health or sickness of the body. The morality of a philosopher indicates "in what order of rank the innermost drives of his nature stand in relation to each other" (BGE 6). Philosophy so far has been "merely an interpretation of the body and a *misunderstanding of the body*. Behind the highest value judgments that have hitherto guided the history of thought, there are concealed misunderstandings of the physical constitution—of individuals or classes or even whole races" (JS Preface 2).

For Nietzsche, philosophy now turns into a practice that uses the interplay of perspectives and interpretations in order to increase one's capacity for bearing truth as emptiness. It aims at enhancing one's ability to become true and truthful [*wahrhaft*]. Philosophy comes close to Buddhist philosophy, especially as it is conceived in Zen.

In section 30 of *Beyond Good and Evil*, Nietzsche goes into the terms *exoteric* and *esoteric*. He explains that in ancient times, not only in Western philosophy but also in various forms of non-Western philosophy, the distinction between exoteric and esoteric was used. Exoteric teachings were for outsiders, the masses; esoteric teachings were for insiders, the selected few who were initiates.

For Nietzsche, this ancient philosophical distinction takes on a new meaning. For him, exoteric refers to a view from below, whereas esoteric refers to a view from above. A philosopher has to write at various levels in order to reach his readers who are capable of digesting his message to various degrees. What is poison for one can be medicine for the other. For many, the term *esoteric* is commonly associated with some form of New Age mysticism, some secret knowledge, a teaching for the initiated that is forbidden for the uninitiated. For Nietzsche, however, the term doesn't have this connotation. For him, the distinction between exoteric and esoteric refers to ways of perceiving, thinking, and writing. Nietzsche's perspectivism allows for a rank of perspectives, ranging from esoteric views from above to exoteric views from below. But, importantly, both exoteric and esoteric ways of seeing are valid perspectives.

In a propositional philosophy, some doctrines are exoteric and others are esoteric. In Nietzsche's non-propositional orthopraxy, however, there are in addition exoteric and esoteric strategies and ways of making use of doctrines and perspectives. It is the task of the philosopher to nourish his readers so that they can become capable of inhabiting and digesting more esoteric perspectives. The philosopher is like a cook preparing meals that will nourish his readers. His doctrines are the ingredients at his disposal.

WILL TO POWER AS AN EXOTERIC NOTION

In his afterword to Nietzsche's late notebook fragments,[1] editor Giorgio Colli calls special attention to an intriguing fragment:

> *Exoteric—esoteric*
> 1. —everything is will against will
> 2. There is no such thing as will
> 1. Causality
> 2. There is no such thing as cause-effect (KSA 12, 5[9])

As Colli notes, it seems that Nietzsche here uses the distinction between exoteric and esoteric in the ancient sense as the distinction between conventional teachings intended for a general audience versus teachings for a smaller circle of those who are in some way initiated. Colli considers this fragment a key to interpreting Nietzsche's late philosophy. In its use of the conceptual pair esoteric/exoteric, it offers an important clue to decipher incompatible and contradictory elements in Nietzsche's thought without having to grasp at all kinds of fanciful interpretative tricks. Generally speaking, Colli considers Nietzsche's anti-metaphysical and anti-epistemological thought as esoteric and Nietzsche's constructive efforts to create a metaphysics of will to power and an epistemology of perspectivism as exoteric. All critical, deconstructive formulations in the notebook fragments should be interpreted as Nietzsche's genuine, esoteric philosophy; all constructive and systematic formations in the notebook fragments should be interpreted as Nietzsche's practicing at designing a system that would convince the general audience.[2]

In the first line in this fragment, "everything is will against will," Nietzsche implies that his doctrine of will to power belongs in the exoteric category. According to Colli, therefore, this fragment shows the will to power to be Nietzsche's attempt at an exoteric explication of his thought, aimed at a large audience, an explication whose philosophical weaknesses were all too clear to Nietzsche himself.[3] But a philosopher who wants to convince his audience needs a system—the anti-metaphysician needs to disguise himself as a metaphysician—for rhetorical reasons. For Colli, this puts an end to all speculation on the will to power as containing Nietzsche's final philosophy. The will to power turns out to be nothing more than a popular fairy tale, a pious lie in the Platonic sense, whose untruth was known to Nietzsche himself. If the will to power is "nothing more than the exoteric expression of [Nietzsche's] thoughts," Colli remarks, how ironic that scholars have struggled for a century to make sense of Nietzsche's magic formula of will to power.[4]

Other Nietzsche researchers have realized the importance of this fragment. Holger Schmid agrees with Colli that the fragment on exoteric–esoteric is very significant for the interpretation of Nietzsche's thought. Schmid assumes a double structure of thought in Nietzsche's work. According to him, Nietzsche consciously distinguished between two spheres of thought.[5] The exoteric sphere of his thought would contain notions and doctrines that Nietzsche has already rejected elsewhere in his work as "metaphysics for the people" [*Volksmetaphysik*]. For Schmid, with the sentence "there is no such thing as will," the real Nietzsche starts.[6] According to Schmid, however, the relationship between esoteric and exoteric is reversed: it is exactly the esoteric that points to Nietzsche's positive, affirmative philosophy. For Schmid, the esoteric is connected to the Dionysian and the tragic in Nietzsche's thought.

For Schmid, Nietzsche's distinction between exoteric and esoteric is connected with his philosophical self-criticism and the continual self-overcoming that characterizes his philosophy. Also the most cherished philosophical notions need to be overcome, as they are still intellectual constructs. According to Schmid, the esoteric doesn't refer to some mystical, unwritten doctrine, hidden in the depths, but rather to the direct experience of the body.[7] As an exoteric notion, the will to power serves as a critical notion to overcome the mechanistic worldview. "Everything is will against will" is the way of thinking that takes the causality of will to its extreme (which means to absurdity).[8] But after it has served its purpose, the will to power needs to be left behind as an instrumental, exoteric notion.[9]

Both Colli and Schmid therefore concur on the relationship between Nietzsche's esoteric and exoteric thought, even if they disagree on what counts as Nietzsche's esoteric thought. Both concur that the will to power is Nietzsche's attempt to inhabit a perspective that he knows to be insufficient, for rhetorical purposes.[10]

Heidegger famously suggested that in the published works, we find Nietzsche the artist, aiming at seducing his audience, whereas in the notebook fragments, we find Nietzsche the philosopher at work in his laboratory, experimenting with various philosophical approaches and positions. From this perspective, Nietzsche's will to power is his main thought that he was perfecting in his laboratory but did not get to publish. Colli has a different interpretation: the exoteric Nietzsche is trying to communicate with his audience and is at work in his laboratory putting together systems that will convince his audience, whereas the esoteric Nietzsche notes down, for himself, all those esoteric truths that cannot be communicated. Colli argues that Heidegger, Nishitani, and others have made the will to power far too central to Nietzsche's thought. The self-overcoming of the will to power does not refer to some essence that needs to overcome itself. It refers to leaving behind the will to power as a perspective on life. To consider whether it is possible for the will to power to overcome itself is still to think in teleological and essentialist terms. The will to power is not a new essence and has no ultimate telos.

THE ESOTERIC TRANSMISSION OF ZEN

As we have seen, the distinction between exoteric and esoteric plays an important role in Buddhism. When many Indian Buddhist sutras came into China during the first centuries CE, the Chinese were confronted with a plethora of contradictory views that could not be assimilated into a coherent doctrine. Their solution consisted of applying the Mahāyāna Buddhist hermeneutic of skill in means (*upāya*), which held that the Buddha used different perspectives (perspectives from different heights) when speaking to different categories of followers. This led to the Chinese Buddhist hermeneutic of doctrinal classification (*panjiao*), a hierarchical classification of Buddhist perspectives. Some perspectives were interpreted as "beginner's perspectives," others as perspectives for more advanced practitioners. Such a range of different perspectives was seen as an expression of the Buddha's skillful means (*upāya*) to help his followers according to their capacity to understand his teachings. The highest perspective could only be transmitted directly from teacher to student in an experiential way.

It was important for Buddhism to be considered a teaching (*jiao*)—a coherent philosophical system or doctrine—otherwise it would be persecuted by the emperor. The many schools of Chinese Buddhism that arose therefore stressed that Buddhism was a *jiao*.[11] The Zen school rebelled against this, and placed an emphasis on *zong*, a personal interpretation or individual perspective.[12] Zen doesn't have sutras, but it has records accounts of meetings and clashes (*agon*) between the personal standpoints (*zong*) of various Zen masters. Rather than containing specific doctrines, the Zen texts are a constant play with masks. The Zen koans are famous for their indecipherable character. They are enhanced with introductions and commentaries that are even more indecipherable. Rather than a fixed notion of what the Way was, the Zen tradition stressed the validity of a plurality of perspectives and even encouraged an agon between these perspectives. They stressed the importance of personal realization. They would agree with Nietzsche when he said, "These are my truths, not everyone is entitled to them." John McRae has argued that the encounter dialogues between Zen practitioners may be considered their soteriology. Rather than indoctrination of Buddhist teachings, they advocated an agon between personal standpoints.[13]

Nietzsche would agree with Zen's rebellion against all kinds of ranking of doctrines. And his way of practicing philosophy can also be described as an agon between his personal standpoint and that of his opponents. However, Nietzsche would probably find another development in the Zen tradition unacceptable. Some followers of Linji famously considered Zen to be "a special transmission outside the teachings (or scriptures)." They claimed that conceptual language is by its very nature dualistic and therefore unfit to describe the inexpressible nondual reality. All linguistic and cognitive perspectives were only of instrumental value, to the extent that they could facilitate a direct experience of emptiness. A popular Zen metaphor speaks of the finger pointing to the moon.

What would Nietzsche think of such a metaphor? He would probably reject it as another instance of the ascetic ideal: setting up some kind of ultimate state that can only be reached by going beyond thought and language. Interestingly enough, Dōgen also rejects such an interpretation of Zen. Dōgen advocates continuing hermeneutical reflection on scripture. Therefore, his Zen is sometimes referred to as the "oneness of Zen and teachings (or scriptures)" (*kyōzen itchi*).[14] For Dōgen, Zen is not about realizing a universal mystical experience or transcending language and thinking, but about the continuing realization-practice of Buddha nature *within* language and thinking. Dōgen follows the Buddhist hermeneutical tradition of using doctrines for pragmatic purposes (*upāya*). In his fascicle *Kattō* (Entangled Vines), for example, he speaks about using thought and language to deconstruct thought and language. Dōgen rejects the metaphor of the finger pointing to the moon because it re-inserts a certain duality in which enlightenment is reestablished as an ultimate insight into reality. Kim puts it as follows:

> Enlightenment is construed as seeing things as they are rather than as they appear; it is a direct insight into, and discernment of, the nature of reality that is apprehended only by wisdom, which transcends and is prior to the activity of discriminative thought. In this view, delusion is defined as all that is opposed to enlightenment.[15]

As Kim points out, various pairs of opposites are implied in this view: "things as they really are" versus "things as they appear to be," "true wisdom" versus "discriminative thought," "enlightenment" versus "delusion." Enlightenment is viewed as the overcoming of delusion. Such an approach, however, suggests a dualistic and teleological opposition between enlightenment as a state beyond language and thinking and our mundane daily experience, steeped in language and thinking.

Dōgen disagrees with those who separate enlightenment from thought and language. In his view, enlightenment is not a liberation of thought and language, but a clarification of it: "Enlightenment, from Dōgen's perspective, consists of clarifying and penetrating one's muddled discriminative thought in and through our language to attain clarity, depth, and precision in the discriminative thought itself. This is enlightenment or vision."[16]

INTERPRETING ACCORDING TO A SCHEME THAT WE CANNOT THROW OFF

Is it possible to speak of a direct esoteric transmission that goes beyond exoteric perspectives that are always bound to thought and language? With this discussion we return to the problem of Nāgārjuna's two truths in chapter 4. Should conventional truths be seen as exoteric perspectives that can be used in a constructive truth practice to make room for the direct esoteric realization of an ultimate truth? Or do we only have conventional truths, and should any claim to ultimate truth be rejected? Nietzsche recognized the same dilemma: if all thinking takes place in exoteric perspectives, can we ever truly escape from thought and language? He explored this dilemma in a series of ten aphorisms (5 [10–19]), written immediately after aphorism 5[9] about exoteric–esoteric.[17] We will therefore interpret them as a commentary on and further explication of 5 [9].[18]

Nietzsche starts his exploration, which he describes as "the coldest kind of rational criticism,"[19] with the question "what is 'knowing?'" This is the theme of the entire text. Nietzsche answers: to reduce something foreign to something that is known. This is why the first instinct of the knower is to find the rule, the regularity: this provides security. Nietzsche explains that the intellect cannot criticize itself. First, we would have to be superior beings with higher knowledge to do that. But more importantly, this assumes that something like a true reality, apart from all perspectives, can be found, which Nietzsche rejects. Nietzsche raises the fundamental question whether the perspectival valuations (the various wills to power) belong to the essence of reality or are just a way of seeing things. Nietzsche gives the Humean argument that, when we repeatedly observe a succession of phenomena, it leads us to the conviction that these phenomena are somehow connected in some fundamental, lawful way (for example, through causality). It seems that science discovers such laws through empirical observation. However, although science intends to reduce the foreign to what is known, it accomplishes exactly the opposite:

> Science prepares us for a *sovereign ignorance*, a sense that "knowing" does not occur at all, that it is a kind of conceit to dream of it, moreover, that we don't retain the slightest understanding to allow "knowing" even as a *possibility*—that "knowing" itself is a very contradictory notion. (5 [14])

Nietzsche criticizes the attempt of metaphysicians to go beyond the perspectival and gain insight into reality in itself: "'*Wisdom*' as an attempt to go *beyond* the perspectival valuations (i.e. the "wills to power"), a principle that is hostile to life and dissociative, symptom as with the Indians, etc. *Weakening* of the capacity for incorporation." (5 [14]) Therefore, we are fundamentally condemned to not knowing. Science can only find regularities in superficial phenomena, those that can be counted and calculated. However, "logic and mechanics *never* touch on causality" (5 [16]). In spite of this, people adopt, for all kinds of reasons, certain systematic conceptions. Nietzsche expresses the fundamental dilemma:

> the world that means anything to us is only apparent, is unreal.—But the notion of "real, truly present" we have distilled from the notion "means anything to us:" the more we are affected in our interests, the more we believe in the "reality" of a thing or being. "It exists" means: it makes me feel that I exist. —Antinomy. (5 [19])

This problematizes the very idea of a "true world." We only give ourselves interpretations of our experience of being affected. Consequently, "things affecting us are experienced and interpreted along the lines of a *delusory causality*: in short, that we measure value and nonvalue, advantage and disadvantage through fallacies, that the world *that means anything to us* is a delusion" (5 [19]). For this dilemma, Nietzsche offers a "fundamental resolution" [*Grundlösung*]:

> Fundamental resolution: we believe in reason: this is however the philosophy of bleak *concepts*, language is built on the most naïve preconceptions[. N]ow we read disharmonies and problems into things, because we *think only* in language form—and thus believe in the "eternal truth" of "reason" (e.g. subject-predicate etc.) [. *W]e cease to think when we don't want to do so under the constraints of language [. . .] Rational thought means to interpret according to a scheme that we cannot throw off.* (5 [22])

The symmetry with 5 [9] is clear. We think that everything is will against will but simultaneously know that actually, there is no such thing as will. We think in terms of cause and effect but simultaneously know that actually causality cannot be proven. Our thinking amounts to a process of interpreting according to a scheme that we know to be insufficient but that we cannot get rid of. This is our fundamental epistemological predicament.

So what is the philosopher to do? If we interpret according to a scheme that we cannot throw off, will we be stuck forever in exoteric perspectives? How is it possible to escape from exoteric perspectives? Doesn't all of our thinking and writing take place in the exoteric realm—including the very distinction of esoteric and exoteric itself? Isn't the conceptual pair esoteric–exoteric itself an exoteric invention?

One possible solution for this dilemma we have encountered in chapter 6 is that the philosopher needs to improve the capacity for incorporation in his readers. One way to do this is to devise thinking exercises for his readers that gradually will open their eyes to the insufficiency of all interpretative schemes. Seen from this perspective, Nietzsche's evocation of the conceptual pair esoteric–exoteric can perhaps be interpreted as a rhetorical move, a way to exhort his readers to continual self-overcoming, a way of saying "what I am saying is not really true, there is a higher perspective that you can ascend to." If a teacher has with everything he writes only the usefulness for his pupils in mind (as Nietzsche writes in KSA 11, 37 [7]), Nietzsche the teacher would be evoking the distinction esoteric–exoteric itself as a teaching tool for the reader (and not so much as a helpful hermeneutical tool for the Nietzsche researcher struggling to interpret his work).[20]

In several notebook fragments, Nietzsche speaks of an esoteric philosophy as an expression of an extraordinary high state of the soul.[21] Yet in spite of having personally experienced such an esoteric "perspective from a height," he finds himself unable to communicate such a perspective unless through translating it into exoteric perspectives that educate his readers. This resembles Nāgārjuna's epistemological predicament that we encountered in chapter 4. Nāgārjuna distinguished between conventional truth and ultimate truth. All views are empty, also Buddhist ones. They belong to the domain of conventional truth. And yet, Nāgārjuna says, ultimate truth is not taught other than through conventional truth. As a solution to Nāgārjuna's dilemma, we have seen that Mahāyāna Buddhism devised the hermeneutical strategy of *upāya*: all Buddhist teachings are attempts to educate the Buddhist practitioners and are perspectivally matched to their capacity for understanding.

Nietzsche's use of the notion of will to power can be interpreted as a form of *upāya*. It is a self-oriented perspective that can be useful in a practice of active nihilism in order to dislodge others from their other-oriented perspectives. In *Human, All Too Human*, Nietzsche writes about the constructive practice of creating "other metaphysical plausibilities":

> How one would like to exchange the false assertions of the priests that there is a God who desires that we do good, is the guardian and witness of every action, every moment, every thought, who loves us and in every misfortune only wants what is best for us—how one would like to exchange these for truths that would be as salutary, pacifying and beneficial as those errors are! Yet such truths do not exist: the most philosophy can do is to set against them other metaphysical plausibilities (at bottom likewise untruths). (HAH I, 109)

The will to power serves as such a metaphysical plausibility that views reality in a non-teleological and non-anthropocentric way. It is an interpretation that helps to overcome other interpretations. This is why Nietzsche can answer to the objection that the will to power is also merely a perspective, "all the better" (BGE 22). Just like the Buddhist notion of emptiness, the will to power is ultimately a conventional truth, pragmatically superior to other conventional truths. Just as the Buddhist who has realized emptiness philosophizes with the hammer of emptiness, in order to deconstruct fixed notions of permanence and essentialism, Nietzsche philosophizes with the hammer of will to power.[22] He uses it as a counter perspective that will help his readers to emancipate themselves from the "thou shalt" of their culture. But although the will to power can be used to smash cultural idols in a practice of active nihilism, eventually it has to be recognized as merely an exoteric perspective. From an esoteric perspective (viewed from above, as Nietzsche explains in

Beyond Good and Evil 30), "There is no such thing as will." The very notion of "will" must ultimately been seen through as illusory.

ZEN MASTER NIETZSCHE?

As we have seen, Dōgen's view of Zen comes close to Nietzsche's perspectivism, and their philosophical *áskēsis* is similar. Dōgen's Zen is a more Nietzschean Zen than the Zen mysticism that has become popular in the West. Can we therefore also speak of Zen master Nietzsche?

One of the hermeneutical strategies of approaching Nietzsche's work is to take him at his word when he speaks about his task as that of a teacher and educator. Especially after his discovery of the eternal recurrence, Nietzsche sees himself as a teacher of eternal recurrence, and he conceives his task as that of educating the reader. In *Ecce Homo*, for example, he says that "Schopenhauer as Educator" should be read as "Nietzsche as Educator."

Sometimes, in his notebook fragments, Nietzsche seems to despair of his task and give up and just philosophize for himself: "Someone who knows 'the reader,' surely doesn't write anymore for readers—but for himself, the writer" (KSA 10, 4 [1]). And "I don't respect the reader anymore: how could I write for readers? [. . .] But I write down myself, for myself" (KSA 12, 9 [188]). But elsewhere he takes his task as a teacher and educator very seriously, both in his published work ("Someone who fundamentally is a teacher, takes all things only seriously with regard to his students—even himself," BGE 63), and in his notebook fragments:

> If we think of the philosopher as a great educator, [. . .] an educator never says what he thinks himself, but always only what he thinks about something with regard to its advantage for whom he educates. In this artificiality he may not be betrayed; it belongs to his mastery that one believes in his sincerity. (KSA 11, 37 [7])

In order to understand Nietzsche's use of esoteric and exoteric, one has to approach this conceptual pair from within the context of the teacher–student relationship. There are not only esoteric and exoteric teachings, each with a very specific content, but there are also esoteric and exoteric *ways* of teaching. These ways of teaching are rhetorical in the original sense of the word. They are not meant to seduce the student, but to educate him, to teach him how to think, to raise him to be capable of a "more divine way of thinking." In order to be capable of such a thing, preliminary exercises are needed. As Nietzsche formulates it, one has to learn to walk before one can dance.

This interpretation can be supported by looking at the way in which Nietzsche presents his theory of will to power in *Beyond Good and Evil* 36. As Paul van Tongeren has pointed out,[23] this aphorism starts out very tentatively with "suppose," the whole section is a sequence of hypotheses, and its conclusion is also only hypothetical. Nietzsche is not out to convince the reader of the viability of his perspective of will to power. On the contrary, he stresses that will to power is "my conviction."[24] *Beyond Good and Evil* 36 is not so much a proposal of a new interpretation; it is a thinking exercise.

Nietzsche the teacher uses a threefold layer of communications with his audience. At the first, literary level, Nietzsche tries to evoke interest in his audience in his teachings. We can recognize this, for example, in his new prefaces of 1886 and in *Ecce Homo*. Nietzsche is advertising himself and his works, just as Plato is advertising himself and his particular view of what it means to philosophize (against the Sophists) in his dialogues. At the second, exoteric level, Nietzsche attempts to educate his readers by presenting them with new perspectives that force them to think through their preconceptions and presuppositions. Examples of this level can be found in *Beyond Good and Evil* and *The Antichrist*.

At the third, esoteric level, Nietzsche attempts to express an experience "from a height" in order to induce it in the reader by presenting him with a symbolic language. In the Dionysian mystery religions, such a symbolic language could be found in the Dionysian dithyrambs. In the mysteries, as Aristotle noted, the aim is not to teach something, but to have the initiated undergo an experience. Examples of this level can be found in *Thus Spoke Zarathustra*, which Nietzsche calls a dithyramb in *Ecce Homo*.

From an epistemological perspective, the movement from exoteric to esoteric can be viewed as a movement toward a more inclusive way of perceiving. From the height, one has a different and more inclusive view. But from an existentialist perspective, the movement from exoteric to esoteric can be viewed as a movement toward an increasing singularity. The esoteric perspective is one's own unique, singular perspective. It is not accessible to others, not because it is "secret" or mystically unknowable, but because it is inherently subjective and personal in nature. The esoteric view is a view from "my height." In order to become capable of an esoteric view, one has to become what one is. Only a Master of Truth can entertain an esoteric view. The teacher is always a *Versucher*, a tempter and an attempter. As a tempter, he tempts the student to advance on the path toward wisdom. As an attempter, his philosophy is not a system but an experimental philosophy; there is no teaching as such.

Among the many ways it can be read, one way to read *Thus Spoke Zarathustra* is as a meditation on what it means to teach self-overcoming.

Richard Schacht, for example, has read it this way.[25] In his three speeches to the crowd in the prologue, Zarathustra tries to tempt them to enter a path to wisdom through holding out the Übermensch as their highest hope in order to evoke a longing for the Übermensch as a telos of human existence. He also appeals to their will to truth. The Zen master tries to tempt the disciple to become a Buddhist practitioner. He may evoke the aspiration toward awakening (*bodhicitta* or *bodaishin*) by holding out enlightenment as the telos of human existence. From an other-oriented perspective, the practice is to revere, honor, and love (the Übermensch in Nietzsche's case, the Buddha in Zen) under the guidance of an educator (the philosopher, as Nietzsche describes him in *Schopenhauer as Educator*, or the Zen master).

From a self-oriented perspective, the practice is to overcome truth and the ascetic ideal and break the reverential heart of the camel. The teacher helps the student to see through his will to truth. In Zen, the realization of emptiness reveals that enlightenment is not an essence and not a telos. The Zen master teaches the disciple to kill the Buddha; he tries to break the revering heart of the Zen Buddhist camel—there is no enlightenment and no realization. Eventually the teacher tempts the student to go under, to forget himself, see through his "I will." Both ego and will to power are recognized as exoteric notions. The Zen master tempts the disciple to drop body and mind, go through the great Death, and realize the emptiness of emptiness. This is the transformation into a world-oriented perspective.

DISCUSSION

This chapter has argued that Nietzsche used the notion of will to power as an exoteric notion that ultimately needs to be left behind. In Zen language, the will to power is empty. Perhaps we can learn from the Zen *áskēsis*: at some point it becomes necessary to "kill the will to power." Nietzsche researchers need to kill the will to power and liberate themselves from the chains of Heidegger's influential Nietzsche interpretation that centered around the will to power.

In chapter 7 we have interpreted the will to power as a cosmic body. This could be seen as a kataphatic formulation of the aim of Nietzsche's *áskēsis*, whereas the will to power as empty could be seen as an apophatic formulation. The Zen tradition can teach us to appreciate and respect the tension between kataphatic and apophatic formulations as a key aspect of any philosophical *áskēsis*. We could interpret Nietzsche's work on a main work called *The Will to Power* as an attempt at a kataphatic formulation of his Dionysian philosophy. Nietzsche left these attempts behind in 1888. In his late notebook fragments, we can follow how his attempts at a de-anthropomorphized, non-essentialist, non-teleological worldview stranded. Eventually he abandoned his project of advancing the notion of will to power as a "dehumanization of nature" and a "naturalization of humanity." He never fully worked out an extramoral, naturalistic perspective on redemption.

Perhaps, however, Nietzsche recognized not only the impossibility but also the shortcomings of such an exercise in propositional philosophy. Perhaps the point is not to come up with another plausible exoteric doctrine, but with a new *way* of doing philosophy. Nietzsche called this project "a revaluation of all values." In 1888, he rebaptized *The Will to Power* as *The Revaluation of All Values*. This work was to contain four parts of which only the first part, *The Antichrist*, was completed by Nietzsche. In *Ecce Homo*, Nietzsche's autobiography that he wrote as an introduction to *The Antichrist*, he even claims that *The Antichrist* constitutes the entire revaluation of all values. Let us therefore investigate this important notion in the next chapter.

NOTES

1. Giorgio Colli, "Nachwort (zu Band 12 und 13)," in KSA 13, 651–68.
2. Colli, *Nachwort*, 651.
3. Colli (*Nachwort*, 653) points out that Nietzsche's use of the label "exoteric" does not come at the end of a theoretical passage, as an apology for the weak spots in a line of reasoning—no, even before Nietzsche develops his "system" of will to power, he knows this to be nothing more than an exoteric elaboration of his thought.
4. Colli, *Nachwort*, 653.
5. Holger Schmid, *Nietzsches Gedanke der tragischen Erkenntnis* (Würzburg: Königshausen und Neumann, 1984), 55.
6. Schmid, *Nietzsches Gedanke der tragischen Erkenntnis*, 56.
7. Schmid, *Nietzsches Gedanke der tragischen Erkenntnis*, 2f.
8. Schmid, *Nietzsches Gedanke der tragischen Erkenntnis*, 62.
9. Aristotle refers eight times in his works to *exoterikoi logoi* (K. Gaiser, "Exoterisch/esoterisch," in *Historisches Wörterbuch der Philosophie II*. Ed. J. Ritter (Basel/Stuttgart: Schwabe & Co Verlag, 1972), 866). In the scholarly literature, the interpretation of the status of such "external teachings," or "teachings with an external origin," or "externally directed teachings" has proven controversial. Generally, "exoteric" has been interpreted as referring to the literary productions of Aristotle's school (like Plato's dialogues), and "esoteric" as referring to what was taught inside the school itself. Recently, a different interpretation distinguishes between three levels of philosophical teachings in Aristotle (as well as in Plato): the literary works (dialogues), exoteric propedeutical exercises for beginning students at the school, and esoteric, strictly scientific-philosophical teachings for members of the school itself

(Gaiser, *Exoterisch/esoterisch,* 866). If we follow this interpretative scheme, will to power could be seen as a propedeutical exercise aimed at educating the reader.

10. Lampert interprets Nietzsche's practice as a new esotericism, different from other esotericisms in the past. Plato's esotericism used the *pia fraus* to mislead the public about his true intentions. The esotericism of Bacon and Descartes attempted to attain "secret knowledge." Nietzsche's esotericism is out in the open. *Thus Spoke Zarathustra* is a book "for all and no one," in principle accessible to anyone, in practice too esoteric for all. (Laurence Lampert, *Nietzsche's Task: An Interpretation of* Beyond Good and Evil (New Haven/London: Yale University Press, 2001, 74f).

11. Yoshizu, *The Relation between Chinese Buddhist History and Soteriology*, 311.

12. The term *zong* has a complex meaning; it can also mean "lineage" or "school." See Jia Jinhua, *The Hongzhou School of Chan Buddhism in Eighth- through Tenth-Century China* (Albany: State University of New York Press, 2006), 1f.

13. Yoshizu, *The Relation between Chinese Buddhist History and Soteriology*, 335–39.

14. Steven Heine, *Dōgen and the Kōan Tradition: A Tale of Two* Shōbōgenzō *Texts* (Albany: State University of New York Press, 1994), 8. As Heine notes, however, such a distinction is more complex than a simple stereotypical polarization.

15. Kim, *Dōgen on Meditation and Thinking*, 1.

16. Kim, *Dōgen on Meditation and Thinking,* 63.

17. It is often difficult to prove conclusively that passages in Nietzsche's notebooks belong together. However, a look at the original Notebook VII 3 seems to confirm this hypothesis. Nietzsche was in the habit of writing in his notebooks from back to front, each time starting on the left page. The aphorism "exoteric–esoteric" appears all by itself on page 179. The opposing page 180 is nearly empty. The text on pages 177–78 corresponds to 5 [10–12]. Pages 175–76 contain 5 [13–14]. Pages 173–74 contain 5 [15–17]. Page 171 contains 5 [18]. The opposing page 172 is empty. Pages 169–70 contain 5 [19]. Page 167 contains an attempt at a poem (5 [20]). Page 168 contains 5 [21], but seemingly in a different handwriting from 5 [10]–[19]. Page 165 contains 5 [22]. This ten-page fragment was divided by Colli and Montinari, the editors of the KSA, into ten separate aphorisms (KSA 12, 5 [10–19]). Their criteria for this decision remain unknown. See KGW IX III, 165–80.

18. Nietzsche used such a procedure more often, for example, in the third essay of *On The Genealogy of Morality*, where the first section, according to some interpretations, consists of an aphorism that is consequently unpacked and interpreted in the remaining sections of the essay.

19. In a letter to Peter Gast from about the same period as these aphorisms (21 January 1887), Nietzsche writes, "I am now delighting and refreshing myself with the coldest kind of rational criticism, which gives one blue fingers (and consequently takes away the pleasure of *writing*). A full-scale attack on the whole idea of 'causality' in philosophy until now will be the result of it, and a few worse things besides" (KSB 8:93).

20. Incidentally, one such teaching tool may be to confront one's readers to perspectives from philosophical traditions in non-Western traditions. We have seen that

Nietzsche suggests in BGE 20 that, perhaps, in other cultures and language families it will prove possible to at least create some more room in the schemes according to which we interpret and think.

21. For example in KSA 11, 26 [239] and [241].

22. For an argument that the eternal recurrence is the hammer that Nietzsche philosophizes with, see Thomas Brobjer, "Götzen-Hammer: The Meaning of the Expression 'To Philosophize with a Hammer.'" *Nietzsche-Studien* 28 (1999): 38–41.

23. Paul J. M. van Tongeren, *Reinterpreting Modern Culture,* 157f.

24. See also BGE 8: "In every philosophy there comes a point at which the 'conviction'" of the philosopher mounts the stage: or, to say it in the language of an ancient mystery: The ass arrived/beautiful and most brave."

25. Richard Schacht, "Zarathustra / *Zarathustra* as Educator," in *Nietzsche: A Critical Reader,* ed. Peter R. Sedgwick, 222–49 (Oxford: Blackwell 1995).

Chapter 12

Revaluation of All Values

According to Nietzsche, after the death of God, all current values will lose their value within the next few hundred years. The current values are in the irreversible process of losing their worth, and Nietzsche is merely the diagnostician of this process. Just as in the case of the death of God, Nietzsche is merely the messenger that announces this coming nihilism. What will come afterward depends on how many people are willing and able to consciously go through such a devaluation of current values and undertake the painful and difficult process of a revaluation of values. Nietzsche describes such a process as an intra-psychic rearranging of perspectives, an individual attainment of the Great Health, an *Einverleibung* of yes-saying judgments and an affirmative relationship to life.

Nietzsche's revaluation of values forms the crucial connection between the no-saying part of his task and the yes-saying part, between his critique of morality and his postmoralism. Nietzsche's two last works, *The Antichrist* and *Ecce Homo*, perfectly combine these two complementary aspects of any revaluation of all values. Nietzsche also expressly wrote them to go together: *Ecce Homo* served to present the context in which *The Antichrist* should be read.

The Antichrist is a radically skeptical exercise. In it, a philosopher with a hammer is at work. It is a no-saying work par excellence. In the preface, Nietzsche begins by announcing the esoteric character of the book: "This book belongs to the fewest. Perhaps even none of them is alive yet" (AC Preface). Being able to read *The Antichrist* requires "new ears for new music. New eyes for that which is farthest" (AC Preface). In section 1, Nietzsche stresses that *The Antichrist* is written by someone "from a height": "We are Hyperboreans [. . .] we have found the exit out of entire millennia of the labyrinth" (AC 1). The author has reached such a height because he embodies a revaluation of all values: "*we ourselves*, we free spirits, are already a 'revaluation of all values,' an *incarnate* declaration of war and triumph against all the old conceptions of 'true' and 'untrue.'" (AC 13).

Ecce Homo embodies Nietzsche's yes-saying relationship to life. It is filled with joy, exuberance, amor fati, and love for life. Nietzsche blesses his whole life, his whole history, nothing excluded. Whereas *The Antichrist* gives a demonstration of what it means to perform a revaluation of all values, *Ecce Homo* describes the inner history of Nietzsche's own development that has made him into the singularly yes-saying person, freed from resentment, who is capable of performing a revaluation of all values: "I am handy at *inverting perspectives*: the foremost reason why for me alone perhaps a 'revaluation of values' is even possible" (EH I, 1). For such a revaluation, a rare collection of capacities is needed:

> The task of *revaluing values* required perhaps more capacities than have ever dwelt together in one individual, above all contradictory capacities, too, without them being allowed to disturb or destroy one another. Hierarchy of capacities; distance; the art of separating without creating enemies; not conflating, not "reconciling" anything; an immense multiplicity which is nevertheless the opposite of chaos. (EH II, 9)

Such capacities Nietzsche has only discovered in himself, and therefore he considers himself singularly qualified for performing a revaluation. Nietzsche claims in his review of earlier writings that he was already performing a revaluation of values in *Human, All Too Human*; *Daybreak*; *Beyond Good and Evil*; *On the Genealogy of Morality*; and in *The Antichrist*.

INTERPRETATIONS SO FAR

In *Ecce Homo*, Nietzsche suggests that the revaluation of all values has been the purpose of his entire life. Given such crucial importance of this project for the late Nietzsche, it has received surprisingly little attention in the Nietzsche research literature. In the only existing monograph on the topic to date, the analytical philosopher E. Sleinis has tried unconvincingly to capture the abstract underlying principles of Nietzsche's revaluation.[1] There are a number of problems with Nietzsche's notion of revaluation of values. It is very difficult to ascertain what it is exactly that Nietzsche means by "revaluation." Aaron Ridley had identified no less than six different interpretations of what it means to re-evaluate values.[2] Among Nietzsche researchers, there have been four different types of interpretation of what the revaluation is, what is revalued into what, and how it is meant to take place. Thomas Brobjer has given an overview[3]:

1. The revaluation means the transvaluation of old values into something new, just like ancient values were transvalued into Christian values (the first revaluation of all values, masterminded by Paul). Brobjer calls this interpretation *utopian*: it is hard to say what these new values will be like, other than that they are different from what has come before. This is the most prominent interpretation among Nietzsche researchers.
2. A second interpretation is the *critical* interpretation: it stresses the genealogical, diagnostic, and skeptical part of Nietzsche's work (in this view he truly is best viewed as primarily a "master of suspicion"). Here it is even less clear what the new values are supposed to look like.
3. A third interpretation sees the revaluation as a *reversal* of the currently popular values into their opposites. What is revered now will be despised tomorrow. What is suppressed now will be celebrated tomorrow. Examples of these pairs of opposites can indeed be found in Nietzsche's work. Negation of life will be reversed into affirmation of life. Selflessness will be reversed into healthy egoism.
4. A fourth interpretation sees the revaluation of all values literally as a revaluation, a return to healthy, pre-Christian ancient values. Brobjer calls this the *dichotomy* interpretation. There are two fundamental value systems: healthy ancient values, and unhealthy Christian values. Whereas the first revaluation of all values was a movement from ancient to Christian values, Nietzsche aims to restore ancient values.

Needless to mention, these four interpretations are ideal types, and a mixture of them probably gives the most insight into the nature of Nietzsche's project. Brobjer concludes, after an examination of the texts in which the revaluation of all values occurs, that the fourth interpretation is the most likely.[4] But this doesn't necessarily have to be interpreted as a return to ancient values. Brobjer suggests that Nietzsche believes that there are two systems of value—life-affirming and life-denying—and that throughout history one or the other has gained prominence. The revaluation of values would entail a switch back to a life-affirming system of value, not necessarily in the form that the ancient Greeks gave to it, but possibly in a new form uniquely fitting for our own time.[5]

Daniel Conway distinguishes between an active *trans*valuation of values (the creation ex nihilo of new values) and a passive *re*valuation of values (returning to a former mode of valuation). He argues that, due to the prevailing decadence in European culture of Nietzsche's age (a decadence which Nietzsche himself also shared), only such a passive revaluation was possible for Nietzsche. Therefore, unlike his celebrated "philosophers of the future," the legislators of new values, Nietzsche can at best hope to reverse the reigning values of his time. So for Conway, Nietzsche's revaluation of values is no more than a precondition for a future transvaluation of values, a clearing the rubble of past millennia before new temples may be raised. Nietzsche's revaluation of values is not ushering in a new age; it is merely creating the right conditions for it. *The Antichrist* merely excavates an exit from the labyrinth of Christianity, but because of his own decadence, Nietzsche himself cannot make use of that exit. Only the philosophers of the future can actually use the exit to escape the labyrinth.

In Conway's interpretation, Nietzsche is stuck in the practice of active nihilism from a self-oriented perspective. However, as the various dialogues with Zen in this study show, the passages in his work that reveal a world-oriented perspective are simply too numerous to be discarded so easily.[6]

REVALUATION OF ALL VALUES AS A PHILOSOPHICAL ÁSKĒSIS

At first sight, it would seem that a dialogue with Zen has little to offer in interpreting Nietzsche's revaluation of all values. In the Zen tradition, there is nothing to be found that corresponds to it—not surprisingly, since Nietzsche's revaluation is closely connected to the crisis of nihilism that he diagnoses in Western culture. However, in this study we have seen that Dōgen, for example, could be seen as engaging in a continuous Buddhist revaluation of values: revaluing the notion of Buddha nature, revaluing the oppositions of delusion and enlightenment, practice and realization, and zazen and ordinary life.

Based on the dialogues between Nietzsche and Zen so far, how would Nietzsche's revaluation of all values fit in with the three perspectives used in this study: other-oriented, self-oriented, and world-oriented? Seen from these perspectives, Nietzsche's practice of revaluation would look as follows:

1. From an other-oriented perspective, self-overcoming takes place within the existing values of one's culture. Initially, there is no sense that a revaluation of values is necessary. However, during this first phase of self-overcoming, the skeptical suspicion grows that these existing values might not only be philosophically untenable, but also psychologically rooted in resentment. The challenge is now to become strong enough for performing a revaluation of values. The thought of the eternal recurrence, as the greatest heavyweight, functions as the most hopeless thought, as the ultimate sparring partner and test case for the camel.

2. The no-saying part of a revaluation of all values: "philosophizing with the hammer" to devalue all existing values even further, and further the inescapable advent of nihilism. Nietzsche calls this "active nihilism." The Nietzsche of *The Antichrist* can be placed at this stage. As a result, all existing values are robbed of their value, and nihilism looms large. Radical skepsis is not enough, however; it has to be followed up by waging war against all virulent threats to psychological well-being (such as Christianity), in order to provide a healthy environment for those few potentially free spirits.
3. The yes-saying part of a revaluation of all values: creating new values, a new normativity, arising from an affirmative relationship to life instead of resentment. Nietzsche planned to dedicate part IV of his *The Revaluation of All Values* to his Dionysian philosophy, but since such a work was never written, let us turn to the last chapter of *Ecce Homo*, "Why I Am a Destiny," as an indication of how the late Nietzsche conceived of the yes-saying part of his revaluation of all values. Nietzsche starts out with describing himself as someone in whom a revaluation of all values has become incarnate: "The truth speaks from me.—But my truth is *terrifying*, for *lies* were called truths so far.—*Revaluation of all values*: that is my formula for the highest act of self-reflection on the part of humanity, which has become flesh and genius in me" (EH IV, 1). He continues to speak about his alter ego Zarathustra and what the name Zarathustra means in his mouth:

   > Zarathustra is more truthful than any other thinker. His teaching and it alone has as its highest virtue truthfulness—in other words the opposite of the *cowardice* of the "idealist," who takes flight from reality; Zarathustra has more bravery in his body than all the other thinkers put together. (EH IV, 3)

   The idealist says no to reality out of cowardice and weakness. The yes-saying part of revaluating all values means to have the strength and courage to say yes where others so far have said no:

   > The kind of man that [Zarathustra] conceives, conceives reality *as it is*: it is strong enough for that—it is not alienated from it, not at one remove from it, it is *reality itself*, it has all its terrible and questionable aspects, too; *that is the only way man can have greatness* . . . . (EH IV, 5)

All three parts of the revaluation of values are closely related to the thought of eternal recurrence. We already find a book title proposal in the notebook fragments of summer 1884: *Philosophy of Eternal Recurrence / An Attempt at Revaluation of all Values* (KSA 11, 26 [259]). If Nietzsche's philosophy of the eternal recurrence is to get off the ground, a revaluation of values is indispensable. Nietzsche describes the revaluation of all values as the means to endure the thought of eternal recurrence (KSA 11, 26 [284]). The revaluation of values is an inner process of transformation. The revaluation of values is not optional; if one doesn't succeed, one will go under, one will get stuck in either passive or active nihilism.

The thought of eternal recurrence as the greatest heavyweight serves as a personal instrument to assist in de-valuing all values. To philosophize with the thought of eternal recurrence as a hammer means to demolish all cultural ideals based on some utopian future. The eternal recurrence is a public, *exoteric* truth here, meant to lessen confidence in other truths. The thought of eternal recurrence as an *esoteric* truth can only be embraced by someone who has become what he is. Only someone who has completed a revaluation of values in himself will be able to fully embrace the thought of eternal recurrence.

The revaluation of all values refers not so much to implementing a new value system, but to a new way of determining what is valuable, a new normativity. Nietzsche increasingly emphasizes in his work that moral criteria of determining value will be a thing of the past. In *Beyond Good and Evil* 32, he gives a mini-genealogy of morality. He distinguishes three periods: the pre-moral, the moral, and the extramoral [*außermoralisch*]. In the pre-moral period, the value of an action was determined by its consequences. In the shift to the moral period, not the consequences of an action, but its origin became of supreme importance for judging its value. This reversal of perspective came about by the first revaluation of values, that of the Christian priests, especially Paul.

But a crucial superstition crept in: it was the intention of an action that determined its values. Nowadays however, thanks to the current "self-reflection and deepening of man," we stand at the brink of a new extramoral period: exactly what is non-intentional in an action determines its value. Nietzsche is working up here to his introduction of the will to power in *Beyond Good and Evil* 36. Entering this new period will be brought about by a second revaluation of all values, similar to the first revaluation that ushered in the present moral period. Nietzsche views such a development as unavoidable.[7]

As a postmoralist, Nietzsche describes and advocates the self-overcoming of morality. Already in his preface of *Daybreak*, Nietzsche writes, "In us there is accomplished—supposing you want a formula—the self-overcoming of morality" (D Preface 4). And in *Ecce Homo*, Nietzsche writes that in Zarathustra, the self-overcoming of morality has become incarnate: "The self-overcoming of morality out of truthfulness, the self-overcoming of the moralist into its opposite—*me*—this is what the name of Zarathustra means in my mouth" (EH IV, 3). The extramoral period will follow this self-overcoming of a morality that says no to life.

BEYOND GOOD AND EVIL?

Nietzsche's self-declared immoralism is echoed by Zen's self-declared moral iconoclasm. Nietzsche and Zen share an interesting predicament in their shared reception as philosophies "beyond good and evil." According to some interpretations of Zen, the nondual enlightenment experience not only transcends the oppositions of bondage and liberation, but also those of good and evil. In the sixties, this led to the popularity of a Zen iconoclasm. A kind of Zen "beyond good and evil" became popular. And just as Nietzsche has been criticized for his immoralism "beyond good and evil," Zen has been criticized for its nondual views that seem to imply that Zen is a religious tradition that ignores morality.

According to Kyoto School member Masao Abe, since discriminating thought is transcended in the pure, enlightened experience of reality, the distinction between good and evil can also be annulled in such an experience. Abe maintains that in enlightenment, one is liberated from the web of causality that conditions one's daily life. He speaks of the religious dimension of life that lies at a much deeper level than the ethical one. Enlightenment is therefore not only a liberation from evil, but from the entire dilemma of good and evil. The distinction between good and evil in the moral dimension is relative, not absolute. Therefore, Abe comes to the conclusion that even the Holocaust is a relative evil.[8] For such views, the Kyoto School has been severely criticized, especially since some Kyoto School members supported the Japanese war effort. As mentioned in the Introduction, in 1995, a collection of critical essays on the Kyoto School appeared, aptly titled *Rude Awakenings*.[9]

Interestingly enough, Fraser uses in his work *Redeeming Nietzsche* very similar arguments to reject Nietzsche's soteriology. For Fraser, Nietzsche's perspective on suffering falls short. Commenting on Nietzsche's anti-Christian soteriology, he ultimately concludes that Nietzsche's redemption fails because Nietzsche is incapable of facing the full horror of human suffering, as manifested, for example, in the evil revealed later in the Nazi death camps.[10] As an alternative to Nietzsche's soteriology—which, according to him, excludes the harsh realities of suffering and evil—Fraser advocates an inclusive Christian soteriology built around the notion of forgiveness.[11]

Should we therefore conclude that for both Nietzsche and Zen, their project of the self-overcoming of morality leads to reprehensible views on good and evil? Let us turn once again to Dōgen. For Dōgen, enlightenment is not a nondualistic state of mind where good and evil have been eradicated; it is a nondual perspective that fully clarifies and penetrates good and evil. Enlightenment doesn't liberate us from good and evil; it increasingly confronts us with good and evil.

In all Buddhist traditions, the precepts (Sanskrit: *śīla*; Jap.: *kai*) serve as guidelines that should be followed by all Buddhists. There is no sanction for breaking them. The monastic rules (Sanskrit: *vinaya*; Jap.: *ritsu*), on the other hand, serve as external regulations regarding the conduct of Buddhist monks. Violating them does have repercussions. Therefore, some argue that the monastic rules serve as a "thou shalt" that can easily lead to conformism and heteronomy, whereas the moral precepts appeal to individual moral autonomy and freedom.[12] We could interpret the monastic rules as an other-oriented Buddhist form of morality and the moral precepts as a somewhat more self-oriented form of morality. Dōgen interprets the Buddhist precepts not as a "thou shalt," but as vows that embody the way of the bodhisattva. For Dōgen, morality and enlightenment are inseparably related to each other. As Kim notes,

> Unadulterated spiritual freedom, the authenticity of which was tested by the samadhi of self-fulfilling activity, paradoxically demanded an equally unadulterated moral commitment of those who interpreted Zen as beyond good and evil. In brief, spiritual freedom and moral commitment were inseparably intertwined in Zen, as far as Dōgen was concerned.[13]

Throughout the Zen tradition, attempts have been made to save morality from conformism and moralism. One of the most famous of these attempts is the following Zen koan:

> Nansen Osho [Chin.: Nanyue] saw monks of the Eastern and Western halls quarreling over a cat. He held up the cat and said, "If you can give an answer, you will save the cat. If not, I will kill it." No one could answer, and Nansen cut the cat in two. That evening Joshu returned, and Nansen told him of the incident. Joshu took off his sandal, placed it on his head, and walked out. "If you had been there, you would have saved the cat," Nansen remarked.[14]

Nansen appears here as a Nietzschean "Zen immoralist" who breaks the Buddhist precept of not killing. In his comments on this koan, Dōgen notes that Nansen's killing of the cat is at once a sinful act and a Buddha act.[15] However, he argues that a Buddha act and a sinful act can coexist in one and the same act. Therefore, an act that violates the Buddhist precepts can be used extra-morally as a teaching device in the hands of someone who has realized "the nonproduction of evil":

> Even though such people of thusness, when authentically enlightened, appear to live, come and go in the environment that is conducive to evil, or encounter circumstances that engender evil, or are associated with those who commit evil, they no longer commit evil. Because the efficacious power of "not to commit [any evil]" unfolds itself, evil loses its character as evil, being deprived of its grounds.[16]

However, Dōgen is strongly opposed to an interpretation of Buddhist ethics as "beyond good and evil." The values of good and evil do not exist in themselves for Dōgen, but are temporary configurations resulting from ever-changing conditions. Therefore, to conform to these values is not a matter of following rules (from an other-oriented perspective) or even of moral deliberation (from a self-oriented perspective). The *Dhammapada* contains a famous verse on good and evil:

> Do no evil (*shoaku-makusa*)
> Do good,
> Purify your own intentions,
> This is the teaching of all Buddhas.[17]

In his essay *Shoaku-makusa*, Dōgen comments on this verse. Thomas Kasulis argues that Dōgen interprets *shoaku-makusa* not as the other-oriented ethical imperative "do no evil," but as a description of the world-oriented enlightened experience of "the nonproduction of evil." He translates Dōgen's comments on *shoaku-makusa* as follows:

> Ordinary people at first construe this as "do no evil," but it is not what they make it out to be. One hears it thus when one is taught about enlightenment as suited for exposition. So heard, it is an expression in which unexcelled enlightenment is verbal. Since it is already the word of enlightenment, it is the stating of enlightenment. In hearing the unexcelled enlightenment be expounded, things are turning around: the resolve to do no evil continues as the act of not producing evil. When it comes to be that evils are no longer produced, the efficacy of one's cultivation is immediately presencing.[18]

In Kasulis's translation of this passage, the ethical injunction "do no evil" may be taught to beginners on the Buddhist path as a moral precept that the practitioner is to follow, but when one is able to see *shoaku-makusa* as "the nonproduction of evil," it is an extra-moral description of the maturity of one's practice of self-cultivation.[19]

As I have argued throughout this study, the other-oriented, self-oriented, and world-oriented perspectives on a philosophical *áskēsis* do not simply refer to stages of development, leading up to a state of redemption that transcends all perspectives. Instead, they point to the increasing capacity to contain an inclusive range of different perspectives on reality. The other-oriented perspective is an ethical perspective, firmly embedded in good and evil. The self-oriented perspective is an emancipation from the "thou shalt" of the ethical and religious cultural authorities, but remains stuck in a Kantian autonomy and sovereignty and the illusion of being able to determine one's own good and evil. From the nondual, self-forgetful world-oriented perspective, any notion of personal determination is recognized as absurd, and reality itself is seen as the sole determinant of one's behavior.

When all trace of enlightenment disappears, we are once again confronted with daily existence, including all its moral dilemmas. We have to apply discriminative thought and language to find our way through duality and deal with the reality of evil. And yet, this traceless enlightenment continues on without end: freed from limiting perspectives, ethical and otherwise, we have a wide range of perspectives at our command to respond to reality in the most inclusive way possible. We could call Dōgen a "postmoralist" in the same sense as Nietzsche: overcoming more limited ethical views doesn't lead to an absence of morality, but to a more severe morality.

For Nietzsche as well as Dōgen, the self-overcoming of morality does not refer to an escape from or relativization of mundane existence (including its evil aspects), but to a more inclusive, affirmative perspective on duality. This could potentially create more openness and sensitivity to evil in all its horrendous aspects, more so than any fixed ethical perspective in which evil can be accorded its proper place and position. It is exactly because evil is radically beyond our comprehension that no ethical perspective can sufficiently grasp it.

STAYING FAITHFUL TO THE EARTH

Zen has become famous in the West for its radical view that in order to realize awakening, there is nothing special that one could or should do. A famous Zen dictum tells the practitioner just to eat when he's hungry and to sleep when he's tired, following his natural inclinations, without running around looking for enlightenment. But Dōgen is critical of such rhetoric, which he calls "Zen naturalism." For him, Zen practice is "the practice of buddhahood" (*butsugyo*): an active recognition of one's own buddhahood and an engagement with it. Practicing buddhahood is for Dōgen not just doing whatever one pleases, but refers to very specific activities modeled on the practice of Shākyamuni Buddha. Such activities include sitting in zazen but also extend to one's daily activities. As Dōgen scholar Dan Leighton explains,

> The point is to enact the meaning of the teachings in actualized practice, and the whole praxis, including meditation, may thus be viewed as ritual, ceremonial expressions of the teaching, rather than as a means to discover and attain some understanding of it. Therefore, the strong emphasis in much of this approach to Zen training is the mindful and dedicated expression of meditative awareness in everyday activities.[20]

Dōgen attempts to rethink the dualistic opposition between ordinary life and enlightenment. In his view, nonduality is not about overcoming duality, but about fully realizing it. This implies the continual uncovering and manifesting of the enlightenment that is already there. "The endeavor to negotiate the Way, as I teach now, consists in discerning all things in view of enlightenment, and putting such a unitive awareness into practice in the midst of the revaluated world."[21]

In Zen, practice and realization in the midst of daily activities constitutes liberation, as reflected in the Zen-saying "ordinary mind is the Way." But one only reaches the ordinary through the non-ordinary. Zen enlightenment, therefore, would refer to a kind of ceaseless activity in the world that is the same and yet different from ordinary ceaseless activity. It is no longer centered on the ego and no longer producing karmic debt. All work takes on the character of play or, as Dōgen calls it, playful samadhi. Dōgen's expression of self-forgetting, as quoted earlier, is at the same time a radical affirmation of ordinary life, as the necessary (and only) habitat in which we live and are enlightened:

> To forget the self is to be verified by the myriad things [of the world]. To be verified by the myriad things is to let drop off the body-mind of the self and the body-mind of others. There is laying to rest the traces of enlightenment, and one must ever again emerge from resting content with such traces.[22]

All traces of enlightenment are wiped out when the dichotomy between "ordinary life" and "enlightenment" has disappeared. Then ordinary life becomes itself the location of sacrality, and Zen comes to be understood not as a way to a pure enlightenment experience but as, in the words of the contemporary Japanese Zen teacher Taizan Maezumi (1931–1995), a way to "appreciate your life."[23]

Interpretations of Zen as a philosophy "beyond good and evil" could therefore perhaps be seen as self-oriented interpretations of Zen. In the world-oriented interpretation of Zen, the bodhisattva vow leads the Zen master back to daily life, back to the marketplace. An existentialist interpretation of either Nietzsche or Zen ignores this "back to the marketplace" aspect. In the end, the philosophical *áskēsis* of both Zen and Nietzsche is about staying faithful to the earth.

NOTES

1. E. E. Sleinis, *Nietzsche's Revaluation of Values: a Study in Strategies* (Urbana: University of Illinois Press, 1994).

2. Aaron Ridley, "Nietzsche and the Re-Evaluation of Values." *Proceedings of the Aristotelian Society* 105/2 (2005), 171–91. Ridley prefers the term *re-evaluation* as a translation of Nietzsche's *Umwertung.*

3. Thomas H. Brobjer, "On the Revaluation of Values." *Nietzsche-Studien* 25 (1996): 342–48.

4. The expression "revaluation of values" occurs in the following texts: BGE 46; BGE 203; GM I, 7; GM I, 8; GM III, 27; TI Foreword (twice), TI 6, 2; TI 7, 4; TI 10, 5; AC 13; AC 61; AC 62; EH Foreword; EH I, 1; EH II, 9; EH III HAH, 6; EH III D, 1; EH III BGE, 1; EH III GM; EH III TI, 3; EH III CW, 4; EH IV, 1; EH IV, 7.

5. The project of the revaluation has therefore also been associated with Nietzsche's ill-fated political plans on a grand scale, his *Grosse Politik* from 1888. The revaluation of all values was to be undertaken by the philosophers of the future, who as lawgivers could present a dying and degenerated civilization with the new values that it so desperately needed. Nietzsche's revaluation could be interpreted as a political project, for which Nietzsche would consider himself, as a self-proclaimed physician of culture, as eminently qualified. In my interpretation, I focus on the re-valuation as a personal project of self-overcoming.

6. Daniel W. Conway, *Nietzsche's Dangerous Game: Philosophy in the Twilight of the Idols* (Cambridge: Cambridge University Press, 1997). In my opinion, Conway takes his provocative argument too far when he argues that Nietzsche's revaluation project is actually a product of resentment and is therefore doomed to fail.

7. See White, *Nietzsche and the Problem of Sovereignty*, 150–73.

8. See Henk Vroom, "Boven goed en kwaad uit? Ethiek in het denken van de boeddhistische Kyoto-filosofie." *Tijdschrift voor Theologie*, 42 (2002): 35–49.

9. Jim Heisig and John Maraldo, eds. *Rude Awakenings.*

10. Fraser, *Redeeming Nietzsche*, 122.

11. Fraser, *Redeeming Nietzsche*, 155.

12. See the discussion in Kim, *Eihei Dōgen—Mystical Realist*, 213.

13. Kim, *Eihei Dōgen—Mystical Realist*, 217.

14. Katsuki Sekida, *Two Zen Classics*, 58f.

15. See Douglas K. Mikkelson, "Who Is Arguing About the Cat? Moral Action and Enlightenment According to Dōgen." *Philosophy East and West,* 47/3 (1997): 383–97.

16. Dōgen, *Zuimonki* II:4. Quoted in: Kim, *Eihei Dōgen—Mystical Realist*, 226.

17. *Dhammapada* IV:183. Quoted in: Kasulis, *Zen Action–Zen Person*, 94.

18. Dōgen, *Shōbōgenzō, Shoaku-makusa.* Quoted in: Kasulis, *Zen Action–Zen Person*, 94f.

19. For a slightly different translation of this passage, see Kim, *Eihei Dōgen—Mystical Realist*, 225.

20. Taigen Dan Leighton, *Zazen as an Enactment Ritual*, 169.

21. Dōgen, *Shōbōgenzō, Bendōwa.* Quoted in: Kim, *Dōgen on Meditation and Thinking*, 21.

22. Dōgen, *Shōbōgenzō, Genjōkōan.* Quoted in: Davis, *The Presencing of Truth*, 257.

23. Taizan Maezumi, *Appreciate Your Life: The Essence of Zen Practice* (Boulder: Shambhala, 2001).

Epilogue

Toward a Philosophy of the Future

The dialogues in this study between Nietzsche and various Zen thinkers can open up new perspectives on what an *áskēsis* of a philosophy of the future could look like. The dialogue between Nietzsche and Nāgārjuna has elucidated the skepticism in both thinkers. It suggests that Nietzsche's skepticism should be interpreted in light of his Dionysian philosophy and that Nāgārjuna's skepticism should not only be studied through a Pyrrhonian, but also through a Nietzschean lens. Linji's Zen deconstruction has shown itself to be in line with Nietzsche's active nihilism. However, when Linji's followers reify Zen as a "direct transmission beyond words and letters," they diverge from Nietzsche. The temptation then arises to view enlightenment as a redemptive state beyond thought and language, a liberation from ignorance and delusion.

Dōgen's Buddhist revaluation of values brings Zen closer to Nietzsche again. Dōgen's *áskēsis* stresses continuous self-overcoming, not attaining some kind of static and final state of redemption. Both Dōgen and Nietzsche take a soteriological term from their own native religious tradition (for Nietzsche, Christian redemption, for Dōgen, Buddhist enlightenment), criticize its orthodox meaning as a final state beyond suffering, purge it of its metaphysical and transcendent connotations, and revalue its meaning out of a thoroughly this-worldly orientation. Rather than present a new version of "the Zen experience" as a new attempt at radical transcendence or a new conception of religious experience, Dōgen's immanent transcendence, his radical phenomenalism, can serve to overcome the implicit dichotomies in Western modes of thought between inner and outer, mind and body, meditation and ritual, individual and society, spiritual and secular, and "religious life" and "ordinary life."

Nishitani has done much for the dialogue between Nietzsche and Zen. However, his Heideggerian interpretation of the will to power has put a premature conclusion to the dialogue. Interpreting the will to power as *upāya* allows us to continue the dialogue. Also, Nishitani's approach of measuring Nietzsche against the Zen standard of emptiness can be complemented with measuring Zen against the standard of Nietzsche's thought. In this way, the dialogue with the philosopher with the hammer may perhaps contribute to the realization of a different, more "Nietzschean" Zen for the West that can assist in Nietzsche's project of revaluation of all values.

For Nietzsche, overcoming the European philosophical tradition was not a goal in itself; the purpose was to remove the barriers for a more encompassing world philosophy:

> I imagine future thinkers in whom European-American indefatigability is combined with the hundredfold-inherited contemplativeness of the Asians: such a combination will bring the riddle of the world to a solution. In the meantime the reflective spirits have their mission: they are to remove all barriers that stand in the way of a coalescence of human beings. (KSA 8, 17 [55])

May the dialogue between Nietzsche and Zen continue, not so much in order to bring the riddle of the world to a solution, but in order to contribute to a Way-seeking philosophy and a coalescence of human beings.

Bibliography

Abe, Masao. *Zen and Western Thought*. Honolulu: University of Hawai'i Press, 1985.

———. *A Study of Dōgen: His Philosophy and Religion*. Albany: State University of New York Press, 1992.

Addiss, Stephen, Stanley Lombardo, and Judith Roitman, eds. *Zen Sourcebook: Traditional Documents from China, Korea, and Japan*. Indianapolis/Cambridge: Hackett Publishing Company, 2008.

Alderman, Harold. *Nietzsche's Gift*. Athens: Ohio University Press, 1977.

Ames, Roger T. "Nietzsche's 'Will to Power' and Chinese 'Virtuality' (*De*): A Comparative Study." In *Nietzsche and Asian Thought*, edited by Graham Parkes, 130–50. Chicago: University of Chicago Press, 1991.

Arifuku, Kōgaku. "The Problem of the Body in Nietzsche and Dōgen." (translated by Graham Parkes). In *Nietzsche and Asian Thought*, edited by Graham Parkes, 214–25. Chicago: Chicago University Press, 1991,

Aschheim, Steven E. *The Nietzsche Legacy in Germany: 1890–1990*. Berkeley: University of California Press, 1990.

Bazzano, Manu. *Buddha is Dead: Nietzsche and the Dawn of European Zen*. Brighton/Portland: Sussex Academic Press, 2006.

Bell, Catherine. *Ritual: Perspectives and Dimensions*. Oxford/New York: Oxford University Press, 1997.

Benson, Bruce Ellis. *Pious Nietzsche: Decadence and Dionysian Faith*. Bloomington/Indianapolis: Indiana University Press, 2008.

Bourget, Paul. "Théorie de la décadence." In *Essais de psychologie contemporaine, vol. I*. Paris: Plon, 1926, 3–33.

van der Braak, André F. M. *Hoe men wordt, wat men is. Zelfvervolmaking, zelfoverwinning en zelfvergetelheid bij Nietzsche*. Budel: Damon, 2004.

———. "Buddhismus." In *Nietzsche-wörterbuch: Abbreviatur–einfach*, edited by Paul van Tongeren, Gerd Schank, and Herman Siemens, 419–33. Berlin/New York: de Gruyter, 2004.

———. "Nietzsche's transcultural hermeneutics: proliferation versus fusion of horizons." In *Nietzsche y la Hermenéutica*, edited by Francisco Arenas-Dolz, Luca Giancristofaro, and Paolo Stellini, 79–88. Valencia: Nau Llibres, 2007.

———. "Enlightenment revisited: Romantic, historicist, hermeneutic and comparative perspectives on Zen." *Acta Comparanda* 19 (2008): 87–97.

———. "Nietzsche, Christianity, and Zen on Redemption." *Studies in Interreligious Dialogue* 18/1 (2008): 5–18.

———. "Nietzsche on Redemption. A Mahāyāna Buddhist Perspective." In *Nietzsche—Philosoph der Kultur(en)?*, edited by Andreas Urs Sommer, 519–27. Berlin/New York: de Gruyter, 2008.

———. "Nietzsche and Japanese Buddhism on the Cultivation of the Body: To What Extent Does Truth Bear Incorporation?" *Comparative and Continental Philosophy* 1/2 (2009): 223–51.

———. "Toward a Philosophy of Chan Enlightenment: Linji's Anti-Enlightenment Rhetoric." *Journal of Chinese Philosophy* 37/2 (June 2010): 231–47.

van Bragt, Jan. "Translator's Introduction." In *Religion and Nothingness,* Keiji Nishitani, xxiii–xlix. Berkeley: University of California Press, 1982.

———. "Foreword." In *On Buddhism*, Keiji Nishitani, vi–ix. Albany: State University of New York Press, 2006.

Braverman, Arthur. *Living and Dying in Zazen: Five Zen Masters of Modern Japan.* New York: Weatherhill, 2003.

Brobjer, Thomas H. "On the Revaluation of Values." *Nietzsche-Studien* 25 (1996): 342–48.

———. "Götzen-Hammer: The Meaning of the Expression 'To Philosophize with a Hammer.'" *Nietzsche-Studien* 28 (1999): 38–41.

———. "Nietzsche's Reading About Eastern Philosophy." *Journal of Nietzsche Studies* 28 (2004): 3–27.

———. "Nietzsche's Reading About China and Japan." *Nietzsche-Studien* 34 (2005): 329–36.

Bronkhorst, Johannes. *Buddhist Teaching in India.* Boston: Wisdom Publications, 2009.

Brusotti, Marco. *Die Leidenschaft der Erkenntnis: Philosophie und ästhetische Lebensgestaltung bei Nietzsche von* Morgenröthe *bis* Also sprach Zarathustra. Berlin/New York: de Gruyter, 1997.

Buswell, Robert E. Jr., and Robert M. Gimello, eds. *Paths to Liberation: The Mārga and Its Transformations in Buddhist Thought.* Honolulu: University of Hawai'i Press, 1992.

Chen, Guying. "Zhuang Zi and Nietzsche: Plays of Perspectives." (translated by James Sellman). In *Nietzsche and Asian Thought*, edited by Graham Parkes, 115–29. Chicago/London: University of Chicago Press, 1991.

Clarke, J. J. *Oriental Enlightenment: The Encounter Between Asian and Western Thought.* London/New York: Routledge, 1997.

Cole, Alan. *Fathering Your Father: The Zen of Fabrication in Tang Buddhism.* Berkeley: University of California Press, 2009.

Colli, Giorgio. "Nachwort (zu Band 12 und 13)." In *Sämtliche Werke, Kritische Studienausgabe (KSA)*. Edited by Giorgio Colli and Mazzino Montinari. Band 13, 651–68. Berlin/New York: de Gruyter, 1967–1977.

Constantinidès, Yannis, and Damien MacDonald. *Nietzsche l'Éveillé*. Paris: Ollendorff & Desseins, 2009.

Conway, Daniel W., and Julie K. Ward. "Physicians of the Soul: Peritrope in Sextus Empiricus and Nietzsche." In *Nietzsche und die antike Philosophie*, edited by Daniel W. Conway and Rudolf Rehn, 193–223. Trier: Wissenschaftlicher Verlag, 1992.

Conway, Daniel W. *Nietzsche & the Political*. London/New York: Routledge, 1997.

———. *Nietzsche's Dangerous Game. Philosophy in the Twilight of the Idols*. Cambridge: Cambridge University Press, 1997.

———. "Beyond Truth and Appearance: Nietzsche's Emergent Realism." In *Nietzsche, Epistemology, and Philosophy of Science, Part II*, edited by B. Babich and R. Cohen, 109–22. Dordrecht: Kluwer, 1999.

———. "Life and Self-Overcoming." In *A Companion to Nietzsche*, edited by Keith Ansell Pearson, 532–47. Oxford: Blackwell Publishing, 2006.

Coomaraswamy, Sir Mutu. *Sutta Nipâta, or Dialogues and Discourses of Gotama Buddha*. London: Trübner, 1874.

Cowherds, The. *Moonshadows: Conventional Truth in Buddhist Philosophy*. Oxford: Oxford University Press, 2011.

Cox, Christoph. *Nietzsche: Naturalism and Interpretation*. Berkeley: University of California Press, 1999.

Dallmayr, Fred. *Beyond Orientalism: Essays on Cross-Cultural Encounter*. Albany: State University of New York Press, 1995.

Davis, Bret W., Brian Schroeder, and Jason M. Wirth, eds. *Japanese and Continental Philosophy: Conversations with the Kyoto School*. Bloomington and Indianapolis: Indiana University Press, 2011.

Davis, Bret W. "Zen After Zarathustra: The Problem of the Will in the Confrontation Between Nietzsche and Buddhism." *Journal of Nietzsche Studies* 28 (2004): 89–138.

———. "Nishitani Keiji's 'The Standpoint of Zen:' Directly Pointing to the Mind." In *Buddhist Philosophy: Essential Readings*, edited by William Edelglass and Jay L. Garfield, 93–102. Oxford: Oxford University Press, 2009.

———. "The Presencing of Truth: Dōgen's Genjōkōan." In *Buddhist Philosophy: Essential Readings*, edited by William Edelglass and Jay L. Garfield, 251–59. Oxford: Oxford University Press, 2009.

———. "The Kyoto School." In *The Stanford Encyclopedia of Philosophy (Summer 2010 Edition)*, edited by Edward N. Zalta. http://plato.stanford.edu/archives/sum2010/entries/kyoto-school (accessed September 15, 2010).

———. "Nishitani after Nietzsche: From the Death of God to the Great Death of the Will." In *Japanese and Continental Philosophy: Conversations with the Kyoto School*, edited by Bret W. Davis, Brian Schroeder, and Jason M. Wirth, 82–101. Bloomington and Indianapolis: Indiana University Press, 2011.

Dōgen, Kīgen. *Shōbōgenzō*, edited by Mizuno Yaoko. Tokyo: Iwanami, 1990.

Dreyfus, Georges, and Jay L. Garfield. "Madhyamaka and classical Greek Skepticism." In *Moonshadows: Conventional Truth in Buddhist Philosophy*, edited by The Cowherds, 115–30. Oxford: Oxford University Press, 2011.

Dreyfus, Georges. "Can a Mādhyamika Be a Skeptic? The Case of Patsab Nyimadrak." In *Moonshadows: Conventional Truth in Buddhist Philosophy*, edited by The Cowherds, 89–113. Oxford: Oxford University Press, 2011.

Droit, Roger-Pol. *The Cult of Nothingness: The Philosophers and the Buddha*. North Carolina: University of North Carolina Press, 2003.

Edelglass, William, and Jay L. Garfield, eds. *Buddhist Philosophy: Essential Readings*. Oxford: Oxford University Press, 2009.

Elberfeld, Rolf. "The Middle Voice of Emptiness: Nishida and Nishitani." In *Japanese and Continental Philosophy: Conversations with the Kyoto School*, edited by Bret W. Davis, Brian Schroeder, and Jason M. Wirth. Bloomington and Indianapolis: Indiana University Press, 2011, 269–85.

Figl, Johann. "Nietzsche's Early Encounters with Asian Thought." (translated by Graham Parkes). In *Nietzsche and Asian Thought*, edited by Graham Parkes, 51–63. Chicago: University of Chicago Press, 1991.

———. "Nietzsche's Encounter with Buddhism." In *Void and Fullness in the Buddhist, Hindu, and Christian Traditions: Sūnya-Pūrna-Pleroma,* edited by B. Bäumer and J. Dupuch, 225–37. New Delhi: D.K. Printworld, 2005.

———. *Nietzsche und die Religionen. Transkulturelle Perspektiven seines Bildungs- und Denkweges*. Berlin/New York: de Gruyter, 2007.

Fischer, Zoketsu Norman. "A Coin Lost in the River Is Found in the River." In *The Art of Just Sitting: Essential Writings on the Zen Practice of Shikantaza*, 149–54. Edited by John Daido Loori. Boston: Wisdom Publications, 2002.

Foucault, Michael. "Friendship as a Way of Life." In *Foucault Live: Collected Interviews, 1961–1984*, 308–12. Edited by Sylvère Lotringer. Translated by Lysa Hochroth and John Johnston. New York: Semiotext[e], 1989.

Fraser, Gilles. *Redeeming Nietzsche: On the Piety of Unbelief*. London: Routledge, 2002.

Freeman, Timothy J. *Zarathustra's Lucid Dream and Asian Philosophy*. Unpublished manuscript.

Froese, Katrin. *Nietzsche, Heidegger, and Daoist Thought: Crossing Paths In-Between*. Albany: State University of New York Press, 2004.

Gaiser, K. "Exoterisch/esoterisch." In *Historisches Wörterbuch der Philosophie II*. Edited by J. Ritter. Basel/Stuttgart: Schwabe & Co Verlag, 1972, 866–67.

Garfield, Jay L., and Graham Priest. "Mountains Are Just Mountains." In *Pointing at the Moon: Buddhism, Logic, Analytic Philosophy*, edited by Mario d'Amato, Jay L. Garfield, and Tom J. F. Tillemans, 71–82. Oxford: Oxford University Press, 2009.

Garfield, Jay L. "Epoche and *Śūnyatā*: Skepticism East and West." *Philosophy East and West* 40/3 (1990): 285–307.

———. *The Fundamental Wisdom of the Middle Way: Nāgārjuna's Mūlamadhyamakakārikā*. Oxford: Oxford University Press, 1995.

———. *Empty Words: Buddhist Philosophy and Cross-Cultural Interpretation.* Oxford/New York: Oxford University Press, 2002.

———. "Nāgārjuna's *Mūlamadhyamakakārikā* (*Fundamental Verses of the Middle Way*): Chapter 24: Examination of the Four Noble Truths." In *Buddhist Philosophy: Essential Readings*, edited by William Edelglass and Jay L. Garfield, 26–34. Oxford: Oxford University Press, 2009.

Gooding-Williams, Robert. *Zarathustra's Dionysian Modernism.* Palo Alto: Stanford University Press, 2001.

Hadot, Pierre. *Philosophy As a Way of Life.* Oxford: Wiley-Blackwell, 1995.

Hall, David L., and Roger T. Ames. *Thinking from the Han: Self, Truth, and Transcendence in Chinese and Western Culture.* Albany: State University of New York Press, 1998.

Han, Béatrice. "Nietzsche and the 'Masters of Truth': the pre-Socratics and Christ." In *Nietzsche and the Divine*, edited by John Lippitt and Jim Urpeth, 115–36. Manchester: Clinamen Press, 2000.

Heidegger, Martin. *Nietzsche I.* Pfullingen: Neske, 1961.

———. *Was heisst Denken?* Tübingen: Niemeyer, 1984.

———. "Wer ist Nietzsches Zarathustra?" In *Vorträge und Aufsätze*, 99–124. Frankfurt am Main: Klostermann, 2000 (Original edition 1954).

Heine, Steven. *Dōgen and the Kōan Tradition: A Tale of Two* Shōbōgenzō *Texts.* Albany: State University of New York Press, 1994.

———. *Zen Skin, Zen Marrow: Will the Real Zen Buddhism Please Stand Up?* Oxford: Oxford University Press, 2008.

Heine, Steven, and Dale S. Wright, eds. *Zen Ritual: Studies of Zen Buddhist Theory in Practice.* Oxford: Oxford University Press, 2008.

Heisig, James, W. *Philosophers of Nothingness: An Essay on the Kyoto School.* Honolulu: University of Hawai'i Press, 2001.

Heisig, Jim, and John Maraldo, eds. *Rude Awakenings: Zen, the Kyoto School, and the Question of Nationalism.* Honolulu: University of Hawai'i Press, 1995.

Heller, Erich. *The Disinherited Mind.* New York: Harcourt Brace Jovanovich, 1975.

Herrigel, Eugen. *Zen in the Art of Archery.* London: Routledge, 1953.

Hershock, Peter D. *Liberating Intimacy. Enlightenment and Social Virtuosity in Ch'an Buddhism.* Albany: State University of New York Press, 1995.

———. *Chan Buddhism.* Honolulu: University of Hawai'i Press, 2005.

Hodge, Charles D. D. *Systematic Theology II.* London: Thomas Nelson and Sons, 1871.

Hoffman, J. N. *Wahrheit, Perspektive, Interpretation. Nietzsche und die philosophische Hermeneutik.* Berlin/New York: de Gruyter, 1994.

Hutter, Horst. *Shaping the Future: Nietzsche's New Regime of the Soul and Its Ascetic Practices.* Lanham, MD: Lexington Books, 2006.

Jia, Jinhua. *The Hongzhou School of Chan Buddhism in Eighth- through Tenth-Century China.* Albany: State University of New York Press, 2006.

Jones, David. "Empty Soul, Empty World: Nietzsche and Nishitani." In *Japanese and Continental Philosophy: Conversations with the Kyoto School*, edited by Bret

W. Davis, Brian Schroeder, and Jason M. Wirth, 102–19. Bloomington and Indianapolis: Indiana University Press, 2011.

Jullien, Francois. *Detour and Access: Strategies of Meaning in China and Greece.* New York: Zone Books, 2000.

Jung, Carl G. *Nietzsche's Zarathustra Vol I and II: Notes of the Seminar Given in 1934–1939.* Princeton: Princeton University Press, 1988.

Kasulis, Thomas P. *Zen Action / Zen Person.* Honolulu: University of Hawai'i Press, 1981.

———. "Editor's Introduction." In Yasuo Yuasa, *The Body: Towards an Eastern Mind-Body Theory,* 1–15. Albany: State University of New York Press, 1987.

———. "Masao Abe as D. T. Suzuki's Philosophical Successor." In *Masao Abe: A Zen Life of Dialogue*, edited by Donald W. Mitchell, 251–59. Boston/Rutland, VT/ Tokyo: Charles E. Tuttle, 1998.

Kee, Alistair. *Nietzsche Against the Crucified.* London: Trinity Press International, 1999.

Keown, Damien. "trikāya." *Encyclopedia.com: A Dictionary of Buddhism.* http:// www.encyclopedia.com/doc/1O108-trikya.html (accessed September 6, 2010).

Kim, Hee-Jin. *Eihei Dōgen—Mystical Realist.* Tucson: University of Arizona Press, 2004 (original edition 1975).

———. *Dōgen on Meditation and Thinking: A Reflection on His View of Zen.* Albany: State University of New York Press, 2007.

Köppen, Carl Friedrich. *Die Religion des Buddha. Vol. 1. Die Religion des Buddha und ihre Entstehung.* Berlin: F. Schneider, 1857.

Koestler, Arthur. *The Lotus and the Robot.* New York: Macmillan, 1961.

Kuzminski, Adrian. *Pyrrhonism: How the Ancient Greeks Reinvented Buddhism.* Lanham, MD: Lexington, 2008.

Ladner, Max. *Nietzsche und der Buddhismus. Kritische Betrachtungen eines Buddhisten.* Zürich: Juchli-Beck, 1933.

Lampert, Laurence. *Nietzsche's Teaching: An Interpretation of* Thus Spoke Zarathustra. New Haven/London: Yale University Press, 1986.

———. *Nietzsche's Task: An Interpretation of* Beyond Good and Evil. New Haven/ London: Yale University Press, 2001.

Large, Duncan. "Introduction." In Friedrich Nietzsche, *Ecce Homo: How To Become What You Are.* Oxford: Oxford University Press, 2007.

Leighton, Taigen Dan, and Shokaku Okamura, trans. *Dōgen's Extensive Record: a Translation of the Eihei Kōroku.* Boston: Wisdom Publications, 2008.

Leighton, Taigen Dan. *Faces of Compassion: Classic Bodhisattva Archetypes and Their Modern Expression.* Boston: Wisdom Publications, 2003.

———. *Visions of Awakening Space and Time: Dōgen and the Lotus Sutra.* Oxford: Oxford University Press, 2007.

———. "Zazen as an Enactment Ritual." In *Zen Ritual: Studies of Zen Buddhist Theory in Practice,* edited by Steven Heine and Dale S. Wright, 167–84. Oxford: Oxford University Press, 2008.

Leiter, Brian. "The Paradox of Fatalism and Self-Creation in Nietzsche." In *Nietzsche*, edited by John Richardson and Brian Leiter, 281–321. Oxford: Oxford University Press, 2001.

Loori, John Daido. "Nanyue Polishes a Tile." In *The Art of Just Sitting: Essential Writings on the Zen Practice of Shikantaza*, edited by John Daido Loori, 127–34. Boston: Wisdom Publications, 2002.

Löwith, Karl. *Nietzsches Philosophie der Ewigen Wiederkunft des Gleichen*. Stuttgart: Kohlhammer, 1956.

Magliola, Robert. *Derrida on the Mend.* West Lafayette: Purdue University Press, 1984.

Mall, R. A. *Philosophie im Vergleich der Kulturen: Interkulturelle Philosophie, eine neue Orientierung*. Darmstadt: Wissenschaftliche Buchgesellschaft, 1995.

Maraldo, John C. "The Practice of Body-Mind: Dōgen's Shinjingakudō and Comparative Philosophy." In *Dōgen Studies*, edited by William R. LaFleur, 112–30. Honolulu: University of Hawai'i Press, 1985.

Maezumi, Taizan. *Appreciate Your Life: The Essence of Zen Practice.* Boulder: Shambhala, 2001.

Martin, Glen T. "Deconstruction and Breakthrough in Nietzsche and Nāgārjuna." In *Nietzsche and Asian Thought*, edited by Graham Parkes, 91–111. Chicago: University of Chicago Press, 1991.

McEvilley, Thomas. *The Shape of Ancient Thought: Comparative Studies in Greek and Indian Philosophies.* New York: Allworth Press, 2002.

Mikkelson, Douglas K. "Who Is Arguing About the Cat? Moral Action and Enlightenment According to Dōgen." *Philosophy East and West* 47/3 (1997): 383–97.

Mishima, Yukio. *The Temple of the Golden Pavilion*. New York: Knopf, 1959.

Mistry, Freny. *Nietzsche and Buddhism: Prolegomenon to a Comparative Study.* Berlin/New York: de Gruyter, 1981.

Moeller, Hans-Georg. "The 'Exotic' Nietzsche—East and West." *Journal of Nietzsche Studies* 28 (2004): 57–69.

Morrison, Robert G. *Nietzsche and Buddhism: A Study in Nihilism and Ironic Affinities*. Oxford: Oxford University Press, 1997.

———."Response to Graham Parkes' Review." *Philosophy East and West* 50/2 (2000): 267–79.

Müller, Max. "Über den Buddhismus." In *Essays, Bd. 1: Beitrage zur vergleichenden Religionswissenschaft*, 162–204. Leipzig: Engelmann, 1869.

Müller-Lauter, Wolfgang. *Nietzsche: His Philosophy of Contradictions and the Contradictions of his Philosophy* (translated by David J. Parent). Urbana/Chicago: University of Illinois Press, 1999.

———. *Heidegger und Nietzsche, Nietzsche-Interpretationen III*. Berlin/New York: de Gruyter, 2000.

Nagatomo, Shigenori. *Attunement through the Body*. Albany: State University of New York Press, 1992.

Nietzsche, Friedrich. *Sämtliche Werke, Kritische Studienausgabe (KSA)*. Edited by Giorgio Colli and Mazzino Montinari. Berlin/New York: de Gruyter, 1967–1977.

———. *Sämtliche Briefe, Kritische Studienausgabe (KSB)*. Edited by Giorgio Colli and Mazzino Montinari. Berlin/New York: de Gruyter, 1986.

———. *Werke, Kritische Gesamtausgabe (KGW)*. Edited by Giorgio Colli and Mazzino Montinari. Berlin/New York: de Gruyter, 1967–.

———. *Thus Spoke Zarathustra: A Book for Everyone and Nobody*. Translated by Graham Parkes. Oxford: Oxford University Press, 2005.

———. *Ecce Homo: How To Become What You Are*. Translated by Duncan Large. Oxford: Oxford University Press, 2007.

———. *The Pre-Platonic Philosophers*. Translated by Greg Whitlock. Urbana/Chicago: University of Illinois Press, 2001.

Nishitani, Keiji. *Religion and Nothingness*. Berkeley: University of California Press, 1982.

———. *The Self-Overcoming of Nihilism*. Albany: State University of New York Press, 1990.

Ōkōchi, Ryōgi. "Nietzsches *amor fati* im Lichte von Karma des Buddhismus." *Nietzsche-Studien* 1 (1972): 36–94.

———. *Wie man wird, was man ist. Gedanken zu Nietzsche aus östlicher Sicht*. Darmstadt: Wissenschaftliche Buchgesellschaft, 1985.

———. "Nietzsche's Conception of Nature from an East-Asian Point of View" (translated by Graham Parkes). In *Nietzsche and Asian Thought*, edited by Graham Parkes, 200–13. Chicago: Chicago University Press, 1991.

Oldenberg, Hermann. *Buddha; Sein Leben, seine Lehre, seine Gemeinde*. Berlin: W. Hertz, 1881.

Osthövener, Claus-Dieter. *Erlösung:Transformationen einer Idee im 19. Jahrhundert*. Tübingen: Mohr Siebeck, 2004.

Parkes, Graham. "The Wandering Dance: Chuang-Tzu and Zarathustra." *Philosophy East and West* 29/3 (1983): 235–50.

———."Nietzsche and Nishitani on the Self through Time." *The Eastern Buddhist* 17/2 (1984): 55–74.

———, ed. *Nietzsche and Asian Thought*. Chicago: University of Chicago Press, 1991.

———. "Nietzsche and Nishitani on the Self-Overcoming of Nihilism." *International Studies in Philosophy* 25/2 (1993): 51–60.

———. *Composing the Soul: Reaches of Nietzsche's Psychology*. Chicago: University of Chicago Press, 1994.

———. "Nietzsche and East Asian Thought: Influences, Impacts, and Resonances." In *The Cambridge Companion to Nietzsche*, edited by Bernd Magnus and Kathleen M. Higgins, 356–83. Cambridge: Cambridge University Press, 1996.

———. "Nietzsche and Nishitani on Nihilism and Tradition." In *Culture and Self: Philosophical and Religious Perspectives, East and West*, edited by Douglas Allen, 131–44. Boulder: Westview Press, 1997.

———. "Nietzsche and Early Buddhism" and "Reply to Robert Morrison." *Philosophy East and West* 50/2 (2000): 254–67 and 279–84.

———. "Nature and the Human 'Redivinized': Mahāyāna Buddhist themes in *Thus Spoke Zarathustra*." In *Nietzsche and the Divine*, edited by John Lippitt and Jim Urpeth, 181–99. Manchester, Clinamen Press, 2000.

"Redemption." *Believe*. mb-soft.com/believe/txw/redempti.htm (accessed September 20, 2010).

Rethy, Robert. "The Tragic Affirmation of *The Birth of Tragedy*." *Nietzsche-Studien* 17 (1988): 1–44.

Ridley, Aaron. "Nietzsche and the Re-Evaluation of Values." *Proceedings of the Aristotelian Society* 105/2 (2005): 171–91.

Roberts, Tyler. *Contesting Spirit: Nietzsche, Affirmation, Religion.* Princeton: Princeton University Press, 1998.

Rorty, Richard. *Philosophy and the Mirror of Nature.* Princeton: Princeton University Press, 1980.

Sadler, Ted. *Nietzsche: Truth and Redemption—Critique of the Postmodern Nietzsche.* London/Atlantic Highlands, NJ: Athlone Press, 1995.

Salome, Lou. *Friedrich Nietzsche in seinen Werken.* Vienna: Carl Konegen, 1894.

"Salvation, Soteriology." *Believe.* mb-soft.com/believe/text/salvatio.htm (accessed September 20, 2010).

Santaniello, Weaver. *Nietzsche and the Gods.* Albany: State University of New York Press, 2001.

Schacht, Richard. "Zarathustra as Educator." In *Nietzsche: A Critical Reader,* edited by Peter R. Sedgwick, 222–49. Oxford: Blackwell 1995.

———, ed. *Nietzsche's Postmoralism.* Cambridge: Cambridge University Press, 2000.

Schank, Gerd. *Dionysos gegen den Gekreuzigten: eine philologische und philoso phische Studie zu Nietzsches "Ecce homo."* Bern: Peter Lang, 1993.

Scheiffele, Eberhard. "Questioning One's 'Own' from the Perspective of the Foreign" (translated by Graham Parkes). In *Nietzsche and Asian Thought,* edited by Graham Parkes, 31–47. Chicago: University of Chicago Press, 1991.

Schipperges, Heinrich. *Am Leitfaden des Leibes: Zur Anthropologik und Therapeutik Friedrich Nietzsches.* Stuttgart: Ernst Klett Verlag, 1975.

Schmid, Holger. *Nietzsches Gedanke der tragischen Erkenntnis.* Würzburg: Königshausen und Neumann, 1984.

Schott, E. "Erlösung." In *Historisches Wörterbuch der Philosophie* II, edited by J. Ritter a.o., 717–18. Basel/Stuttgart: Schwabe & Co Verlag, 1972.

Schroeder, Brian. "Dancing Through Nothing: Nietzsche, the Kyoto School, and Transcendence." *Journal of Nietzsche Studies* 37 (2009): 44–65.

Scott, Jacqueline, and A. Todd Franklin, eds. *Critical Affinities: Nietzsche and African American Thought.* Albany: State University of New York Press, 2006.

Sekida, Katsuki, transl. *Two Zen Classics: The Gateless Gate and the Blue Cliff Records.* Boston: Shambhala, 2005.

Shaner, David Edward. *The Bodymind Experience in Japanese Buddhism: A Phenomenological Study of Kūkai and Dōgen.* Albany: State University of New York Press, 1985.

Shang, Ge Ling. *Liberation as Affirmation: The Religiosity of Zhuangzi and Nietzsche.* Albany: State University of New York Press, 2006.

Skowron, Michael. "Nietzsches Weltliche Religiosität und ihre Paradoxien." *Nietzsche-Studien* 31 (2002): 1–39.

———. *Nietzsche, Buddha, Zarathustra: Eine West-Ost Konfiguration.* Daegu: Kyungpook National University Press, 2006.

———. "Rezensionen: Neuerscheinungen zu Nietzsches Philosophie der Religion und der Religion seiner Philosophie." *Nietzsche-Studien* 36 (2007): 425–39.

Sleinis, E. E. *Nietzsche's Revaluation of Values: a Study in Strategies.* Urbana: University of Illinois Press, 1994.

Sommer, Andreas Urs. *Friedrich Nietzsches 'Der Antichrist.' Ein philosophisch-historischer Kommentar.* Basel: Schwabe, 2000.

Soll, Ivan. "Schopenhauer, Nietzsche, and the Redemption of Life through Art." In *Willing and Nothingness: Schopenhauer as Nietzsche's Educator*, edited by Christopher Janaway, 79–115. Oxford: Clarendon Press, 1998.

Sprung, Mervyn. "Nietzsche's Trans-European Eye." In *Nietzsche and Asian Thought*, edited by Graham Parkes, 76–90. Chicago: University of Chicago Press, 1991.

Stambough, Joan. "Thoughts on the Innocence of Becoming." *Nietzsche-Studien* 14 (1985): 164–78.

Stern, J. P. *A Study of Nietzsche.* Cambridge: Cambridge University Press, 1979.

Stone, Jacqueline I. *Original Enlightenment and the Transformation of Medieval Japanese Buddhism.* Honolulu: University of Hawai'i Press, 1999.

Suzuki, Daisetz Teitaro. *An Introduction to Zen Buddhism.* Kyoto: Eastern Buddhist Society, 1934.

Taishō shinshū daizōkyō, ed. Takakusu Junjirō and Watanabe Kaigyoku, 100 vols. Tokyo: Taishō issaikyō kankōkai, 1924–1932.

Tanahashi, Kazuaki, ed. *Moon in a Dewdrop: Writings of Zen Master Dōgen.* New York: North Point Press, 1985.

Taylor, Charles. *A Secular Age.* Cambridge: The Belknap Press, 2007.

Theierl, Herbert. *Nietzsche: der Verkünder einer Erlösungslehre.* Unpublished Dissertation. Heidelberg: Ruprecht Universität, 1949.

———. *Nietzsche: Mystik als Selbstversuch.* Würzburg: Königshausen und Neumann, 2000.

von Tongeren, Paul J. M., Gerd Schank, and Herman Siemens, eds. *Nietzsche-Wörterbuch Band 1: Abbreviatur–einfach.* Berlin/New York: de Gruyter, 2004.

von Tongeren, Paul J. M. "Nietzsche's Symptomatology of Skepticism." In *Nietzsche, Epistemology, and Philosophy of Science*, edited by Babette Babich and Robert S. Cohen, 61–71. Dordrecht: Kluwer Academic Publishers, 1999.

———. *Reinterpreting Modern Culture: An Introduction to Friedrich Nietzsche's Philosophy.* Lafayette: Purdue University Press, 2000.

Tönnies, Ferdinand. *Der Nietzsche-Kultus.* Leipzig: O. R. Reisland, 1897.

Tuck, Andrew. *Comparative Philosophy and the Philosophy of Scholarship.* Oxford/New York: Oxford University Press, 1990.

Urpeth, Jim, and John Lippitt, eds. *Nietzsche and the Divine.* Manchester: Clinamen Press, 2000.

Victoria, Brian Daizen. *Zen At War.* New York: Weatherhill, 1997.

Vroom, Henk. "Boven goed en kwaad uit? Ethiek in het denken van de boeddhistische Kyoto-filosofie." *Tijdschrift voor Theologie*, 42 (2002): 35–49.

Waddell, Norman, and Masao Abe, trans. *The Heart of Dōgen's Shōbōgenzō.* Albany: State University of New York Press, 2002.

Walser, Joseph. *Nāgārjuna in Context: Mahāyāna Buddhism and Early Indian Culture.* New York: Columbia University Press, 2005.

Wang, Youro. *Linguistic Strategies in Daoist Zhuangzi and Chan Buddhism: The Other Way of Speaking*. London: Routledge, 2003.

Watson, Burton, trans. *The Zen Teachings of Master Lin-Chi: A Translation of the Lin-chi lu*. New York: Columbia University Press, 1993/1999.

Welbon, G. R. *The Buddhist Nirvana and Its Western Interpreters*. Chicago: University of Chicago Press, 1968.

Welter, Albert. *Monks, Rulers, and Literati: The Political Ascendancy of Chan Buddhism*. Oxford: Oxford University Press, 2006.

———. *The Linji lu and the Creation of Chan Orthodoxy: The Development of Chan's Records of Sayings Literature*. Oxford: Oxford University Press, 2008.

Westerhoff, Jan. *Nāgārjuna's Madhyamaka: A Philosophical Introduction*. Oxford: Oxford University Press, 2009.

White, Richard J. *Nietzsche and the Problem of Sovereignty*. Urbana/Chicago: University of Illinois Press, 1997.

Wilkerson, Dale. *Nietzsche and the Greeks*. London/New York: Continuum, 2005.

Willers, Ulrich. *Friedrich Nietzsches antichristliche Christologie. Eine theologische Rekonstruktion*. Wien: Tyrolia Verlag, 1988.

Wohlfart, Günter. "Also sprach Herakleitos." *Heraklits Fragment B52 und Nietzsches Heraklit-Rezeption*. Freiburg/München: Alber, 1991.

———. "Nachwort. Wille zur Macht und ewige Wiederkunft: die zwei Gesichter des Aion." In *Friedrich Nietzsche: Die nachgelassenen Fragmente, eine Auswahl*, 295–314. Stuttgart: Reclam, 1996.

———. "The Death of the Ego: An Analysis of the 'I' in Nietzsche's Unpublished Fragments." *Journal of Chinese Philosophy* 26:3 (September 1999): 323–41.

Wright, Dale S. *Philosophical Meditations on Zen Buddhism*. Cambridge: Cambridge University Press, 1998.

———. "Introduction: Rethinking Ritual Practice in Zen Buddhism." In *Zen Ritual: Studies of Zen Buddhist Theory in Practice*, edited by Steven Heine and Dale S. Wright, 3–19. Oxford: Oxford University Press, 2008.

Yamada, Shōji. "The Myth of Zen in the Art of Archery." *Journal of Japanese Religious Studies* 28/1–2 (2001): 1–30.

———. *Shots in the Dark: Japan, Zen, and the West*. Chicago: University of Chicago Press, 2009.

Yampolsky, Philip B. *The Platform Sutra of the Sixth Patriarch*. New York: Columbia University Press, 1967.

Yoshizu Yoshihide. "The Relation between Chinese Buddhist History and Soteriology." In *Paths to Liberation: The Mārga and its Transformations in Buddhist Thought*, edited by Robert Buswell and Robert Gimello, 309–38. Honolulu: University of Hawai'i Press, 1992.

Young, Julian. *Nietzsche's Philosophy of Religion*. Cambridge: Cambridge University Press, 2006.

Yuasa, Yasuo. *The Body: Toward an Eastern Mind-Body Theory*. Albany: State University of New York Press, 1987.

Zotz, Volker. *Auf den glückseligen Inseln: Buddhismus in der deutschen Kultur*. Berlin: Theseus, 2000.

Index

About the Author

André van der Braak is associate researcher at the department of Philosophy at Radboud University, Nijmegen. He has been a member of the Nietzsche Research Group in Nijmegen since 1998 and is a coworker of the Nietzsche Dictionary Project. He is the author of *Enlightenment Blues* (Monkfish Publishing 2003), *Hoe men wordt, wat men is: Zelfvervolmaking, zelfoverwinning en zelfvergetelheid bij Nietzsche* [How One Becomes, What One Is: Self-cultivation, Self-overcoming and Self-forgetting in Nietzsche] (Damon 2004), *Goeroes en charisma* [Gurus and Charisma] (Altamira 2006), and various articles on Western and Buddhist philosophy. From 2007 to 2009, he served as a director of the Dutch Philosophy East West Foundation.